VAJRAYANA BUDDHISM

VAJRAYANA BUDDHISM

A K Mishra

MD PUBLICATIONS PVT LTD
NEW DELHI
www.mdppl.com

Published by :

MD Publications Pvt Ltd
"MD House", 11, Darya Ganj,
New Delhi - 110 002
Phone : +91-11-45355555
E-mail : contact@mdppl.com
Website: www.mdppl.com

ISBN: 978-81-7533-289-8

Published and Printed by Mr. Pranav Gupta on behalf of MD Publications Pvt Ltd at Times Press, Delhi.

Preface

Vajrayana, or Tantric Buddhism, has been described as the latest phase in the development and evolution of Buddhist thought. Vajrayana metaphysics is, like Indian Tantra, a hybrid affair: a coming together of Indian Tantrism, Mahayana Buddhism, and the original aboriginal shamanism - the Bon tradition - of Tibet itself. Like the Nathas, Shaktas, and Shaivites, the Vajrayanists postulated a subtle or iconographic body, made up of chakras, nadis, and subtle winds (vayu). And like their Indian counterparts they worked on manipulating the forces of this subtle body through yoga in order to attain spiritual enlightenment. But Vajrayana tantra diverged very early from Indian tantra. Instead of the later seven-chakra model, they retain an earlier four chakra schema of navel, heart, throat, and head centres. Starting from this four-chakra foundation, the Vajrayanists-like the Indian tantics - built up a very elaborate system of correspondences.

Vajrayana Buddhism, also known as Tantric Buddhism, Mantrayana, Tantrayana, Esoteric Buddhism, '"Diamond Vehicle" or "True Words Sect", is often viewed as the third major school of Buddhism, alongside the Theravada and Mahayana schools. The Vajrayana is actually a subset of Mahayana Buddhism. Vajrayana Buddhists themselves often classify their school as the final stage in the evolution of Indian Buddhist theory. Although Vajrayana practices vary from school to school; they all place a strong emphasis on esoteric transmission from teacher to student. Initiation is an inportant component, and the ongoing non-verbal transmission of teachings is considered essential. These transmissions are believed to speed practitioners' progress, enabling them to achieve insights through contact with a teacher that might otherwise take them much longer to realize on their own.

Vajrayana relies on various tantric techniques rooted in scriptures known as tantras, written in India. The most important aspect of the tantric path is to 'use the result as the Path'; which means that rather than placing full enlightenment as a goal far away in the future, one tries to identify with the enlightened body, speech and mind of a Buddha. The buddha-form which one can best relate to is called the yidam (Tibetan) or (Sanskrit: ishtadevata) or 'personal buddha-form'. In order to achieve this self-identification with a buddha-form, much symbolism and visualization is used in Buddhist tantric techniques.

Vajrayana Buddhism had mostly died out in India by the 13th century, its practices merging with Hinduism, and both tantric religions experiencing pressure from the rising importance of Islam. By that time, the vast majority of the practices were also made available in Tibet, where they were preserved until recently. In the second half of the 20th century a sizeable number of Tibetan exiles fled the oppressive anti-religious rule of the Communist Chinese to establish Tibetan Buddhist communities in northern India, particularly around Dharamsala. They remain the primary practitioners of Tantric Buddhism in India and the entire world.

I am very grateful to Mr. Pranav Gupta, Director of MD Publications Pvt Ltd, New Delhi, for his kind cooperation and support for this book.

A K Mishra

Contents

1

Vajrayana Buddhism

An Introduction

Vajrayana, or Tantric Buddhism, has been described as the latest phase in the development and evolution of Buddhist thought. For a long time, Western scholars dismissed Vajrayana as the final "degenerate phase" of Buddhist thought. This attitude was due to the fact that these materialistic scholars had only a Christian or a secular way of seeing the world. They could appreciate ordinary Buddhism (Theravada, etc), seeing the Buddha as the Christ of the East teaching an essentially moral message, or as a sort of spiritual humanist; but when faced with a system of knowledge and practice that embraced all the magical and occult elements that Western rationalism had rejected centuries ago, could only explain it as some sort of degenerate end phase. Fortunately, in more recent times other Westerners have studied Tantric Buddhism first hand, at the feet of actual Tibetan Masters, and so have a more mature appreciation and respect for that noble tradition.

Indeed, if anything good has come out of the terrible Chinese invasion and oppression of the Tibetan homeland in the 2nd half of the 20th century, it has been that this has driven Tibetan lamas and teachers to the West, and encouraged them to spread their tradition among sympathetic Westerners. Vajrayana metaphysics is, like Indian Tantra, a hybrid affair: a coming together of Indian Tantrism, Mahayana Buddhism, and the original aboriginal shamanism - the Bon tradition - of

Tibet itself. Like the Nathas, Shaktas, and Shaivites, the Vajrayanists postulated a subtle or iconographic body, made up of chakras, nadis, and subtle winds (vayu). And like their Indian counterparts they worked on manipulating the forces of this subtle body through yoga in order to attain spiritual enlightenment. But Vajrayana tantra diverged very early from Indian tantra. Instead of the later seven-chakra model, they retain an earlier four chakra schema of navel, heart, throat, and head centres.

Starting from this four-chakra foundation, the Vajrayanists - like the Indian tantics - built up a very elaborate system of correspondences. There are a number of other important differences to Indian (Shakta) Tantra as well. In Indian tantra one starts form the base chakra and progresses up. In Tibetan tantra one starts from the head, which is the "lowest" level of consciousness (body, waking consciousness, wrathful deities), and progresses down to the heart, which is the highest level of consciousness. With Indian Tantra the kundalini is awakened through specific breathing practices and yoga-postures. The prana or vital-force of the subtle body is thus manipulated through the breath and the physical body; through an extension of Hatha yoga which, the reader will recall, was associated from the beginning with Indian Tantra. In contrast, Vajrayana practice involves manipulating the vital force through the mind and concentration.

Through intense visualisation of deities and so on, one activates the inner "winds" (= prana = ch'i) and "drops". The Instead of the Kundalini-Shakti or "Serpent Fire" of Shakta Tantrism, Vajrayana has the *Tumo* (literally "fierce woman"). Through intense visualisation of deities and concentration upon the "lower tip" (the minor chakra at the tip of the sex-organ), the winds (prana) are drawn into the lower opening of the central channel (sushumna), producing an intense heat, called tumo. In her fascinating book, *Magic and Mystery in Tibet* Alexandra David-Neel popularised stories of Tibetan yogis drying icy sheets with their naked bodies outside in the middle of winter. That is a showy exhibition of tumo. Real tumo of course is the tantric meditation itself.

As a result of the tumo-heat, the drops melt and enter the central channel. The red "female" drops in the navel chakra ascend to the heart chakra, while the white drops in the crown chakra descend to the same chakra. The bliss of the drops flowing in the central channel is said to be a hundred times greater than that of orgasm. The drops, moving up or down the central channel, finally enter the "indestructable drop" in the heart chakra, so called because it is said to be drop that passes from life-time to life-time, taking with it the "very subtle mind" and "very subtle wind". The entire visualisation or meditation stage itself is called the stage of Generation, as its purpose is to construct or generate an actual enlightenment or Buddha-body, the stage of Completion.

The result of all this is that one rises in an "illusory body", so called because it is a spirit body rather than a physical body, and at death, rather than be caught up by the bardo and reincarnation, one remains in full consciousness in the illusory body, so attaining Buddhahood. Mystical practices and esoteric sects are found in all forms of Buddhism. The mystical tendency that Buddhism inherited from Indian religion became increasingly pronounced. Following the codification of the Theravada canon-which according to tradition emerged orally shortly after the Buddha's death and was written down by the late 1st century BCE -and the subsequent emergence of Mahayana (1st century CE), this mystical element slowly developed into discrete schools of thought. Buddhist mysticism (including the philosophical school of Chan), like other forms of mysticism, insists on the ineffability of the mystical experience, because it is not intelligible to anyone who has not had a similar experience.

Mystical knowledge is not intellectual but is "felt knowledge" that views things in a different perspective and gives them new significance. The experience is both ineffable and timeless, which means that the mystic seems to be outside time and space, oblivious to his surroundings and the passage of time. Early Buddhist mysticism was concerned with the emptying of subjective being, considered to be the greatest obstacle to the individual's spiritual growth. This passing into a new dimension of reality is described in terms of a flame going out. In this emptying process the limits of the individual's being are supposedly transcended. The experience of this new dimension of reality is a vision that goes far beyond the reach of "mere logic" and normal perception.

While Theravada Buddhism was analytic in its attempt to free reality from the imposition of subjectivity, Mahayana extended the analytic process to objective reality. In its rejection of subjectivism and objectivism, it emphasized the nature of reality-as-such, which was experienced in enlightenment (Pali and Sanskrit: *bodhi*). While the various philosophical trends associated with Mahayana dealt with the intellectual problem of reality, the tantras (Sanskrit: "treatises"), which form the distinctive literature of Esoteric Buddhism, dealt with the existential problem of what it is like or how it feels to attain the highest goal.

ORIGINS

Vajrayana (Sanskrit: "Diamond Vehicle" or "Thunderbolt Vehicle") or Mantrayana (Sanskrit: "Path of the Sacred Formulas"), also known as Tantric Buddhism, first emerged in various parts of India and Sri Lanka. The esoteric nature of Tantric doctrine and practice makes identifying the origins of the Vajrayana school difficult, but some Buddhist traditions associate them with Nagarjuna and Asanga and therefore suggest that Vajrayana began to develop quietly in the 2nd or 4th century CE . Vajrayana was prominent in India and Tibet, and a form of it, which does not seem to have emphasized sexoyogic practices, spread to China and then to Japan, where it became associated with the Tendai and Shingon schools. Although Vajrayana texts describe numerous yogic or contemplative stages that must be experienced before enlightenment can be achieved, they preserve the Mahayana identification of nirvana and samsara as a basic truth.

Moreover, Vajrayana teaches that nirvana as *shunyata* ("voidness") is one side of a polarity that must be complemented by *karuna* ("compassion of the bodhisattva").

Shunyata, according to the Vajrayana tradition, is the passive wisdom (*prajna*) that possesses an absolutely indestructible or diamond-like (*vajra*) nature beyond all duality and *karuna* is the means (*upaya*) or dynamic aspect of the world. Enlightenment arises when these seeming opposites are understood to be one. This realization, which is known experientially and not cognitively, is portrayed in Vajrayana imagery and practice as the union of the passive female deity, which signifies wisdom or voidness, with the dynamic male, signifying compassion without attachment. Such a union, *yab-yum* (Tibetan: "father-mother"), is a symbol of the unity of opposites that brings the "great bliss," or enlightenment.

Vajrayana Buddhists believe that, as all things are in truth of one nature-the void-physical-mental processes can be used as a vehicle for enlightenment. According to the *Kalacakra Tantra*, the Buddha taught that, in this age of degeneration, enlightenment must be achieved through the body, which contains the whole cosmos. Vajrayana specialists warn, however, that the first step toward enlightenment is taken by undergoing instruction by a master who has been initiated into the mysteries and can teach the correct use of the body's process. The master directs every step so that the pupil learns to control mental and physical processes instead of being dominated by them. The master, it is believed, leads the student to compassion through meditation on the transitoriness of life, the relation of cause and effect of one's actions, and the suffering of humanity.

After sympathy for human suffering has been aroused, the student is taught yogic, or contemplative, exercises that help to produce inner experiences corresponding to the various stages of spiritual growth. Advancement toward enlightenment involves the identification of the initiate with deities that represent various cosmic forces. These gods are first visualized with the help of mudras (meditative gestures and postures), mantras (sacred syllables and phrases), and icons portrayed in a mandala, all of which are believed to possess the essence of the divinities to be invoked. After this visualization the initiate identifies with the divinities and finds that each in turn is *shunyata* ("voidness"). According to Vajrayana traditions, the culmination of this process, called vajrasattva yoga, gives the initiate a diamond-like body beyond all duality.

The four stages in the process are described in four different groups of tantras (the *Kriya-tantra, Carya-tantra, Yoga-tantra,* and *Anuttarayoga-tantra*) that are compared with the fourfold phases of courtship (the exchange of glances, a pleasing or encouraging smile, the holding of hands, and consummation in the sexual act). The first stage involves external ritual acts, and the second combines these outward acts with contemplation. The third stage involves only contemplation, and the fourth is the unification of all dualities in the sexual act, symbolically or effectively. The last stage is divided into two phases. In the first the initiate uses controlled imagination to experience the union on an ideational level.

The second phase is the *maithuna,* or sexual coupling. Unlike the ordinary sexual act, which gives only momentary pleasure, the *maithuna* is considered a technique to attain enlightenment and eternal bliss because the initiate has already realized the voidness of all things, allowing perfect control over emotions and a complete absence of attachment. These Vajrayana practices have been condemned by some Buddhists and some modern scholars as degenerate, a view ostensibly borne out by the *Guhyasamaja-tantra,* which states that adultery and eating of human flesh are actions of the bodhisattva.

Vajrayana practices and the imagery of its texts, however, were designed to shock the complacency and self-righteousness of more traditional Buddhists. Moreover, the imagery of the texts was based on the belief that voidness alone exists and that it is beyond good or evil in the usual sense. The imagery is also based on the belief that any acts that bring about this realization are acts that benefit the practitioner and all sentient beings.

VAJRAYANA LITERATURE

The tantras, the genre of texts unique to the Vajrayana tradition, are written in a highly figurative and symbolic language to enable individual spiritual development. Because of this symbolic character, the tantras have usually been kept secret, and a literalist interpretation of such texts has usually failed to make any sense out of them. The *Guhyasamaja-tantra* ("Treatise on the Sum Total of Mysteries"), also called the *Tathagataguhyaka* ("The Mystery of Tathagatahood [Buddhahood]"), is the earliest-known tantra and is traditionally ascribed to Asanga (*c.* 4th century CE), the renowned Indian scholar and propounder of the Yogacara philosophy. Unlike most tantras, which do not explain the technical or symbolic terms that they employ, the *Guhyasamaja-tantra* devotes a very long chapter to the elucidation of these terms.

An important feature of all tantras is a polarity symbolism, which appears on the physical level as the union of male and female, on the ethical level as the union of beneficial activity and an appreciation of what there is as it is, and on the philosophical level as the synthesis of absolute reality and absolute compassion. The richness of this symbolism is apparent in the opening of the *Guhyasamaja*, where the absolute, which is depicted as a polarity, manifests itself in various mandalas (circular diagrams that have both a psychological and a cosmic reference), each related to one of the celestial Buddhas-Aksobhya, Vairocana, Ratnasambhava, Amitabha, and Amoghasiddhi. Each of these Buddhas again represents a polarity that is often portrayed in iconographic works through their union with female consorts.

The tantras may emphasize either "beneficial activity" or "appreciative awareness" or their "unity," and, therefore, Tantric literature has been divided into the so-called Father Tantra (emphasizing activity), the Mother Tantra (emphasizing appreciation), and the Nondual Tantra (dealing with both aspects unitively). The original Sanskrit versions of most of these works have been lost, but their influence is noticeable in works such as *Jnanasiddhi* ("Attainment of Knowledge") by the great Vajrayana teacher Indrabhuti (*c.* 687–717), *Prajnopayavinishcayasiddhi* ("The Realization of the Certitude of Appreciative Awareness and Ethical Action") by the 8th-century writer Anangavajra, and the songs of the 84 *mahasiddhas* ("masters of miraculous powers," who were considered to have attained the Vajrayana goal). One of the last Sanskrit works to have been written in Central Asia was the *Kalacakra-tantra* ("Wheel of Time"), which probably entered India in 966 CE. It taught that the Adi-Buddha-primeval Buddhahood-manifested itself as a continuum of time (*kala*) and space (*cakra*).

VAJRAYANA SCHOOLS IN TIBET

When Tibet was converted to Buddhism (7th to 11th century), the most dynamic form in India was Vajrayana; thus, it was this tradition that became established in Tibet. Little is known about the early stages of the conversion (7th to 9th century), however, and the role of Vajrayana in the conversion before the 11th century, when several identifiable schools emerged, remains unclear.

RNYING-MA-PA

Among the Vajrayana schools of Tibet and neighbouring regions, the Rnying-ma-pa claims to preserve most purely the teachings of Padmasambhava, the 8th-century Indian miracle worker who helped convert Tibet by using his magical prowess, it is believed, to quell the local demons. The Rnying-ma-pa makes fuller use than any other school of the "discovered" texts of Padmasambhava. These texts are believed to have been hidden since the early 9th century, when persecution began in Tibet, and their discovery began in the 11th century and continued until the late 20th century. Their importance to this school is reinforced by the Rnying-ma-pa notion that "hidden treasure" has strong spiritual and historical overtones.

The Rnying-ma-pa order divides Buddhist teaching into nine progressively superior groups and subdivides the tantras in a manner different from that of other Vajrayana schools. The six groups of tantras are: Kriya, or ritual; Upayoga, which involves the convergence of the two truths and meditation on the pentad of Buddhas; Yoga, which involves the evocation of the god, the identification of the self with the god, and meditation on the mandala; Mahayoga, which involves meditation on the factors of human consciousness (*skandhas*) as divine forms; Anuyoga, which involves secret initiation into the presence of the god and his consort and meditation on "voidness" in order to destroy the illusory nature of things; and Atiyoga, which involves meditation on the union of the god and his consort, leading to the experience of bliss.

Members of the order believe that those initiated into the Kriya can attain Buddhahood after seven lives, the Upayoga after five lives, the Yoga after three lives, the Mahayoga in the next existence, the Anuyoga at death, and the Atiyoga in the present existence. One of the most profound thinkers of the Rnying-ma-pa tradition, Klong-chen rab-'byams-pa (1308–63), is the author of the *Klong-chen-mdzod-bdun* (Tibetan: "Seven Treasures of Klong-chen"). In modern times Mi-'pham of Khams (1846–1914) wrote important Vajrayana commentaries on the canonical texts.

SA-SKYA-PA, BKA'-BRGYUD-PA, AND RELATED SCHOOLS

Several Tibetan schools that developed during the 11th and 12th centuries traced their lineage back several centuries to particular Indian Vajrayana saints. The Sa-skya-pa and the Bka'-brgyud-pa orders were the most prominent, and they gave rise to many others, including the descendant of Bka'-brgyud-pa, the Karma-pa (Tibetan: "Black Hat"), which has its major centre at the monastery of Mtshur-phu. Although the Sa-skya-pa order traces its lineage back to Virupa, its founder was the Tibetan 'Brog-mi (992–1072), who went to India and received training in the Vajrayana. The order places great emphasis on the *Hevajra-tantra,* which 'Brog-mi translated into Tibetan.

The Sa-skya-pa order had an important impact on the society around it. The order produced many great translators, and its scholars also contributed original works on Vajrayana philosophy and linguistics. On the ecclesiastical and political level, the order sometimes exerted considerable power. During the 13th century, for example, the Sa-skya-pa abbot 'Phags-pa (1235–80?) initiated Kublai Khan (founder of the Yüan, or Mongol, dynasty in China) into the tradition of the

Hevajra-tantra. 'Phags-pa was then appointed *dishi* (Chinese: "imperial preceptor") and invested with the authority to govern Tibet, though under the control of the Mongol court. The Bka'-brgyud-pa school developed from the teachings of the Indian master Tilopa, who transmitted them to the Indian yogi Naropa, the master of Mar-pa, the 11th-century householder-teacher, who was in turn the master of Mi-la-ras-pa (1040–1123).

The school preserved a collection of songs attributed to the founder and a hagiographic account of his life. Sgam-po-pa (1079–1153), who was Mi-la-ras-pa's greatest disciple, systematized the school's teaching and established the basis for its further development. His most famous work, *Thar-rgyan* (Tibetan: "The Jewel Ornament of Liberation"), is one of the earliest examples of the Tibetan and Mongolian Vajrayana literary tradition Lam Rim (Tibetan: "Stages on the Path"), which presents Buddhist teachings in terms of gradations in a soteriological process leading to the attainment of Buddhahood.

Bka'-brgyud-pa teachers stressed the exercises of hatha yoga and posited as the supreme goal the *mahamudra* ("the great seal"), or the overcoming of dichotomous thought in the emptiness of Buddhahood. The Bka'-brgyud-pa made frequent reference to the "Six Teachings of Naropa," which set forth techniques for attaining enlightenment, either in this life or at the moment of death. These techniques are associated with self-produced heat (the voluntary raising of the body temperature), the illusory body, dreams, the experience of light, the state of existence intermediate between death and rebirth (Tibetan: Bardo), and the movement from one existence to another.

THE BKA'-GDAMS-PA AND DGE-LUGS-PA

The Bka'-gdams-pa school was founded by 'Brom-ston (*c.* 1008–*c.* 1064), who based his school's teachings on those of Atisha (an Indian monk who went to Tibet in the 11th century). The school produced the *Bka'-gdams gces-bsdus* (Tibetan: "Collection of the Sayings of the Bka'-gdams-pa Saints"), which preserves the poetic utterances of the founder's disciples. The central practice of the school was the purification of the mind, which required the elimination of intellectual and moral blemishes in order to obtain a clear vision of emptiness (Sanskrit: *shunyata*). The school relied on the *Prajnaparamita* and made use of mantras. It was absorbed in the 15th century by the reform movement that became the Dge-lugs-pa school.

Members of the Dge-lugs-pa (Gelugpa; the "Virtuous") are commonly known as Yellow Hats, in reference to the colour of their head cover. Their founder, Tsong-kha-pa, attended the important Sa-skya-pa, Bka'-brgyud-pa, and Bka'-gdams-pa schools, and his own school is considered the continuation of the Bka'-gdams-pa. Tsong-kha-pa initiated monastic reforms in response to what he deemed a general laxity of morals, increasingly less-rigorous observance of monastic rules, and deviations in the interpretation of the tantras. He imposed respect for the traditional rules of the *Vinaya* and reemphasized dogmatics and logic as aids to salvation. His treatise, the *Lam-rim chen-mo* (Tibetan: "The Great Gradual Path"), based on the *Bodhipathapradipa* by Atisha, presents a process of mental purification ascending through 10 spiritual levels (*bhumi*) that lead to Buddhahood. The essential points of such a process are the state of quiescence and the state of enhanced vision.

Tsong-kha-pa instituted regular debates at monasteries. Competing monks sought to reach, by means of formal logic and in the presence of an abbot of great learning, an unassailable conclusion on a chosen topic. Various ranks of monks were established on the basis of examinations, the highest being that of *dge-bshes* (Tibetan: "philosopher"). The attention to doctrinal and logical problems did not exclude interest in the tantras, and Tsong-kha-pa's *Sngags-rim chen-mo* (Tibetan: "The Great Gradual Tantric Path") deals with Tantric ritual. Tantric initiation, however, was open only to students who had already acquired extensive learning.

The literature of the Dge-lugs-pa is enormous, including the gigantic collections of the Dalai and Panchen lamas, both of whom are members of this school. The Dge-lugs-pa asserts that the nature of the mind element is light, which constitutes the cognitive capacity. The continuum of each person, therefore, is a thinking and luminous energy, which is in either a coarse or a subtle state, the latter state being achieved only after purification through meditation and contemplation.

ESOTERIC TRADITIONS IN CHINA AND JAPAN

During the 7th, 8th, and 9th centuries, Indian Esoteric Buddhism spread to Southeast Asia and East Asia. In East Asia, Esoteric Buddhism became established in the Zhenyan ("True Word") school in China and in the Tendai and Shingon schools in Japan.

ZHENYAN

According to the Zhenyan tradition, Esoteric Buddhism was taken from India to China by three missionary monks who translated the basic Zhenyan texts. The first monk, Shubhakarasimha, arrived in China in 716, and he translated the *Mahavairocana-sutra* and a closely related ritual compendium, the *Susiddhikara*, into Chinese. The other two monks, Vajrabodhi and his disciple Amoghavajra, arrived in 720 and produced two abridged translations of the *Sarvatathagatatattvasamgraha* ("Symposium of Truth of All the Buddhas"), also known as the *Tattvasamgraha*. Between the arrival of Shubhakarasimha and the great persecution of 845, the Zhenyan School enjoyed amazing success.

The tradition of Shubhakarasimha and the *Mahavairocana-sutra* merged with that of Vajrabodhi and the *Tattvasamgraha*. The Chinese disciples of this new tradition, such as Huiguo, contributed to an emerging Zhenyan synthesis. The combination of sophisticated doctrinal instruction and miracle-working powers supposedly conferred by the esoteric rituals enabled Zhenyan leaders to gain the confidence of the court, especially of Emperor Tai-tsung (762–779/780), who rejected Daoism in favour of Zhenyan Buddhism. Although Zhenyan lost its position of prominence in China after the persecution of 845, it maintained spiritual vitality and communal visibility through the Song dynasty (960–1279). Moreover, the Zhenyan School contributed a great deal that has endured in the larger fabric of Chinese religion.

SHINGON

Although Esoteric Buddhism played a much greater role in China than is usually recognized, it was in Japan that it became most influential. Esoteric elements, called *taimitsu* in Japanese, have been an important element in the Japanese Tendai School, which was founded by the monk Saichô (764–822), who studied with Zhenyan and Tiantai masters in China. The most systematized and elaborated expressions of the esoteric tradition, however, were developed in the Shingon School, the Japanese version of Zhenyan. The founder of the Shingon school in Japan was Kûkai, better known by his posthumous name, Kôbô Daishi (Japanese: "Great Master Who Understood the Dharma"). An exceptional scholar, poet, painter, and calligrapher, he wrote a treatise comparing Confucian, Daoist, and Buddhist thought and naming the latter as superior. Although trained for government service, he experienced a change of heart and became a Buddhist monk.

Like many monks in pursuit of the pure Buddhist doctrine, he journeyed to China, where he met the master Huiguo, who recognized Kûkai's potential and taught him Zhenyan Buddhism. After the death of Huiguo, Kûkai returned to Japan, where he received many governmental honours and established a monastery on Mount Kôya as the centre of Shingon Buddhism. In propagating the teachings of his school, Kûkai wrote many important texts, including the *Jûjû shinron* (Japanese: "The Ten Stages of Consciousness"). In this work Kûkai presented a model of the development of the spiritual life that arranged Buddhist teachings and those of other religions into a hierarchical system. He taught that the first stage of human spiritual development was one in which humans are controlled by their instincts.

In the second stage, which Kûkai identifies with Confucian teachings, human beings attempt to live a proper moral existence. The third stage, in which the individual strives for supernatural powers and heavenly rewards, is that of Brahmanism and Daoism. The fourth and fifth stages of spiritual development are taught by the Hinayana schools and are characterized by the striving for self-enlightenment. Stages six to nine, identified with the Mahayanist teachings of Hossô,

Sanron, Tendai, and Kegon, lead the individual to compassion for others. The zenith of spiritual development is identified by Kûkai with the esoteric teachings of Shingon.

The Shingon School claimed that its doctrine was the purest because it was not based on the teachings of the historical Buddha, Shakyamuni, who expounded his doctrine with the limitations of his audience in mind, but on the timeless and immutable teachings of the Buddha in his *dharma-kaya*, or cosmic body. This Buddha, named Mahavairocana, was felt to be beyond all earthly dualism and impurity but at the same instant to be within all things as their Buddha nature. In Shingon the realization that one's own Buddha nature is identical with Mahavairocana is enlightenment. This enlightenment, as depicted in Kûkai's treatise *Sokushin-jôbutsugi* (Japanese: "The Doctrine of Becoming a Buddha with One's Body during One's Earthly Existence"), can be achieved in this world while possessing a human body.

To achieve this enlightened state, however, the aspirant must receive the secret doctrine of Shingon orally and directly from a Shingon master. The truth that the master reveals is founded on the ritual mysteries of the body, speech, and mind; these mysteries invoke cosmic forces embodied in the Buddhas and bodhisattvas with which the aspirant identifies before becoming one with Mahavairocana. The experience of the mystery of the body involves the use of mudras: devotional gestures of the hands and fingers, postures of meditation, and the handling of such sacred instruments as the *vajra* ("thunderbolt" or "diamond") and the lotus. The mystery of speech involves the recitation of *dharanis* or mantras, mystical verses and sounds believed to be the essence of the cosmic forces with which one wishes to commune. Attaining the mystery of the mind involves yogic contemplation of and absorption in the Buddha Mahavairocana and his attendants.

The aspirant is further helped in his quest to identify his Buddha nature with the Cosmic Buddha by means of two mandalas, often placed on the Shingon altar. The mandalas, believed to contain all the power of the cosmos, were drawn in accordance with the teaching of Huiguo, who maintained that the Buddha Mahavairocana's doctrines were so profound that their meanings could be conveyed only in art. One mandala, called the "Diamond Mandala" (based on the *Tattvasamgraha* and known in Japanese as *kongô-kai*), portrays the Buddha Mahavairocana sitting upon a white lotus in deep contemplation, surrounded by the Buddhas of the four regions. This symbolizes Mahavairocana's indestructible, immutable, or potential aspect. The second mandala, called the "Womb Mandala of Great Compassion" (based on the *Mahavairocana-sutra* and known in Japanese as *taizô-kai*), reveals Mahavairocana sitting on a red lotus surrounded by innumerable Buddhas, bodhisattvas, and Indian gods, with consorts.

This represents the Cosmic Buddha's dynamic manifestation in which he is immanent in everything. It was believed that, by meditating correctly on these two mandalas, the aspirant would realize the unity beyond the diversity of the world. The emphasis of Shingon upon ritual, symbolism, and iconography, coupled with the government's praise of Kûkai and the bestowal upon him of the shrine for the protection of the country, made Shingon very popular in Japan. Shingon's popularity was a cause of the growth of Ryôbu Shintô (Japanese: "Two Aspects Shintô"), which identified Shintô *kami* (object of worship or sacred power) with bodhisattvas. Moreover, believing that Shingon rites controlled the forces of the cosmos, many people used them to ward off evil and bring supernatural help in everyday life.

While this combination of Esoteric Buddhism with more this-worldly concerns caused schisms, Shingon maintains its position as one of Japan's strongest Buddhist schools. Vajrayana (Sanskrit: "Diamond Vehicle" or "Thunderbolt Vehicle") or Mantrayana (Sanskrit: "Path of the Sacred Formulas"), also known as Tantric Buddhism, first emerged in various parts of India and Sri Lanka. The esoteric nature of Tantric doctrine and practice makes identifying the origins of the Vajrayana school difficult, but some Buddhist traditions associate them with Nagarjuna and Asanga and therefore suggest that Vajrayana began to develop quietly in the 2nd or 4th century CE . Vajrayana was prominent in India and Tibet, and a form of it, which does not seem to have emphasized sexoyogic practices, spread to China and then to Japan, where it became associated with the Tendai and Shingon Schools.

Although Vajrayana texts describe numerous yogic or contemplative stages that must be experienced before enlightenment can be achieved, they preserve the Mahayana identification of nirvana and samsara as a basic truth. Moreover, Vajrayana teaches that nirvana as *shunyata* ("voidness") is one side of a polarity that must be complemented by *karuna* ("compassion of the bodhisattva"). *Shunyata,* according to the Vajrayana tradition, is the passive wisdom (*prajna*) that possesses an absolutely indestructible or diamond-like (*vajra*) nature beyond all duality and *karuna* is the means (*upaya*) or dynamic aspect of the world. Enlightenment arises when these seeming opposites are understood to be one.

This realization, which is known experientially and not cognitively, is portrayed in Vajrayana imagery and practice as the union of the passive female deity, which signifies wisdom or voidness, with the dynamic male, signifying compassion without attachment. Such a union, *yab-yum* (Tibetan: "father-mother"), is a symbol of the unity of opposites that brings the "great bliss," or enlightenment. Vajrayana Buddhists believe that, as all things are in truth of one nature-the void-physical-mental processes can be used as a vehicle for enlightenment. According to the *Kalacakra Tantra,* the Buddha taught that, in this age of degeneration, enlightenment must be achieved through the body, which contains the whole cosmos.

Vajrayana specialists warn, however, that the first step toward enlightenment is taken by undergoing instruction by a master who has been initiated into the mysteries and can teach the correct use of the body's process. The master directs every step so that the pupil learns to control mental and physical processes instead of being dominated by them. The master, it is believed, leads the student to compassion through meditation on the transitoriness of life, the relation of cause and effect of one's actions, and the suffering of humanity. After sympathy for human suffering has been aroused, the student is taught yogic, or contemplative, exercises that help to produce inner experiences corresponding to the various stages of spiritual growth. Advancement toward enlightenment involves the identification of the initiate with deities that represent various cosmic forces.

These gods are first visualized with the help of mudras (meditative gestures and postures), mantras (sacred syllables and phrases), and icons portrayed in a mandala, all of which are believed to possess the essence of the divinities to be invoked. After this visualization the initiate identifies with the divinities and finds that each in turn is *shunyata* ("voidness"). According to Vajrayana traditions, the culmination of this process, called vajrasattva yoga, gives the initiate a diamond-like body beyond all duality. The four stages in the process are described in four different groups of tantras (the *Kriya-tantra, Carya-tantra, Yoga-tantra,* and *Anuttarayoga-tantra*) that are compared with the fourfold phases of courtship (the exchange of glances, a pleasing or encouraging smile, the holding of hands, and consummation in the sexual act).

The first stage involves external ritual acts, and the second combines these outward acts with contemplation. The third stage involves only contemplation, and the fourth is the unification of all dualities in the sexual act, symbolically or effectively. The last stage is divided into two phases. In the first the initiate uses controlled imagination to experience the union on an ideational level. The second phase is the *maithuna,* or sexual coupling. Unlike the ordinary sexual act, which gives only momentary pleasure, the *maithuna* is considered a technique to attain enlightenment and eternal bliss because the initiate has already realized the voidness of all things, allowing perfect control over emotions and a complete absence of attachment.

These Vajrayana practices have been condemned by some Buddhists and some modern scholars as degenerate, a view ostensibly borne out by the *Guhyasamaja-tantra,* which states that adultery and eating of human flesh are actions of the bodhisattva. Vajrayana practices and the imagery of its texts, however, were designed to shock the complacency and self-righteousness of more traditional Buddhists. Moreover, the imagery of the texts was based on the belief that voidness alone exists and that it is beyond good or evil in the usual sense. The imagery is also based on the belief that any acts that bring about this realization are acts that benefit the practitioner and all sentient beings.

FROM HINAYANA TO VAJRAYANA

THE THREE VEHICLES- THERAVADA, MAHAYANA AND VAJRAYANA

The paths outlined by the Buddha in his teachings are grouped into three principal vehicles. The first is the vehicle of the Theravada or 'elders', which is mainly focused on the path of renunciation and follows the teaching of the four noble truths. The quintessence of the second vehicle, the Mahayana or great vehicle taught by Buddha Shakyamuni, comes down to two central practices, the practice of loving-kindness and the practice of compassion. Let us try to understand together the meaning of these. As an example of loving-kindness, we can reflect on the kindness received from our own mother until a feeling of gratitude and appreciation naturally arises. We can reflect that from the day we were born into this world, we were utterly helpless, and could have easily been abandoned.

Yet our own kind mother protected us from every danger, fed and clothed us, taught us what to do and what to avoid. She gave us everything we needed, sacrificing her own needs for ours. To help loving-kindness grow inside of us, we contemplate the kindness received from our own dear mother. With this in mind, we give rise to the genuine wish that she be happy, and further generate the wish that we ourselves be able to provide her with the causes of happiness. From this benevolent wish, we proceed to cultivate a very creative, positive energy of loving-kindness. In so doing, we both increase our affection for others and strengthen the wish to repay the kindness shown to us by our own mother, the wish to expand her happiness.

This is what is known as loving-kindness. Anyone can reflect on this example, and then begin to extend the feeling they generate through remembering their mother's kindness to include other living beings. Similarly, compassion arises when, through appreciating the kindness and love shown by one's own mother, one feels indebted to her and finds it impossible to even bear the thought of her suffering and undergoing hardships. Whether our mother is living or has moved on to another life, we would never want to see her experiencing any troubles or difficulties. If such situations befall her, one would make sincere efforts to rescue her from even the smallest infirmity, from even the most trifling circumstance that might cause her pain.

We learn active compassion by empathizing with the sufferings of our own mother and by truly trying to reduce this as well as to eliminate whatever is causing her pain. Active compassion is the wish and intent to relieve others from misery and from whatever is causing them anguish. These two are the very core of the teachings of the Mahayana, the great vehicle, which is the Buddha's second turning of the wheel of the teachings. No matter what esoteric meditations of the Vajrayana one may engage in, we must base ourselves in the essence of Mahayana Buddhist teaching, the practice of loving-kindness and compassion. This will lead to a point where we are actually able to renounce our own self-interest in favor of cherishing the welfare of others. This is genuine altruism. Even if one is not quite ready or able to adopt such a noble attitude, we train ourselves step by step to really consider what will help others as much as we look out for our own welfare.

You really can try to be an instrument of happiness for other living beings, even in the smallest ways. It is equally important that we never ignore or turn a blind eye to any causes that might bring suffering to others. As long as there is suffering, and it doesn't need to be yours, it still needs to be resolved or healed. One who has this attitude is able to develop an active or engaged compassion. If there is happiness in a family or between couples, this happiness hinges for the most part on how loving, caring, and giving the family members and partners are toward one another. It does not depend on their accumulation of wealth and their material success. It is exactly the same as far as the well being of one's community, as far as the level of happiness in the greater world around us, is concerned.

Whether or not a leader can set a good example that others can follow depends for the most part on how much they really care about others. It depends on how giving he or she is able to be when conducting their daily affairs. This type of leadership sets a noble standard that people will admire and will naturally wish to emulate. It cannot help but benefit us if we are able to live according to the teaching and practice of loving-kindness toward whomever we share our lives with. Whether we are at home or out in the world, if we show more love and empathy for others, we will find more happiness in our lives. If individuals are able to dedicate themselves to a life of loving-kindness and compassion, then such people will make a great contribution to the well-being of the world, as a whole, to the cause of peace and happiness.

What is called 'world peace' only depends on how the citizens of the world behave toward one another. Love and compassion lead to the happiness of the individual, and this will naturally bring about a peaceful world. Although in this particular lifetime each of us has received the kindness of our own mother, this does not mean that there is only one person to whom we should feel indebted. It has been said by the Buddha that there have been countless occasions on which we have been reborn. We ourselves have experienced births in all the six realms of existence, in every possible situation, in every possible circumstance. In each of these lives, we have had a kind mother, so in fact we are indebted to all of those mothers just as much as we are to the mother of our present life.

Bearing this in mind at all times can lead us to genuine concern for other beings. Due to our involvement with the karmic activities of this present life, we cannot recognize around us those who actually were our mothers in the past. Even so, we still can choose to conduct ourselves so as to repay each of them for all the good they have shown us. This is the way to develop loving-kindness. There is great variety among the different religions in regard to how to approach the spiritual path, as well as in regard to their doctrines and their assertions of what is true. But one thing that we can find in common is that all religions promote love and compassion and caring for one another.

Without a doubt the spirit of Christianity is the same as that of Buddhism in promoting and upholding the value of love. The Christian teaching says that god is love, and, remembering this, one should show love toward others. This must be the most essential belief of Christians, and they try to practise it in their daily lives. It is no different with Buddhism. The Buddhist teachings guide us in how to treat one another. They teach us to understand and resolve for ourselves the moral and ethical choices we make, since only these choices will become the causes for whatever results we ourselves will experience.

This practice of mindfullness attentiveness to one's conduct emphasised in the Buddhist teachings encourages us to cultivate beneficial causes, and these good causes arise from our intention to benefit others. Any deed that is performed with a good intention to benefit others will eventually bear fruits of happiness. This will come about due to what is known as the law of cause and effect, the law of karma. Whether one believes in God, or whether one believes in the law of cause and effect, both teach us to be good people. It is doing well which promotes the happiness of others. When we ourselves shun and avoid negative conduct, the suffering of others is also avoided.

Both views accept the same fact, that we ought not to do things which create the causes of unhappiness, and that rather we should sow seeds of virtue that become causes for the happiness of others. All religions teach love between oneself and others, and that one ought to be a source of benefit to others rather than being a cause of pain for them. It is important to see that these teachings of loving-kindness and compassion are not some sort of formal doctrine that one has to profess loyalty to or belief in. They are concerned with the way we live. What determines our happiness or lack of it is what we do with ourselves. We can conduct ourselves in a way that shows care and concern for whatever sufferings we see around us, however small or apparently insignificant.

We see suffering in the lives of others, and we wish that they did not have to experience such discomfort and unhappiness. We wish that we ourselves might be instruments in freeing them from suffering. We also wish that they will be happy, and that we ourselves can help them to be happy, that we may contribute to their well-being. For example, in the lives of a couple, if each partner wishes the best for the other, and each wishes that the other not have to experience pain and misery, then there will be greater harmony between husband and wife, between partners.

Likewise, if such a relationship exists for example between an employer and those who work for him or her, this promotes happiness in those situations where some are in a leadership role and others are following their directions. It is through each individual who assumes his or her share of this basic responsibility toward other beings, and conducts their relationships based on love and compassion, that it is possible for us to make our world a different place. People speak about world peace. Peace only comes about when people are extending love towards one another. These are essential points of the Mahayana Buddhist teaching.

Having understood what is the basis of the Mahayana or greater vehicle of Buddhism, one may now ask where the Vajrayana, the esoteric tantric vehicle, fits in to the Buddhist tradition. Vajrayana, the diamond vehicle, is a branch of the Mahayana tradition. If one has developed a good basis of loving-kindness and compassion, one may make use of the methods that are the special skillful means of the Vajrayana. The benefit of these methods is that they provide a far more skillful and much swifter means of attaining enlightenment than can be gained by relying on the other vehicles on their own.

It is said that even if one follows the perfection of wisdom or Prajnaparamita of the Mahayana, still it will require three incalculable aeons to attain enlightenment. On the other hand, resorting to the skillful methods of the Vajrayana diamond vehicle, it is taught that it is even possible to attain enlightenment in one lifetime. There have been a great number of practitioners of India and Tibet who through following Vajrayana Buddhism have indeed attained complete enlightenment in a single lifetime. It is for this purpose of greatly accelerating the path to enlightenment that the Vajrayana path is available as a special means within the great Mahayana vehicle.

If one has a heart that overflows with love and compassion as a stable foundation, then resorting to esoteric practices will guarantee rapid spiritual development. In this way, one may gain the capacity to benefit so many more sentient beings so much more quickly. Within the esoteric vehicle of the Vajrayana teachings of the 'new schools' of Tibet, there are four general levels of tantras or scriptures. The highest, ultimate of these four is known as Anuttarayoga tantra or 'Highest Yoga' tantra. The Anuttarayoga tantras themselves are classed as Father Tantras, Mother Tantras, and Non-dual Tantras. In the category of Non-dual Tantras, there are only two scriptural traditions, that of Buddha Hevajra and that of Buddha Kalachakra. In order to understand a little bit about Buddhist tantra, let us consider for example the tradition of Kalachakra.

The empowerment of the Kalachakra Tantra has been widely given throughout the world in recent times. As a non-dual tantra, Kalachakra is the quintessence of all the Anuttara, or Highest Yoga tantras. Kalachakra itself is divided into four types of tantra, giving us an elaborate framework to understand the specifics of the tantra. First there is the outer Kalachakra and relates to the study of and meditation on the outer cosmos of our realm of existence. Outer Kalachakra teaches us how all the physical appearances of this world are the manifestation of our collective karma. In this way, it teaches us the causes that bring about this universe. Outer Kalachakra describes the outer universe and how it directly corresponds with, and reflects the inner propensities and karmic vision of all the beings within this universe.

Second is the inner Kalachakra. Inner Kalachakra addresses itself to applying the profound internal meditations upon the subtle channels, vital winds, elements, and essential drops which make up the subtle or psychic body. The third section of Kalachakra, secret Kalachakra, refers to meditating upon and within the ultimate meaning of the truth of emptiness. The fourth subject within Kalachakra is 'other' or 'alternative' Kalachakra, in large part, these sections are concerned with visualizing and meditating on the Buddha in the form of the meditational deity Kalachakra, and chanting his mantra, as well as practices of the completion stage of tantric meditation.

Thus the Kalachakra tantra contains the deepest meanings of four types of tantras all within one single tradition. Due to its profound meaning and the blessing it carries, it is very good if one can receive the Kalachakra initiation or at least the oral transmission of the mantra of Buddha Kalachakra. As an example of the power and benefits of mantras of the Highest Yoga Tantras of the Vajrayana, it is said that by merely hearing the sound of the Kalachakra mantra, with the proper attitude and faith, many difficulties and obstacles are removed for us. If you take the opportunity to recite the Kalachakra mantra during the course of your life, this will allay outer obstacles and create peace within you. Even reciting the mantra once definitely has the power to pacify one's afflictions and promote a general sense of happiness and well-being.

The expressions Tantric Buddhism and Vajrayana are not exactly synonymous, but they are often used interchangeably. The kind of Buddhism that is most often associated with the Vajrayana is Tibetan Buddhism. That is because Vajarayana plays an important role in it. People can make progress by relying on the written word, ie. teachings that come to us through scripture ("sutra,") and/or they can rely on direct methods that have proven successful and so have been passed from teacher to student, sometimes over centuries ("tantra.") Both play important roles in traditional Buddhism and Himalayan Buddhism is no different in this regard.

Mingyur Dorje Rinpoche explains the distinction between the two methods by giving the traditional example illustrative of the difference between sutra and tantra:

Let's say there is a person walking along carrying some stones. He sees a dog, and throws his stones at the dog. He also sees a lion and he throws his stones at the lion, too.

What does the dog do? At the sight of the stone, the dog immediately tries to bite or chase it. Then the person gets to throw another stone at the dog. The dog again tries to follow the new stone and bite it. Now this guy has got a big collection of stones, so they are not going to run out any time soon. The dog becomes very tired. Now when the man throws a stone at the lion, the lion does not look at the stone. Rather, he thinks, "Where did that stone come from? Who threw that stone?" When he sees the person who threw it, he pounces on him. A person only gets to throw one stone at a lion.

The historical Buddha, more than 2500 years ago, addressed the objective of Enlightenment from four different perspectives. He is held to have used many different approaches and techniques to do so in order to help all types of sentient beings. Tradition says that he taught 84, 000 different ways, but that not all of those were given by his "ordinary" self. The bodhisattva who was to emanate as Prince Siddhartha Gautama, and who eventually would be Buddha Shakyamuni, had attained the Tenth Bhumi without any Vajrayana practices. While dwelling in the Akanistha Realm in a state of deep samadhi, he was snapped out of that state by the Tathagatas of the ten directions and three times, who all gathered together to say "This samadhi of yours is not sufficient for attainment of Bodhi!"

So, having invited the Devis to participate, the Buddhas bestowed upon the bodhisattva the last two of Four Empowerments. On engaging in the practices related to these empowerments, the final objective was attained. In His example, we understand that Buddhahood cannot be attained without going through the Vajrayana or Resultant Path. Furthermore, it is possible for someone to complete the Causal Path of Shravakayana and Paramitayana, which in this case took more than three aeons, and then to enter the Resultant Path for that final segment of the Way. We should understand, though, that Lord Buddha was actually a complete and perfect Buddha before his appearance in this world as Prince Siddhartha.

It is only due to His prior aspiration and the need to set an example for sentient beings whose karma had ripened sufficiently for them to be born in this Good Aeon, that He: appeared to be born, get married, have a child, leave home, practiced asceticism, renounce wrong paths and attained Enlightenment after subduing the Maras. After that, He turned the *Dharmachakra* three times and, having taught and lived for 80 years, He eventually passed beyond existence (Skt. *parinirvana,*) in order to teach the lesson of Impermanence. It is clear that this achievement was not a case of "self-empowerment" and an invention of [the] Vajrayana.

He was a Hindu practitioner until the time of his bodhi. He unequivocally pointed out the flaws of those spiritual traditions then. Many of those ideas are mirrored in some spiritual cocktails currently being concocted. Since Buddhism faded from India, authentic Vajrayana teachings owe their existence today to translators such as Marpa (11th century) who undertook a number of arduous journeys from the Tibetan plateau periodically to retrieve them. The texts and methods that were being preserved in the monasteries of Tibet until the mid-twentieth century are now being collected and preserved by us.

Vajrayana (*the thunderbolt vehicle*) is the Buddhist system that incorporating tantric methods. It means that exercises, practices and rituals are handed down directly from teacher to student by word of mouth, though often with the aid of teaching materials in the form of pamphlets and pictures. Even though Buddha Shakyamuni rejected the notion of a permanent Self, he acknowledged the belief in rebirth. He said that this was not inevitable and he taught the methods that he, himself, had used to achieve enlightenment and release from the bonds of the wheel of rebirth (Skt. *sangsara* or samsara) in a single lifetime.

Vajrayana works to transmute one's "imperfections" and ordinary awareness by means of un-ordinary and also, some extraordinary methods. For example, the system of *chakras* and *nadis* that some people know about from other contexts are also utilized in this system, where it is often called "working with the winds and drops." An advanced initiated student with an agreeable partner or consort can receive instruction in working with this energy as a couple. It must be stressed that the primary objective is not enhancement of physical sensation.

THE GURU

Every Buddhist takes refuge regularly in the Three Jewels: Buddha, Dharma, and Sangha. The Vajrayanist adds three others of which the first and foremost is the guru. That is because without a mentor or lama, access to any of the special methods would not be possible. We have seen (*The Meaning of Tantra*) that even to begin the so-called preliminaries, it is not sufficient to have read about them.

KINDS OF GURU

Tibetans say that each lama has his or her way of teaching. This is an ancient idea deriving from Indian tradition holding that there are various types of guru (Tib. *lama*.) They range from "vidya gurus," teaching through knowledge of scripture, to charismatic or "diksha gurus," who directly transmit realization.

CREATION AND COMPLETION

One of the main techniques used of any tantric practice is the use of the imagination. That is, we imagine in great detail, using the "mind's eye." There are usually two or three parts to a tantric practice: the visualization of the deity, the visualization of the self as deity, and then the dissolution or resolution of the visualization into Emptiness. For example, one imagines the form, colors, clothes, and ornaments of Chenrezi not as a material body, but as a translucent form similar to that of a rainbow, or a virtual image like the moon in water. In the same way, the mantras, or speech element are understood as the union of sound and emptiness.

Finally, the mental activity - the imagination and the thought-is understood as empty Tantric "creation" uses techniques that work with body, speech and mind in new ways involving the insubstantial union of appearance and emptiness. "Completion' is the result of this play, after which awareness rests in the union of intelligence and emptiness to various degrees.

SAMAYA

As it is said: Tantric Buddhists are in the position of a snake inside a bamboo tube; one hole faces up to the Dharmakaya, the other down toward Vajra Hell. There are only two options-up or down; no in-between. Keeping *samaya* (commitment) determines which way the snake slides. In Tibetan Buddhism, it is generally held that the paths of the Hinayana, Mahayana, and Vajrayana are a progression. "There is an analogy concerning three pots: the "hinayana" vows are like a clay pot-you drop it once, it's broken ... gotta get a new pot!

The Bodhisattva vows are like a brass pot-drop it, and it'll take some work to hammer out the dents, but it's fixable, with some elbow grease and sweat ... and maybe you may have to take it back to a "licensed pot-mender!" The Vajrayana vows are like a pure gold pitcher. Since this type of pot is made of the softest metal, it is the one most susceptible to dents! Realistically, for those who have truly received the Highest vows, they are all constantly breaking them ... Well, maybe most of them, at least. These Anuttarayoga vows are really only properly attempted in a closed retreat, I would say-at least until one has achieved a solid experience in maintaining divine pride.

Of course, for those who wish to dispense with all vows, there's the invisible pot of the Mahamudra and/or Dzokchen ... no pitcher to even worry about! Find your water at the source ...."

~ CB, the Kagyu email list, who adds, "May we keep whatever vows is appropriate to us."

For those that embark upon the Vajra path, there are 14 precepts to observe.

THE 14 VAJRAYANA PRECEPTS

We are considered to have broken our *samaya* or tantric commitments if we

1. Show disrespect for the Guru in body, speech, or mind
2. Having no regard for the rules laid down by the Buddha
3. Condemn and/or create problems with one's Vajra brothers and sisters
4. Abandon love for sentient beings
5. Relinquish Bodhicitta due to difficulties
6. Slander the scriptures of Mahayana and Vajrayana
7. Transmit tantric teaching without having the proper empowerment and credentials
8. Abuse and/or foster attachment to the five skandhas, *ie.* world of appearances
9. Harbour skepticism or doubt about the doctrine of Emptiness
10. Maintain ties to beings with cruel intentions towards Buddha and his teachings
11. Indulge in accomplishments forgetting the purpose of Vajrayana practice
12. Fail to transmit authentic Dharma
13. Fail in performance of tantric ritual practices
14. Despise/or condemn Women

Even accomplished masters sometimes have problems keeping their vows. Jonang Taranatha, one of the greatest saints and historians of Tibetan Buddhism, told (*The Seven Instruction Lineages*) how Vajrayogini appeared to about one of his spiritual grandfathers, Abhayakaragupta, three times in his life: once when he was a Tirthika (Hindu practitioner,) once when he was a Buddhist monk, and finally after he had become an accomplished Tantrika. Each time she offered something for him to do or to eat. Three times he refused, thus breaking one or more of the Tantric vows and precepts.

After each time someone was kind enough to let him know what had happened, but it was not until the third time that he realized his mistake. He confessed his error to Vajrayogini, who appeared to him once again and said, "In your manifold births you have intoned mantras to me and made me offerings. Although I have offered you *siddhi* (accomplishments, powers) on three occasions, you have not accepted it. You will not attain the highest siddhi in this life. You must write many *shastras*, preach dharma to many people and then, in the after-death state you will attain perfect siddhi."

BB comments:

"Somewhat happy ending, right? Well, sometimes not as so-it is said that breakage of the 14 and the 8, if not confessed or mended, buys one a ticket on the express to Vajra Hell. One may not always get all those chances like Abhayakaragupta did. Having said all that, if even accomplished masters are vulnerable, I guess I would not feel too bad about breaking a couple of these vows and precepts-I should however be more diligent in applying those restorations and antidotes.

To really maintain these vows, which means either not breaking them in the first place or applying the restoration within the proper time-frame, one really has to almost be in a closed retreat situation.... Divine pride must be maintained every second. The Vajrasattva or Samayasattva Purification has to be done a set number of times each day. Sadhana practices involving empowerment must be done daily if one is doing mainly the Kye Rim; self-initiation must be done daily if Dzog Rim. One must be mindful and re-exam oneself every session of the day to ensure everything is all right or mended. In our everyday life, that's close to impossible.

But Vajrayana is not supposed to be a safe and cozy path anyway; any attempt to hang it out as something as peaceful and comfortable (like the Shravakayana and, to a lesser degree, Paramitayana) is doing nobody a favour. A correct understanding of its gravity and rigor would enable one to:

1. Make an intelligent decision as to whether to undertake it- remember that Vajrayana is not the only game in town;
2. Not be influenced by charlatans and fake Vajrayana "masters" who spin a whole lot more out of "Samaya"

and use it to abuse and exploit; and

3. Strive and make real progress on the Path, instead of cheating oneself with the false-comfort that all vows are intact and one is on the express to Bhumi-land.

See, we are not all right-otherwise we would not be here in Samsara-but it is all right to be not all right. We just need to work at it harder.

CLASSIFICATION OF BUDDHIST TANTRAS

Traleg Kyabgon Rinpoche's *Essence of Buddhism* includes *Levels of Tantra* (138) from a Kagyu point of view:

LEVELS OF TANTRA

Vajrayana practices, or tantric teachings, have been systematized into four categories, and practitioners are encouraged to follow them in a systematic and gradual way. The relationship that exists between the visualized deities and the practitioner will go through different transitions, depending upon the level of Tantra with which the person engages. Even the natures of the visualized deities are different; they may be wrathful or peaceful, for example.

KRIYA TANTRA

The first level of Tantra is Kriya Tantra, or *bya gyü* in Tibetan. Kriya emphasizes the performance of rituals. Three different Buddha families are mentioned at the Kriya tantric level: the Padma, or Lotus family; the Vajra family; and the Tathagathas or family of the Buddhas. At this level, the relationship between practitioner and deity is essentially unequal. We see ourselves as being deluded, while the deity is worshipped as having all the power to impart wisdom.

CHARYA TANTRA

The next stage is Charya Tantra, or *chö gyu*. Charya emphasizes the importance of both meditative states and ritual observances. At that level, there is no longer the same sense of inequality as with Kriya Tantra. The deities are seen as friends' more than exalted beings, even while having little in common with the practitioner in terms of qualities. At that Charya level, deities are visualized as having two aspects, relative and absolute. The absolute nature of visualized deities is understood to be no different from one's own Buddha-nature, or the nature of Mind. The basic point is that the visualizations are not absolute since they are understood as projections of the mind.

ANUYOGA TANTRA

The next level is Anuyoga Tantra, or *jesu naljor gyü*. Here one relies less and less on relative truth and aims towards absolute truth. At the Anuyoga level, it is said that one must have developed bodhichitta and taken the Bodhisattva vow, for without it one cannot continue the practice. Anuyoga deals with delusions and defilements directly, so that they can be transformed into the Five Wisdoms.

When understood properly, these very delusions can be transformed into wisdom, and therefore the delusions are the very material that constitutes what is meant by wisdom. There is no sharp distinction between what should be abandoned and what should be cultivated at this stage. If one knows how to deal with things that normally give rise to delusions, one can gain insight and wisdom instead.

SUPREME YOGA TANTRA: BECOMING A TOTAL PERSON

The final level of Tantra is Mah'anuttarayoga Tantra, or *la-me chenpo'i gyü*, is considered to be the supreme level. It is also the most difficult one to practice. Unlike the other Tantras, on this level the practitioner deals directly with his or her conflicting emotions through practices such as the visualization of wrathful deities.

SYSTEMS OF CLASSIFICATION

Je Tsongkhapa wrote extensively about the issue of the several ways of classifying the tantras in his *Ngakrim Chenmo* and some other important works. He showed that there is not only one system, but many, and none is necessarily better than another. Amongst contemporary teachers and writers, Vidyadhara Chogyam Trungpa dealt with the topic several times, in books such as *Journey Without a Goal* and *The Lion's Roar*.

The Nyingma denominations organizes the tantras into 6 levels (3 Outer and 3 Inner) based on the level of accomplishment and the view of Emptiness/awareness. In the Kagyu tradition, the way the Outer Tantras are classed and labeled is not much different from that of the Nyingma; for the Inner Tantras, the differences are more pronounced. To begin with, the Tantras referred to by Nyingmapa as Inner Tantras are not even the same as those included in the Kagyupa's Anuttarayoga Tantra, a label that adds to the confusion since the Nyingma use it to refer to their Inner Tantras.

This is only natural, for the collections came to Tibet in two separate periods of translation. The Anuttarayoga Tantras include the five major ones: *Guhyasamaja* (Secret Gathering), *Yamantaka* (Death Conqueror), *Hevajra* (Hail, Vajra!), *Mahamaya* (Great Play of Illusion) and *Chakrasamsavra* (Wheel of Great Bliss.) The now famous *Kalachakra Tantra* (Wheel of Time) was apparently a later addition, but is in no way inferior to the others." The second difference lies in the way the classification is done. Unlike [method of classification of] the Nyingmapas, the further sub-division of the Anuttarayoga Tantras is not based on view or accomplishment; instead it is based on the object and method.

Since we are troubled by the Three Poisons [*kleshas*] of Ignorance, Passion and Aggression, and since the Tantras are to help us "get over" them, certain Tantras were taught and developed to focus more on one Poison versus another. However, it should be pointed out that it is all a matter of emphasis-ultimately, it does not mean that a Tantra is somehow "lacking" in any particular way.

Anuttarayoga Tantras are classified as either *Mother*, *Father* or *Non-dual*.

Father Tantra [comprises]: Anuttarayoga Tantra practices utilizing mainly aggression as the path, focusing on the emptiness aspect of Buddhanature. Examples of Father

Tantras include Guhyasamaja and Yamantanka, as well as the practices of "illusory body" and of dream yoga.

Mother Tantra: Anuttarayoga Tantra which utilize desire as the path, focus on the luminosity of Buddha-nature. Examples include *Chakrasamvara, tummo* [heat/energy generation], and clear light yoga.

Non-dual Tantra: Anuttarayoga Tantra practices utilizing equally, desire and anger, act as an antidote to the 3rd poison which is ignorance. They place equal focus on the luminosity and emptiness aspects of Buddha-nature. Examples include Kalachakra, Hevajra and the yoga of the Bardo.

So, for example, if you are a person with a short fuse, who gets angry all the time, it is sometimes beneficial to take advantage of that "natural" propensity by pursuing the Father Tantras. Then, in some of the illusory body practices... you don't have to exert yourself too much to gain accomplishments.

When it gets to the top [advanced tantras] however, there is little if any difference between taking the aggression path versus taking the passion path-it is all the same: non-duality of luminosity and emptiness. Also, different traditions interpret and classify the Tantras differently. For example, Je Rinpoche puts Hevajra under "Mother" instead of "Non-dual." Furthermore, the labels used for these practices may be different, e.g., in *Dzogrim* practices, the Guhyasamaja mentions Speech Isolation, Body Isolation, and so on, instead of 'Six Dharmas.'

While the Kagyu Lineages are especially adept at *Chakrasamvara,* they also maintain lineages of Guhyasamaja, Hevajra and Kalachakra Tantras. Whether they have Mahamaya and Yamantaka, I am not sure. One last point about the Nyingma/Kagyu difference is that the Nyingma also talk about Father, Mother and Non-dual Tantras, using them to refer to the three yogas within the Inner Tantras-Father for Maha-, Mother for Anu- and Non-Dual for Ati-. [For us, this may be] Kind of confusing, but they have their valid points there too."

REQUIREMENTS

Kyabje Kalu Rinpoche, who served for many years as the Chief of Meditation of the Kagyu denomination explained, in his *Gently Whispered* (New York: Station Hill, 1994):

"Most tantrayana or vajrarana visualization and mantra practices require that an initiation and subsequent authorization and instruction be given by a qualified lama before the *sadhana,* or ritual practice, can begin. However, a few practices, those that were given publicly by Lord Buddha Shakyamuni, do not fall under such restrictions. Very definitely, all the practices given in the Sutras have the full blessing of the Buddha and therefore can be practiced if one has the aspiration to do so.

Such practices include those of the noble Chenrezig and of the mother of the Buddhas, Green Tara. Naturally, whenever it is possible for you to take the vajrayana initiation of Chenrezig or Green Tara, you are encouraged to do so. Right now, however, the practice in which I am giving you instruction can be practiced straight away, due wholly to the blessing of Buddha Shakyamuni. When you finally do get around to receiving the Chenrezig initiation, it will deepen your practice and strengthen your connection with your *tsaway* [root] lama and with Yidam Chenrezig." The book, whose title appears at the start of this quotation, has a complete *sadhana* of Chenrezi.

Samaya is the bond, commitment or duty that is the consequence of any initiation or empowerment. It ties the practitioner to his or her teacher, to the practice and to the tantric deity. There are levels of *samaya.* In the narrowest sense, it may be the commitment to do the practice regularly, to say a series of mantras or do some other activity.

2

The Vajrayana in the Perspective of the three Vehicles

Tibetan Buddhism has many techniques of meditation practice. All of these practices are concerned with defusing our ego, negative emotions, and fixed ideas, and revealing our Buddha Nature. Tibetan Buddhism has developed an orderly, integrated system of practice that has been tried and verified in the experience of meditators and enlightened beings for over a thousand years. This approach can be summed up in the Three Vehicles (Yanas) of Buddhism. These vehicles are practiced simultaneously, but can also be presented sequentially as a guide to learning the practices of Tibetan Buddhism.

In general, it is suggested that you lay a good foundation for yourself by progressing gradually. None of this is set in stone, but for someone seeking some guidance for how to begin and continue with Buddhist practice, the following is offered as a rule of thumb. Best of all is to make contact with teachers and practicioners in an authentic lineage of Buddhism and learn from them.

This overview of Buddhist practice is presented in three sections:

1. Getting Started (Hinayana)
2. Going Deeper (Mahayana)
3. Entering the Mandala (Vajrayana)

and finally, a section on How Do I Know If Practice Is Working for Me?

GETTING STARTED (HINAYANA)

The Hinayana is the foundation of all Buddhist practice. Generally, we begin with meditation as a way to calm our minds and experience peace. As we begin to extend the peace we find in meditation into our daily lives, the practice of ethics becomes important as a way to maintain and develop our spiritual growth. Meditation and ethics are practiced by anyone, but someone who begins to have a certain level of understanding and appreciation of the Buddhist teachings may choose to formally become a Buddhist, through the ceremony called "taking Refuge".

SITTING MEDITATION

We begin to defuse our attachment, aggression and ignorance and to dissolve our ego through sitting meditation, called shamatha (Tib. shinay) or "Calm Abiding". Shamatha meditation is the basic practice of sitting meditation common to all Buddhist traditions. Normally our minds are very busy and restless, thinking about what we want to happen or worrying about what we are afraid might happen, or we just get bored and "tune out". When we are upset, we find it very difficult to control our minds, to let go of what's bothering us and just be happy.

Through shamatha meditation, you learn to relax and calm your mental restlessness, and gain more control over your mind. When you let go of distractions and worries, you can experience a state of happiness and inner contentment that doesn't depend on whether things are going OK in your life or not. Another result of meditation is that as your mind becomes calmer, you see things more clearly. Through meditation you develop a more relaxed perspective on life that is known as vipashyana (Tib. lhagtong) or "insight".

BUDDHIST ETHICS

The main practice in daily life (which we can call "post-meditation" practice) is to behave in a mindful and ethical manner at all times. Buddhist ethics primarily involve not harming other beings. Through meditation, we develop *mindfulness*, and through *restraint*, we refrain from acting on our harmful impulses. Sometimes people formalize their commitment to ethical behavior by taking Lay Precepts, which encourage the practitioner not to (1) kill, (2) lie, (3) steal, (4) commit sexual misconduct or (5) take intoxicants, as a way to reduce the harm we cause ourselves and others, and to pacify much of the agitation in our minds for meditation.

A famous summary of the Buddha's teachings, given by the Buddha himself, goes:

"Abandon non-virtue;

Practice virtue;

Purify the mind-

This is the teaching of the Buddha."

REFUGE

Basic sitting meditation can be practiced by anyone, whether you are Buddhist or not. However, after practicing a while and learning more about Buddhism, some people decide to make a more formal commitment to studying and practicing the Buddhist tradition. This commitment is called "Taking Refuge". It represents a decision to orient your life to spiritual practice, based on confidence in the Buddha and his teachings.

This commitment is symbolized by the Refuge Ceremony, which is the formal ceremony that "officially" makes you a Buddhist. The tradition of receiving refuge from a teacher goes all the way back to the Buddha himself. When you take refuge, you become part of a 2,500 year old tradition of Buddhist practicioners. Through the ceremony, you are acknowledging your confidence in the Buddha as a teacher, the Dharma as the path, and the Sangha or community of realized teachers as the support along the path.

The commitments of refuge include:

1. To respect images of the Buddha and not to take refuge in beings that causes you to harm others. From the Buddhist point of view, there is nothing wrong with a

Christian taking refuge in Buddhism, because these approaches are very compatible. But animal sacrifice is out!

2. To respect Dharma texts, and not to harm any living being, to the best of your ability. The ideal of non-violence is the fundamental principle shared by all Buddhists.
3. To respect Buddhist practicioners, and to avoid associating with people who undermine your spiritual practice. Your own spiritual practice will benefit tremendously by associating with other people who are also genuinely committed to the spiritual path. And while it is possible to get started learning about Buddhism through books, you will eventually need to find a qualified teacher to take your farther on the path.

GOING DEEPER (MAHAYANA)

Shamatha meditation tames the mind, and provides a "vacation" from negative emotions. But to really permanently uproot the negative habits of mind that cause us suffering, we need to go farther and train the mind in compassion and emptiness, which are the true antidotes to ego, the root of all suffering. The mind that realizes compassion and emptiness is called bodhicitta, and one powerful practice for developing bodhicitta is tonglen or "sending and receiving" meditation.

BODHICITTA

Once we have some experience of the nature of our minds settled in peace through meditation, we realize that all beings share this same nature equally. All beings become equally dear to us, and we wish for all beings to be happy and free from suffering. This marks an important turning point in the maturity of the spiritual practitioner, who up until now may have been focused primarily on their own peace and happiness. The generation of the compassionate wish to benefit other beings is called bodhicitta, and also contributes to our own spiritual growth. It powerfully defuses our ego, removing negativity and helping our positive qualities to shine out.

We develop compassion through reflecting that all beings are equally dear to us. They are all exactly like us in wanting happiness and wanting to be free from suffering, although in their confusion they only create the causes of more suffering in their lives. And from the Buddhist perspective of rebirth, all beings have been our mothers, fathers, children and dear ones in countless lifetimes, so they all deserve our love and compassion now. Bodhicitta involves both intention, which is developed through meditation, and action. In our daily lives, we practice compassion in action through the Six Perfections (paramitas) of generosity, ethics, patience, effort, meditation, and wisdom. The practice of compassion and the six perfections helps to counteract ego-clinging and purify the mind, so that wisdom spontaneously arises.

The Kagyu lineage teaches two main meditation techniques to develop compassion for beginners: Sending and Receiving (Tonglen) and the Chenrezig sadhana. Sending and receiving is discussed next, while Chenrezig is discussed in the section on Vajrayana.

SENDING AND RECEIVING (TONGLEN)

After you have some grounding in Shamatha meditation and some taste of the tranquility of mind that results from meditation, you generally begin working with practices to develop compassion. One of the main practices is called "Sending and Receiving" or Tonglen. Through this meditation practice, we practice exchanging ourselves for others, putting ourselves "in their shoes" and developing compassion for them. Tonglen is a simple meditation practice where you imagine taking on the sufferings of others and sending them your own merit and happiness.

It is a powerful practice for dissolving ego, which wants exactly the opposite, of course-to keep all happiness for ourselves and send all negativity to others! The main post-meditation practice accompanying Tonglen is called "Mind Training" (Tib. Lojong). It consists of a series of slogans to study and integrate into your daily life.

ENTERING THE MANDALA (VAJRAYANA)

Through practicing meditation and developing compassion, our view of the world begins to change. Our ordinary, confused perception of the world is called "samsara". In a very real sense, "nirvana" is just a change in perspective-developing a more enlightened outlook. Achieving nirvana doesn't mean that we abandon this world for a better one. In fact, two beings can be sitting side by side, whether on a peaceful retreat or in the middle of a traffic jam in a busy city, and one could be experiencing samsara while the other experiences nirvana.

Vajrayana practice is based on the recognition that nirvana is here now, if we could only change our perception. Our confused perception actually is not based in how things really are. By developing pure perception of our world and the beings in it, a practice known as deity yoga, we can rapidly transform our perception and unlock our enlightened potential. We also practice resting in the nature of the mind, which is called mahamudra (or dzogchen in the Nyingma tradition).

Because these practices are so powerful, they are generally preceded by ngondro or the preliminary practices which help prepare the mind of the practitioner so that these practices can be effective. In the Kagyu lineage, these practices may also be supplemented by advanced yoga practices known as the Six Yogas of Naropa, which are primarily taught in retreat settings. Mahamudra and the Six Yogas of Naropa are held to be the distinctive teachings of the Kagyu lineage.

DEITY YOGA

The main way that we transform our perception in Vajrayana is through practicing sadhanas. A sadhana is a guided meditation that is usually chanted in Tibetan. Sadhanas include prayers to yidams, usually translated as "deities". These deities are not gods in the Western sense, but are enlightened beings that represent the potential for enlightenment that we all have. There are many different yidams, male and female, and each one represents a different aspect of enlightenment.

For example, Chenrezig (Skt. Avalokiteshvara) is the bodhisattva of compassion. No matter how confused, hurt, or angry you might feel now, we all have the potential to be wise, calm and compassionate. This is what Chenrezig represents. Through visualizing Chenrezig, reciting his mantra "OM MANI PEME HUNG", and meditating on compassion and wisdom, you can awaken the compassionate nature of enlightenment that is inherent in your own mind.

Other Sadhana practices you may see at our centers include Green Tara, the female bodhisattva who represents the enlightened activity of the Buddhas, and Medicine Buddha, a Buddha of healing.

MAHAMUDRA: THE NATURE OF MIND

The goal of all Vajrayana practice is recognizing the fundamental enlightened nature of the mind. In the Kagyu lineage, this is known as mahamudra (Tib. Chag Chen), the "Great Seal", which refers to the experience emptiness which "seals" all phenomena. Mahamudra is experiencing the nature of mind as complete openness to experience, without grasping at ego or object. All the practices of the Kagyu lineage aim at developing the experience of Mahamudra in practicioners.

In fact, the goal of ALL Buddhist practice is to experience this basic nature of mind, though it may be called by different names. The Nyingma refer to it as Dzogchen, the "Great Perfection". This experience is also referred to as Prajnaparamita (Transcendent Wisdom), Madhyamaka (the Middle Way), Emptiness (Shunyata), and the Clear Light (Tib. Osel), and so forth.

NGONDRO: THE PRELIMINARY PRACTICES

The practice of Mahamudra or Dzogchen is traditionally preceded by the Preliminary Practices (Ngondro). Ngondro includes extensive repetitions to eliminate negative habits and build up positive habits of mind. In the Kagyu lineage, it includes 100,000 repetitions of each of the following:

1. Prostrations
2. Vajrasattva mantra

3. Mandala offering
4. Guru Yoga.

Ngondro may take several years to complete for Westerners who are busy with jobs and families.

THE 6 YOGAS OF NAROPA

In order to enhance the experience of Mahamudra, the Kagyu lineage has preserved a series of exercises known as the Six Yogas of Naropa. The 6 Yogas include: tummo (heat), clear light, dream yoga, illusory body, bardo and phowa. These advanced teachings are normally restricted and taught during retreat. It is extremely important to learn these practices directly from your teacher, rather than from books.

Buddhist practice will definitely have effects if you practice regularly, with a good motivation. It's a lot like exercising the body. You can't practice once in a while when you feel like it and expect to see progress. And merely reading books about exercise sure won't get you in shape. But if you do even a little bit each day, you will see results.

Although people make progress at different rates, there are several signs that your practice is headed in the right direction:

- You become more relaxed, peaceful, and happy, even in the middle of all the ups and downs of your life;
- You become more patient, tolerant, forgiving, and understanding of others;
- You begin to relax your opinions and fixed ideas about how things are "supposed to be";
- You become more committed to spiritual practice, and your wish to benefit beings grows stronger;
- You begin to experience moments of inspiration and spiritual fulfillment more frequently, and these gradually become a more regular way of being for you.

On the other hand, if your practice makes you more inflexible, opinionated, judgmental and intolerant, this is a sign that you have misunderstood the teachings. Beware-you are moving towards "Ego-hood", not Buddhahood! You need to re-examine your motivation for spiritual practice.

It is a common mistake to do a little practice, and think you are a great practitioner; understand a little bit, and think you understand a lot; accumulate intellectual knowledge, and think you don't have to practice; have a few intense experiences, and think you have realization.

Instead of using the Dharma to build up our ego and self-importance, we need to have the attitude that we are like patients, and the Dharma is like medicine. If we want to see any benefit from our practice, we must actually take the medicine and apply the teachings to ourselves in our daily life.

The most important test of your spiritual practice is to look at your own life and see whether your self-centeredness, negative emotions, and fixed opinions are diminishing, and whether you are becoming more peaceful, loving, and compassionate in your daily life. If our spiritual practice makes us more judgmental of others, it is only a sign of our own lack of compassion and spiritual maturity. It is said that we must use the teachings as a mirror, to examine ourselves, not as a window, to judge others.

However, don't get discouraged when you look in the mirror! We all have a lot of negativity and confusion. That's exactly why we need to practice-otherwise we would already be Buddhas. It is important to remember that no matter how much confusion and negativity you may see in your life, your basic nature is loving and compassionate and wise and pure. Through practice you will gradually get in touch with that nature more and more. You've been confused for a long time-don't expect instant results! As a Kagyu teacher once said, "I make mistake after mistake, but I know I'm on the right path!"

IMPORTANCE OF LAMA

The tantric texts often mention that all realisations come from the guru. This is true, but we have to understand that 'guru' has two different levels of meaning. The relative, objective guru is the teacher who, by communicating with us in different ways, shows us how to act so that we can discover our own totality. But on a deeper, more subjective level, our guru is none other than our own inner wisdom, our own fundamental clarity of mind. Look at the different ways in which people respond to the same spiritual teachings by the same teacher. One person may not even understand intellectually the concepts contained in the teaching.

Another may be able to understand them but be unable to penetrate their inner meaning. And there are those who can reach beyond the mere words and concepts and experience total unification with the teacher's wisdom and compassion. These reactions are all due to the various individuals' have achieved different levels of intellectual and spiritual evolution. The more in touch they are with their own internal guru, the more profound their understanding of the teachings will be. Practically speaking, there is only so much the relative, external guru can do for us; he or she cannot guarantee that we gain insight and realisations. But our inner guru, our own clear wisdom, can accomplish everything. The practice of guru-yoga, therefore, is primarily a method for learning how to listen to this inner guru.

Ordinarily, even though we do posses this inner voice of wisdom, we do not listen to it. We do not even hear it! We are too busy listening to the garbage conversation of our gross dualistic minds. We are so accustomed to this that even when wisdom does arise, as an intuitive insight, we often reject it. By practising guru-yoga we are able progressively to cut through our superficial ways of relating to the world and make contact with the innate wisdom at the heart of our being. When we have done this, then we can communicate deeply with the outer guru as well. But as long as we are out of touch without inner guru, no matter how profound the teachings of the outer guru may be, we will never be able to integrate them.

But we should not interpret this to mean that the external, relative guru is unimportant. This is not true; he or she is vitally important. Although it is true that the tantric teachings of Shakyamuni Buddha have been in existence for 2500 years, do they exist for us if we have not yet met a qualified tantric master? Are they real for us or not? Despite the extensive explanations of such realised adepts as Naropa, Marpa and Tsong Khapa, can we say that tantra is a reality for us before someone has introduced it to us?

Of course not. And the same is true for the teachings of sutra as well; the fact that Buddha taught the Four Noble Truths a long time ago does not make them true for us. They only become part of our reality once we have realised them, and this depends upon having met a guru who can show us their truth clearly in a way we can understand. If we do not have the living example and inspiration of the external guru, our inner wisdom remain weak and undeveloped.

THE SPIRITUAL GUIDE AND MODEL

For the teachings of enlightened beings to reach us and for their insights to make an impression on our mind, there should be an unbroken lineage of successive gurus and disciples carrying these living insights down to the present day. As a member of this lineage, the spiritual guide who makes the Four Noble Truths come alive for you does so through his or her inspiration or blessings. Familiar with your character and aptitudes, such a guide can make these noble truths so clean clear for you that your mind itself becomes the path of realisation.

This is what is meant by inspiration or blessing, just this. And the practice of guru-yoga, or guru devotion, is nothing more than opening ourselves to this inspiration. Furthermore, we need an experienced guide to show us exactly how to put the teachings we receive into practice. We will not get anywhere if we try to learn from a book, hoping to figure things out by ourselves. The information may all be there, but nearly all tantric texts are cryptic, revealing their meaning only when studied together with the explanations of skilled practitioners, and it is not easy to know just how to go about implementing this information.

We need someone to show us, to give us a practical demonstration. This person is the guru. The need for such an experienced guide is crucial when it comes to following tantra because tantra is a very technical, internally technical, system of development. We have to be shown how everything fits together until we actually feel it for ourselves. Without the proper guidance we would be as confused as someone who instead of getting a Rolls Royce gets only a pile of unassembled parts and an instruction book. Unless the person was already a highly skilled mechanic, he or she would be completely lost.

The main reason that religion in both the East and the West has degenerated so much nowadays is the rarity of meeting good spiritual examples. If people never meet highly realised beings they have no way of knowing the limitless possibilities of their own human consciousness. It is not enough that there are texts recording the deeds and accomplishments of past masters. By themselves, such stories cannot inspire us very much. In fact, they may only increase our feeling of remoteness: 'Buddha and Jesus lived such a long time ago', we may think, 'and their purity belongs to another age. It is impossible for someone like me living in this degenerate twentieth century to attain anything resembling their level of purity.' Or we may reject these accounts of past masters completely, dismissing them as fairy tales fit only for gullible children. The only way we can lay to rest these feelings of doubt, incapability and cynicism is by coming face-to-face with someone who has activated his or her highest potential. Only then do we have an example of purity and spiritual evolution that we can actually see and relate to ourselves. Thus the outer guru is of utmost importance.

We need the example of someone who, while human like ourselves, has developed beyond the bounds of what we presently think possible. When we see someone who has reached beyond selfishness, who has transcended the petty concerns of this world while still living in the world, who speaks and acts from intuitive wisdom and who is truly dedicated to the welfare of others, then we can have faith and conviction that these attainments are possible for ourselves as well. Otherwise, if our only models are those of greed and aggression, our vision of what we are and what we can become will be sadly limited. A good model is important not only for those interested in following a spiritual path.

The most urgent need in the world today is for peace and harmony, and we all feel this need, whether we call ourselves religious or not. But peace cannot be brought about through mere words, and it certainly will not come about through force. Instead, we need the example of those who have made peace and harmony the centre of their lives. It is only the example of such people, living lives of strength and purity that will convince a disillusioned world that peace - internal and external - is truly possible here and now. So far the broad masses of the public in Tibet have remained in a distressed state as a result of the deprivation of their freedoms.

Nevertheless, even when faced with dangers to their lives, they have, in every respect, remained steadfast in upholding the higher cause of their ethnicity and the common faith in their future prospects, keeping in mind their rights as a people. It is for these reasons that we have an audience on the world stage to which we can speak about the tragedy and well being of Tibet and what we say are received with respect as true. The principal asset for our credibility on the world stage is the people back in Tibet-their dedication to the common cause, indefatigable courage, and steadfast stand. It is because of these that the truth of our position stands proven.

We therefore owe gratitude to the people in Tibet for their genuine dedication to the common cause and unassailable commitment to the common faith that binds them with us. In future, too, the question whether in this world a unique people called the inhabitants of the Snowland of Tibet, and the profound culture and religion connected with them, would survive and thrive depends mainly on the people living in Tibet.

Thinking from the opposite end, it is not impossible that the situation of the Tibetan people in Tibet will take such a tragic turn that they will become a minority in their own land. In such a situation, if those in Tibet fail to uphold the common aspiration of the Tibetan race, it will be extremely difficult for us in exile to be able to maintain the Tibetan ethnic identity and to carry out things like keeping, defending and spreading the Tibetan religion and culture beyond some generations. Things will be just all right during my generation in exile.

After that, there will be another generation. It is possible that the situation will be fairly all right during their time. But it is impossible to say whether beyond that generation the situation will be good or bad. Extreme dangers lurk us in our future. The essential point is that the people living in Tibet are extremely important. In view of this, what is most important is that everyone should act with diligence, without any loss of determination. One of the main ways of being diligent is to pay particular attention to the pursuit of knowledge. The world is undergoing an enormous transformation today.

Even in the communist ruled countries, knowledge is considered important. Previously, during the Cultural Revolution, it was as if knowledge had lost all respect and value. But today, in the case of China, the situation is nothing like in the 1960s. Reports have also been emerging that even North Korea has, for example, been compelled to give importance to the value of modern knowledge. So, when I say that we should make efforts without loss of courage, the essence of it is that we must bring emphasis particularly on education.

Our freedom campaign is based on non-violence. Following the path of non-violence is the business capital and pride of our campaign. If we do not have truth on our side, we will have no alternative but to keep suffering. Having truth on one's side gives one the pride to be transparent about everything and to speak reason in a face-to-face exchange. It is on the basis of knowledge that truth must be vindicated by non-violent means. There is no way this task can be accomplished by just an act of taking a solemn oath. In the area of modern knowledge, Tibetans have lagged extremely behind. Not only was the imperative for it not felt from the very beginning, there has also been no deliberately established system for pursuing it.

His Holiness the 13th Dalai Lama visited China in 1907, 1908, etc., and India during the period of 1910-1911 and witnessed many things about the outside world. As a result, from 1915 to 1920, he made such sound beginnings as sending some Tibetan students to countries like England with plans to have them study English and to acquire related modern mechanical skills and knowledge. However, he did not succeed in continuing these. These are matters of extreme regret. Anyway, although the 13th Dalai Lama had a broad vision for reforms, there were many internal and external elements and obstacles that rendered his efforts fruitless.

In 1960, the year after we arrived in exile in India in April 1959, we were able to speedily set up our first school in Mussoorie. Considerable effort was made to set up schools to give opportunities for modern education to the Tibetans in exile. In particular, in the early 1960s, many initiatives were taken to give more importance to setting up schools than monasteries in the Tibetan community in exile. The main reason why we especially devoted more attention to setting up schools was because it was extremely obvious that one cause of the miserable situation in which the Tibetan race found itself in was attributable to our major failure of being up to the standard in the field of modern knowledge.

This resulted in our inability to set out strategies as a people at par with the rest of the world; it exposed us as too backward to be able to meet the challenges of modern times. It was in view of this that we considered setting up schools to be more important than building religious centres. The public back in Tibet too should draw lessons from this and consider paying attention to the pursuit of modern knowledge as extremely important. In Tibet today there is a big problem in this area, including the fact that one has to pay high fees for educating one's children.

Nevertheless, undaunted by both the internal and external hardships, they continue to send their children to schools, whether they are being run by the Chinese government or by private Tibetans. Everywhere in Dotoe, Domey and U-Tsang, Tibetans in large numbers are emerging, putting in their best efforts and bringing out whatever capabilities they have in the field of learning. To them all I express rejoice and offer praise for efforts well made. Whatever be the case, making efforts in the field of education is highly important.

In the case of schools in Tibet set up by the Chinese, it would be extremely narrow-minded to show disdain for them by such actions as not sending one's children to study there. Schools, even if set up by the Chinese government, are good. In order to ensure good standard of the teaching of Tibetan and other subjects in them, it should be possible to discuss the matter with concerned persons and entities. Whatever be the case, all Tibetans should make efforts in every possible way. There are many aspects of modern education.

They include science, law, economics, environment, etc. Nevertheless, the Tibetan language has not progressed in these numerous subjects. In India, efforts are being made to teach the Tibetan children all the subjects in Tibetan language from Grade I onwards. But, leave alone Tibetans, even the Indians find it most difficult to gain expertise in specialised modern subjects without pursuing it in English. In Tibet too, one has no choice but to rely on Chinese language to gain expertise in a specialised field of modern knowledge. Whether for becoming a professional or an expert researcher, in the different fields of modern knowledge in Tibet today, it is extremely important to use the Chinese language to achieve the required specialisations.

We are today struggling for a meaningful autonomy for Tibet. But in order to achieve an appropriate standard of it, our own people should be able to fully take responsibility in every possible area of undertaking related to it and to be able to produce results. There is no way merely engaging in debates will be sufficient. We ourselves must be able to argue for and administer the autonomy. The essence of this is that we must be able to do our own work by ourselves. In order to achieve both internal and external progresses appropriate for modern times, having modern education is extremely important.

The reality of the situation in Tibet today is such that one has no choice but to rely on Chinese language if one is to become modern educated. One thing that comes to my mind is this: Suppose there are a hundred Tibetan students. Seventy or eighty such students could study Tibetan language as their main subject and achieve excellence in projecting one's national identity and in preserving our cultural heritage. Twenty or thirty such students could study Chinese language as their main subject and make efforts to achieve professional qualifications in modern specialised subjects.

14TH DALAI LAMA

His Holiness the Dalai Lama was born in a peasant family on July 6th, 1935, in a small village called Taktser in north eastern Tibet. His Holiness was recognised at the age of two as the reincarnation of his predecessor the 13th Dalai Lama. When the 13th Dalai Lama passed away in 1935, the task that confronted the Tibetan Government was not simply to appoint a successor but to search for and discover a child in whom the Buddha of Compassion would incarnate. In 1935 the Regent of Tibet went to the sacred lake of Lhamo Lhatso at Chokhorgyal, about 90 miles south east of Lhasa, the capital of Tibet. For centuries the Tibetans had observed that visions of the future could be seen in this lake.

The Regent had a vision of three Tibetan letters, Ah, Ka, and Ma, followed by a picture of a monastery with roofs of jade green and gold, and a house with turquoise tiles. In 1937 high lamas and dignitaries carrying the secrets of the vision were sent to all parts of Tibet in search of the place that the Regent had seen in the waters. The search party that headed east was under the leadership of Lama Kewtsang Rinpoche of Sera Monastery. When they arrived in Amdo, they found a place matching the description of the secret vision. The party went to the house with Kewtsang Rinpoche disguised as the servant, and junior official Lobsang Tsewang disguised as the leader. The Rinpoche was wearing a rosary that had belonged to the 13th Dalai Lama, and the little boy of the house recognised it and demanded that it be given to him.

Kewtsang Rinpoche promised to give it to him if he could guess who he was, and the boy replied that he was "Sera aga", which means in the local dialect "a lama of Sera". Then the Rinpoche asked who the leader was and the boy gave his name correctly; he also knew the name of the real servant. This was followed by a series of tests that included the choosing of correct articles that had belonged to the 13th Dalai Lama. With these tests they were further convinced that the reincarnation had been found and their conviction was enhanced by the significance of the three letters that had been seen in the lake of Lhamo Lhatso: Ah could stand for Amdo, the name of the province; Ka for Kumbum, one of the largest monasteries in the neighbourhood; and the two letters Ka and Ma for the monastery of Karma Rolpai Dorje on the mountain above the village. In 1940 the XIVth Dalai Lama was enthroned.

Jetsun Jamphel Ngawang Lobsang Yeshe Tenzin Gyatso is the 14th Dalai Lama. He is a spiritual leader revered among Tibetans, and the head of the government-in-exile based in Dharamshala, India. Tibetans traditionally believe him to be the reincarnation of his predecessors. The Dalai Lama was born fifth of 16 children to a farming family in the village of Taktser, in the Qinghai province of the Republic of China. His first language was the regional Amdo dialect. He was proclaimed the *tulku* or rebirth of the 13th Dalai Lama at the age of two. In 1950 the army of the People's Republic of China invaded the region.

One month later, on 17 November 1950, he was formally enthroned as Dalai Lama. He thus, at the age of fifteen, became the region's most important spiritual leader and political ruler. In 1951, the Chinese military pressured the Dalai Lama to ratify a seventeen-point agreement which permitted the People's Republic of China to take control of Tibet. He fled through the mountains to India following the failed 1959 uprising, and the effective collapse of the Tibetan resistance movement. In India he set up a government-in-exile.

The most influential figure of the Gelugpa or Yellow Hat Sect, he has considerable influence over the other sects of Tibetan Buddhism. The Chinese goverment regards him as the symbol of an outmoded theocratic system. Along with the 80,000 or so exiles that followed him, the Dalai Lama strives to preserve traditional Tibetan education and culture. Circumstances in Tibet have in more recent years sparked an international protest movement, including the attempted disruption of the 2008 Olympic Games. In March 2008 the Dalai Lama called for an international inquiry into China's treatment of Tibet, which he said amounted to cultural genocide.

A noted public speaker worldwide, the Dalai Lama is often described as charismatic. He is the first Dalai Lama to travel to the West, where he seeks to spread Buddhist teachings and to promote ethics and interfaith harmony. In 1989 he was awarded the Nobel Peace Prize. He was given honorary Canadian citizenship in 2006, and was awarded the United States Congressional Gold Medal in October 2007. He has received more than 100 honorary conferments and major awards. On 17 December 2008, after months of speculation, the Dalai Lama announced his semi-retirement.

He said that the future course of the movement he had led for nearly five decades would now be decided by the elected parliament-in-exile under the Prime Minister Samdhong Rinpoche. The 73-year-old Nobel laureate, who had recently undergone surgery, told reporters in Dharamshala, "I have grown old.... It is better if I retire completely and get out of the way of the Tibetan movement."

Lhamo Döndrub (or *Thondup*) was born on 6 July 1935 to a farming family in the small hamlet of Taktser in the Tibetan region of Amdo (administered officially since 1928 as part of Qinghai province of China.) He was one of nine to survive childhood. The eldest was his sister Tsering Dolma, eighteen years older. His eldest brother, Thupten Jigme Norbu, had been recognised at the age of eight as the reincarnation of the high lama Taktser Rinpoche. His sister Jetsun Pema years later depicted their mother in the 1997 film *Seven Years in Tibet*.

Tibetans traditionally believe Dalai Lamas to be the reincarnation of their predecessors, each of whom is believed to be a human emanation of the bodhisattva Avalokitesvara. A search party was sent out to locate the new incarnation when the boy who was to become the 14th was about two years old. It is said that, amongst other omens, the head of the embalmed body of the thirteenth Dalai Lama, at first facing south-east, had mysteriously turned to face the northeast-indicating the direction in which his successor would be found.

The Regent, Reting Rinpoche, shortly afterwards had a vision at the sacred lake of Lhamo La-tso indicating Amdo as the region to search-specifically a one-story house with distinctive guttering and tiling. After extensive searching, the Thondup house, with its features resembling those in Reting's vision, was finally found. The little boy was presented with various relics, including toys, some of which had belonged to the 13th Dalai Lama and some of which had not. It was reported that he had correctly identified all the items owned by the previous Dalai Lama, exclaiming, "That's mine! That's mine!"

Lhamo Thondup was formally recognized as the reincarnated Dalai Lama and renamed Jetsun Jamphel Ngawang Lobsang Yeshe Tenzin Gyatso (*Holy Lord, Gentle Glory, Compassionate, Defender of the Faith, Ocean of Wisdom*). Tibetan Buddhists normally refer to him as Yishin Norbu (*Wish-Fulfilling Gem*), Kyabgon (*Saviour*), or just Kundun (*Presence*).

Monastic education commenced at the age of six, his principal teachers being Yongdzin Ling Rinpoche (senior tutor) and Yongdzin Trijang Rinpoche (junior tutor). At the age of 11 he met the Austrian mountaineer Heinrich Harrer, having spotted him in Lhasa through his telescope. Harrer effectively became one of the young Dalai Lama's tutors, teaching him about the outside world. The two remained friends until Harrer's death in 2006. In 1959, at the age of 23, he sat his final examination at Lhasa's Jokhang Temple during the annual Monlam or *prayer* Festival. He passed with honours and was awarded the Lharampa degree, the highest-level *geshe* degree, roughly equivalent to a doctorate in Buddhist philosophy.

As well as being the foremost religious figure in Tibet, the Dalai Lama has traditionally been the country's absolute political ruler. In 1939, at the age of four, he was taken in a procession of lamas to Lhasa:

"On 25 November 1939 a nine-member delegation, consisting of staff from the Mongolian and Tibetan Affairs Commission, arrived in Lhasa, and were later joined by Wu Zhongxin, the Commission's director of Tibetan Affairs. The arrival in Lhasa was carefully planned to coincide with the enthronement ceremony for the 14th Dalai Lama. On 22 February 1940, Wu Zhongxin and other foreign representatives attended the ceremony in the Potala..." Later the Kuomintang and the Communists claimed that Wu had *presided* over the ceremony and that his involvement was essential to the recognition of the new Dalai Lama.

"There is no evidence to suggest that Wu Zhongxin presided over the installation of the Dalai Lama. However, the delegation managed to establish a permanent office in Lhasa, and installed a direct radio communication with Nanjing."

The remainder of the Dalai Lama's childhood was spent between the Potala and Norbulingka, his summer residence:

"On 8 July 1949, the Kashag [Tibetan Parliament] called Chen Xizhang, the acting director of the Mongolian and Tibetan Affairs Commission office in Lhasa. He was informed that the Tibetan Government had decided to expel all Chinese connected with the Guomingdang Government. Fearing that the Chinese might organise protests in the streets of Lhasa, the Kashag imposed a curfew until all the Chinese had left. This they did on 14, 17 and 20 July 1949. At the same time the Tibetan Government sent a telegram to General Chiang Kai-shek and to President Liu Zongren informing them of the decision."

On 17 November 1950, with the country facing possible conflict with the People's Republic of China, the 15-year-old Jetsun Jamphel Ngawang Lobsang Yeshe Tenzin Gyatso was formally enthroned as the temporal leader of Tibet.

His governorship was short. In October of that year the army of the People's Republic of China entered the country, breaking through Tibetan defenses with ease. The Dalai Lama sent a delegation to Beijing and, although under PLA military pressure, ratified the subsequent Seventeen Point Agreement for the Peaceful Liberation of Tibet and tried to work with

Beijing. In September 1954, the Dalai Lama and the 10th Panchen Lama went to Beijing to attend the first session of the first National People's Congress, meeting Mao Zedong.

The Dalai Lama was even elected to be the *Vice Chairman* of the Congress. However, during 1959, there was a major uprising among the Tibetan population. In the tense political environment that ensued, the Dalai Lama and his entourage began to suspect that China was planning to kill him. Consequently, he fled to Tawang, India, on 17 March of that year, entering India on 31 March during the Tibetan uprising. Central Intelligence Agency paramilitary teams from their Special Activities Division were responsible for the Dalai Lama's successful clandestine escape from Tibet and the initial resistance fighters in Tibet to the Chinese communist forces.

The Dalai Lama met with the Prime Minister of India, Jawaharlal Nehru, to urge India to pressure China into giving Tibet an autonomous government, as relations with China were not proving successful. Nehru did not want to increase tensions between China and India, so he encouraged the Dalai Lama to work on the Seventeen Point Agreement Tibet had with China. Eventually, after the failed uprising in 1959, the Dalai Lama fled Tibet and set up the Government of Tibet in Exile in Dharamshala, India, which is often referred to as "*Little Lhasa*".

After the founding of the exiled government he reestablished the approximately 80,000 Tibetan refugees who followed him into exile in agricultural settlements. He created a Tibetan educational system in order to teach the Tibetan children the traditional language, history, religion, and culture. The Tibetan Institute of Performing Arts was established in 1959 and the Central Institute of Higher Tibetan Studies became the primary university for Tibetans in India. He supported the refounding of 200 monasteries and nunneries in an attempt to preserve Tibetan Buddhist teachings and the Tibetan way of life. The Dalai Lama appealed to the United Nations on the question of Tibet. This appeal resulted in three resolutions adopted by the General Assembly in 1959, 1961, and 1965.

These resolutions required China to respect the human

rights of Tibetans and their desire for self-determination. In 1963, he promulgated a democratic constitution which is based upon the Universal Declaration of Human Rights. A Tibetan parliament-in-exile is elected by the Tibetan refugees scattered all over the world, and the Tibetan Government-in-Exile is likewise elected by the Tibetan parliament. In 1970, he opened the Library of Tibetan Works and Archives in Dharamshala which houses over 80,000 manuscripts and important knowledge resources related to Tibetan history, politics and culture. It is considered one of the most important institutions for Tibetology in the world.

At the Congressional Human Rights Caucus in 1987 in Washington, D.C., he proposed a Five-Point Peace Plan regarding the future status of Tibet. The plan called for Tibet to become a "zone of peace" and for the end of movement by ethnic Han Chinese into Tibet. It also called for "respect for fundamental human rights and democratic freedoms" and "the end of China's use of Tibet for nuclear weapons production, testing, and disposal." Finally, it urged "earnest negotiations" on the future of Tibet. He proposed a similar plan at Strasbourg on 15 June 1988. He expanded on the Five-Point Peace Plan and proposed the creation of a self-governing democratic Tibet, "in association with the People's Republic of China."

This plan was rejected by the Tibetan Government-in-Exile in 1991. In October 1991, he expressed his wish to return to Tibet to try to make a mutual assessment on the situation with the Chinese local government. At this time he feared that a violent uprising would take place and wished to avoid it. The Dalai Lama has indicated that he wishes to return to Tibet only if the People's Republic of China sets no preconditions for his return, which they have so far refused to do. The Dalai Lama celebrated his seventieth birthday on 6 July 2005.

About 10,000 Tibetan refugees, monks and foreign tourists gathered outside his home. Patriarch Alexius II of the Russian Orthodox Church said, "I confess that the Russian Orthodox Church highly appreciates the good relations it has with the followers of Buddhism and hopes for their further development." Taiwan's President, Chen Shui-bian, attended an evening celebrating the Dalai Lama's birthday that was entitled "Travelling with Love and Wisdom for 70 Years" at the Chiang Kai-shek Memorial Hall in Taipei. The President invited him to return to Taiwan for a third trip in 2005. His previous trips were in 2001, and 1997. In Tibet there is a popular song calling for his return to Tibet called Aku Pema.

TEACHING ACTIVITIES

The Dalai Lama chief spiritual practice is Dzogchen, a subject he teaches and writes about extensively. He has conducted numerous public initiations in the Kalachakra, and is the author of a great number of books. His teaching activities in the US include:

- In July 2008, the Dalai Lama had held a public lecture and conducted a series of teachings at Lehigh University in Bethlehem, Pennsylvania.
- He visited the U.S. in April 2008, when he gave lectures on engaging wisdom and compassion, and sustainability, at the University of Michigan in Ann Arbor and at Colgate University in Hamilton, N.Y.
- In February 2007, the Dalai Lama was named *Presidential Distinguished Professor* at Emory University in Atlanta, Georgia, United States, the first time that the leader of the Tibetan exile community has accepted a university appointment. The appointment is in part an expansion of a program begun in 1998 called the Emory–Tibet Partnership. As Presidential Distinguished Professor, he will:
    - provide opportunities for university community members to attend his annual teachings,
    - make periodic visits to Emory to participate in programmes, and
    - continue the Emory–Tibet Partnership practice of providing private teaching sessions with students and faculty during Emory's study-abroad programme in Dharamshala.

- The Dalai Lama has strong ties with University of Wisconsin-Madison in Madison, Wisconsin, United States, and is a frequent visitor there. He visited the university in 1981 and again in 1989, the year in which he won the Nobel Peace Prize. In May 1998, he addressed a large audience at the Kohl Center and received an honorary degree from the university. He visited Madison again during the summers of both 2007 and 2008, making public appearances at The Kohl Center and Alliant Energy Center, as well as more intimate sessions at the nearby Deer Park Buddhist Center, where Geshe Sopa (the first Tibetan tenured in an American university), whom the Dalai Lama sent to America in 1959 to bridge cultures, resides.
- In May 2001, he met with a group of neuroscientists who conduct research on the effects of meditation on brain function, emotions and physical health.

Since 1967, the Dalai Lama has initiated a series of tours in 46 nations. He has frequently engaged on religious dialogue. He met with Pope Paul VI at the Vatican in 1973. He met with Pope John Paul II in 1980 and also later in 1982, 1986, 1988, 1990, and 2003. In 1990, he met in Dharamsala with a delegation of Jewish teachers for an extensive interfaith dialogue.

He has since visited Israel three times and met in 2006 with the Chief Rabbi of Israel. In 2006, he met privately with Pope Benedict XVI. He has also met the late Archbishop of Canterbury Dr. Robert Runcie, and other leaders of the Anglican Church in London, Gordon B. Hinckley, late President of the Church of Jesus Christ of Latter-day Saints (Mormons), as well as senior Eastern Orthodox Church, Muslim, Hindu, Jewish, and Sikh officials. During the runup to the Beijing Olympics of 2008, the Dalai Lama visited Japan on 10 April 2008 on his way to the United States, amid protests around the world over China's handling of the 2008 Tibetan unrest.

The Dalai Lama, whom Beijing claimed fomented the unrest, called for calm, but the protests showed little sign of abating. The Dalai Lama said he did not support a boycott of the 2008 Summer Games outright. Japan's government had been relatively quiet about the violence in Tibet and, out of deference to Beijing, does not deal officially with the Dalai Lama. Tokyo does, however, grant visas to the spiritual leader, who has visited Japan fairly frequently.

INTERNATIONAL CHILDREN'S VILLAGES

The Dalai Lama has long been a supporter of SOS Children's Villages organization. He often visits the villages, and has maintained a friendship with the founder, Hermann Gmeiner.

He has said of SOS's efforts:

"The splendid work done by SOS Children's Villages is charity where deeds speak louder than words. The revolutionary idea and the general concept developed by Hermann Gmeiner for providing orphaned and abandoned children with a new family and a permanent home has had a great influence on child welfare world-wide, and SOS Children's Villages have become a model on every continent. Above all, SOS Children's Villages shows that it is possible to create a community of brothers and sisters comprising children of all races, creeds and nationalities. The ties that develop and holds these communities together and form the basis of their upbringing is love."

TIBETAN INDEPENDENCE MOVEMENT

The Dalai Lama accepted the 1951 Seventeen Point Agreement for the Peaceful Liberation of Tibet with the People's Republic of China. However, he moved to Kalimpong in India and, with the help of American government organized pro-independence literature and the smuggling of weapons into Tibet. Armed struggles broke out in Amdo and Kham in 1956 and later spread to Central Tibet.

The movement was a failure and was forced to retreat to Nepal or goes underground. Following normalisation of relations between the United States and the People's Republic of China, American support was cut off in the early 1970s. The Dalai Lama then began to formulate his policy towards a peaceful solution in which a democratic autonomous Tibet would be established. In October 1998, the Dalai Lama's administration acknowledged that it received US$1.7 million a year in the 1960s from the U.S. Government through the Central Intelligence Agency (CIA), and had also trained an army in Colorado (USA).

The Dalai Lama has on occasion been denounced by the Chinese government as a supporter of Tibetan independence. Over time, he has developed a public position stating that he is not in favour of Tibetan independence and would not object to a status in which Tibet has internal autonomy while the PRC manages some aspects of Tibet's defense and foreign affairs. In his 'Middle Way Approach', he laid down that the Chinese government can take care of foreign affairs and defense, and that Tibet should be managed by an elected body.

The Dalai Lama on 16 March 2008 called for an international inquiry into China's treatment of Tibet, which he said amounted to cultural genocide. He has stated that he will step down as leader of Tibet's government-in-exile if violence by protesters in the region worsens, the exiled spiritual leader said 18 March 2008 after China's premier Wen Jiabao blamed his supporters for the growing unrest. On 20 March 2008, he claimed he was powerless to stop anti-Chinese violence.

The Dalai Lama 28 March 2008 rejected a series of allegations from the Chinese government, saying he does not seek the separation of Tibet and has no desire to "sabotage" the 2008 Summer Olympics. Critics of the news and entertainment media coverage of the controversy charge that feudal Tibet was not as benevolent as popularly portrayed. The penal code before 1913 included forms of corporal punishment and capital punishment. In response, the Dalai Lama agreed many of old Tibet's practices needed reform. His predecessor had banned extreme punishments and the death penalty.

And he had instituted key reforms like removal of debt inheritance before the Chinese invaded in 1951. On 4 June 2008, Dalai Lama said that Tawang in Arunachal Pradesh, a territory that is called Southern Tibet in mainland China and still claimed by the People's Republic of China, is part of India, acknowledging the validity of the McMahon Line as per the 1914 Simla Agreement signed by Tibetan and British representatives. On 25 October 2008, the Dalai Lama announced he had given up negotiating for increased autonomy for Tibet within the People's Republic of China. He stated that from now on Tibetans themselves should decide how to continue a dialogue with the Chinese government.

INTERFAITH DIALOGUE

On 6 January 2009, at Gujarat's Mahuva, the Dalai Lama inaugurated an interfaith "World Religions-Dialogue and Symphony" conference convened by Hindu preacher Morari Bapu. This conference explored « ways and means to deal with the discord among major religions », according to Morari Bapu.

The Dalai Lama endorsed the founding of the Dalai Lama Foundation in order to promote peace and ethics worldwide. The Dalai Lama is not operationally involved with this foundation, though he suggests some overall direction and his office is routinely briefed on its activities. He has also stated his belief that modern scientific findings take precedence over ancient religions.

The Dalai Lama reminds that according to Buddhist precepts abortion is an act of killing, although he has taken a nuanced position, as he explained to the New York Times:

"Of course, abortion, from a Buddhist viewpoint, is an act of killing and is negative, generally speaking. But it depends on the circumstances. If the unborn child will be retarded or if the birth will create serious problems for the parent, these are cases where there can be an exception. I think abortion should be approved or disapproved according to each circumstance."

"Of all the modern economic theories, the economic system of Marxism is founded on moral principles, while capitalism is concerned only with gain and profitability. Marxism is concerned with the distribution of wealth on an equal basis and the equitable utilization of the means of production. It is also concerned with the fate of the working classes-that is, the majority-as well as with the fate of those who are underprivileged and in need, and Marxism cares about the victims of minority-imposed exploitation. For those reasons the system appeals to me, and it seems fair. I just recently read an article in a paper where His Holiness the Pope Benedict XVI also pointed out some positive aspects of Marxism (though dissapproving of it on the whole).

As for the failure of the Marxist regimes, first of all I do not consider the former USSR, or China, or even Vietnam, to have been true Marxist regimes, for they were far more concerned with their narrow national interests than with the Workers' International; this is why there were conflicts, for example, between China and the USSR, or between China and Vietnam. If those three regimes had truly been based upon Marxist principles, those conflicts would never have occurred.

I think the major flaw of the Marxist regimes is that they have placed too much emphasis on the need to destroy the ruling class, on class struggle, and this causes them to encourage hatred and to neglect compassion. Although their initial aim might have been to serve the cause of the majority, when they try to implement it all their energy is deflected into destructive activities. Once the revolution is over and the ruling class is destroyed, there is not much left to offer the people; at this point the entire country is impoverished and unfortunately it is almost as if the initial aim were to become poor. I think that this is due to the lack of human solidarity and compassion. The principal disadvantage of such a regime is the insistence placed on hatred to the detriment of compassion.

The failure of the regime in the former Soviet Union was, for me, not the failure of Marxism but the failure of totalitarianism. For this reason I still think of myself as half-Marxist, half-Buddhist."

He has also expressed his concern for environmental problems:

"On the global level, I think the ecology problem is very serious. I hear about some states taking it very seriously. That's wonderful! So this blue planet is our only home, if something goes wrong at the present generation, then the future generations really face a lot of problems, and those problems will be beyond human control; so that's very serious. Ecology should be part of our daily life."

In recent years, he has been campaigning for wildlife conservation, including a religious ruling against wearing tiger and leopard skins as garments.

In 2001, he discussed firearms and self-defense, and Hal Bernton, a staff reporter of *The Seattle Times*, reports that:

One girl wanted to know how to react to a shooter who takes aim at a classmate. The Dalai Lama said acts of violence should be remembered, and then forgiveness should be extended to the perpetrators. But if someone has a gun and is trying to kill you, he said, it would be reasonable to shoot back with your own gun. Not at the head, where a fatal wound might result. But at some other body part, such as a leg.

In his view, oral, manual and anal sex (both homosexual and heterosexual) is not acceptable in Buddhism or for Buddhists, but society should tolerate gays and lesbians from a secular point of view. In 1997 he explained that the basis of that teaching was unknown to him and that he at least had some "willingness to consider the possibility that some of the teachings may be specific to a particular cultural and historic context" while reiterating the unacceptable nature saying, "Buddhist sexual proscriptions ban homosexual activity and heterosexual sex through orifices other than the vagina, including masturbation or other sexual activity with the hand... From a Buddhist point of view, lesbian and gay sex is generally considered sexual misconduct".

In a 1994 interview with OUT Magazine, the Dalai Lama explained "If someone comes to me and asks whether homosexuality is okay or not, I will ask 'What is your companion's opinion?'. If you both agree, then I think I would say 'if two males or two females voluntarily agree to have mutual satisfaction without further implication of harming others, then it is okay'". However, in his 1996 book Beyond Dogma, he clearly states, "A sexual act is deemed proper when the couples use the organs intended for sexual intercourse and nothing else....Homosexuality, whether it is between men or between women, is not improper in itself. What is improper is the use of organs already defined as inappropriate for sexual contact." He has said that sex spelled fleeting satisfaction and trouble later, while chastity offered a better life and "more independence, more freedom." He says that problems arising from conjugal life could even lead to suicide or murder.

In Tibet, meat being the most common food, most monks have historically been omnivores, including the Dalai Lamas. After leaving Tibet the Dalai Lama attempted vegetarianism after seeing his cook kills a chicken for his meal. However, after getting jaundice, his doctors advised him to return to eating meat. Since then, he abstains from meat every other day.

British journalist Christopher Hitchens criticised the Dalai Lama in 1998, questioned his alleged support for India's nuclear weapons testing, his statements about sexual misconduct, his suppression of Shugden worship, as well as his meeting Shoko Asahara, whose cult Aum Shinrikyo released sarin nerve gas in the Tokyo subway system. Hitchens proclaims that he "makes absurd pronouncements about sex and diet and, when on his trips to Hollywood fund-raisers, anoints major donors like Steven Segal and Richard Gere as holy."

Despite protest from China, German Chancellor Angela Merkel met with the Dalai Lama in the Berlin Chancellery on 25 September 2007. The meeting was characterized as "*private and informal talks*" in order to avert potential retaliation by China such as the severance of trade ties. In response to the meeting, China cancelled meetings with German officials including Justice Minister Brigitte Zypries.

Several Tulkus or "reincarnate Lamas" have criticized Tenzin Gyatso. Two months after the 2008 Tibetan unrest and before the 2008 Beijing Olympics, news carried by *Xinhua*, the Chinese official government news agency, said that the twelfth Samding Dorje Phagmo (considered to be Tibet's "only female living Buddha,") who is also the vice-chairwoman of the standing committee of the Tibetan Autonomous Regional People's Congress, was quoted saying that "The sins of the Dalai Lama and his followers seriously violate the basic teachings and precepts of Buddhism and seriously damage traditional Tibetan Buddhism's normal order and good reputation."

She told Xinhua that "Old Tibet was dark and cruel; the serfs lived worse than horses and cattle." The Dalai Lama's talks in the UK, May, 2008, were attended by Chinese protestors who oppose Tibetan independence. During a teaching tour of the UK in May, 2008, there were demonstrations by the Western Shugden Society and Chinese students. The Western Shugden Society say they are protesting the ban of a prayer to Dorje Shugden, which they argue constitutes religious persecution.

Similar protests occurred in Sydney when the Dalai Lama arrived in Australia in June 2008. The Dalai Lama says he had not banned the practice, but strongly discourages it as he feels it promotes the spirit as being more important than Buddha, and that it may encourage cult-like practices and sectarianism within Tibetan Buddhism. The Shugden worshipers in India say they are denied admission to hospitals, stores, and other social services provided by the local Tibetan community.

RECOGNITION OF THE 17TH KARMAPA

Another controversy associated with the Dalai Lama is the recognition of the seventeenth Karmapa. To briefly sum up this controversy, two sides of the Kagyu school of Tibetan Buddhism have chosen two different Karmapas, leading to a deep division within the Kagyu School. The Dalai Lama has given his support to Urgyen Trinley Dorje, while supporters of Trinley Thaye Dorje claim that the Dalai Lama has no authority in the matter, nor is there a historical precedent for a Dalai Lama involving himself in an internal Kagyu dispute.

In his 2001 address at the International Karma Kagyu Conference, Kunzig Shamar Rinpoche - one of the four Karma Kagyu regents - accused the Dalai Lama of adopting a "divide and conquer" policy to eliminate any potential political rivalry arising from within the Kagyu School. For his side, the Dalai Lama accepted the prediction letter presented by Tai Situ Rinpoche (another Karma Kagyu regent) as authentic, and therefore Tai Situ Rinpoche's recognition of Urgyen Trinley Dorje, also as correct.

Tibet observer Julian Gearing suggests that there might be political motives to the Dalai Lama's decision: "The Dalai Lama gave his blessing to the recognition of [Urgyen] Trinley, eager to win over the formerly troublesome sect [the Kagyu school], and with the hope that the new Karmapa could play a role in a political solution of the 'Tibet Question.' ...If the allegations are to be believed, a simple nomad boy was turned into a political and religious pawn." However, according to Tsurphu Labrang, articles by Julian Gearing on this subject are biased, unverified and without crosschecking of basic facts.

CIA BACKING

In October 1998, The Dalai Lama's administration acknowledged that it received $1.7 million a year in the 1960s from the U.S. Government through the Central Intelligence Agency (CIA), and also trained a resistance movement in Colorado (USA). When asked by CIA officer John Kenneth Knaus in 1995 whether the organization did a good or bad thing in providing its support, the Dalai Lama replied that though it helped the morale of those resisting the Chinese, "thousands of lives were lost in the resistance" and further, that "the U.S. Government had involved itself in his country's affairs not to help Tibet but only as a Cold War tactic to challenge the Chinese."

REFUSAL OF VISA TO ENTER SOUTH AFRICA

In March 2009, the Dalai Lama was denied a visa to enter South Africa in order to attend an international peace conference. The South African government initially stated that it denied his visa to avoid distracting attention from South Africa and its hosting of the 2010 FIFA World Cup, although the visa-refusal precipitated precisely such a distraction. South African government officials later acknowledged that his visa had been denied to maintain close relations with China. Chinese officials had urged the South African government to not admit him.

Two other Nobel Peace Prize laureates, Arch Bishop-emeritus Desmond Tutu and former South African President FW de Klerk, criticised the denial and pulled out of the conference. Current Minister of Health Barbara Hogan was critical of the decision, accusing the Government of "being dismissive of human rights". Opposition parties to the ruling African National Congress, including the Democratic Alliance, Inkatha Freedom Party and Congress of the People, also expressed disgust.

"The recent shameful denial of entry to South Africa to a peace icon and Nobel laureate, the Dalai Lama, is a demonstration of the ANC government's willingness to sacrifice the standing of South Africa on the altar of political expediency," said Mvume Dandala, leader of the last-mentioned, as well as former presiding bishop of the Methodist Church of Southern Africa and former head of the All Africa Council of Churches. "This is especially so if the rumours are true that this was because of the funding arrangements between the ANC and the Communist Party of China."

Conference organisers, including the grandson of Nelson Mandela, also expressed outrage over the refusal to issue the Dalai Lama a visa. The conference was subsequently cancelled. The South African government defended its decision as a matter of sovereignty. One South African official publicly criticised the Dalai Lama and lamented a taboo on criticism of him, while another publicly criticised the government for denying his visa.

The Dalai Lama has been successful in gaining Western sympathy for Tibetan self-determination, including vocal support from numerous Hollywood celebrities, most notably the actors Richard Gere and Steven Seagal, as well as lawmakers from several major countries.

In 2005 and 2008 *Time* placed the Dalai Lama on its list of the world's 100 most influential people. On 22 June 2006, the Parliament of Canada voted unanimously to make The Dalai Lama an honorary citizen of Canada. This marks the third of four times in history that the Government of Canada has bestowed this honour, the others being Raoul Wallenberg posthumously in 1985, Nelson Mandela in 2001 and Aung San Suu Kyi in 2007.

In September 2006, the United States Congress voted to award the Dalai Lama the Congressional Gold Medal, the highest award which may be bestowed by the Legislative Branch of the United States government. The actual ceremony and awarding of the medal took place on 17 October 2007. The Chinese Government has reacted angrily to the award, which it merely refers to as "the extremely wrong arrangements". Chinese Foreign Minister Yang Jiechi said: "It seriously violates the norm of international relations and seriously wounded the feelings of the Chinese people and interfered with China's internal affairs".

In June 2007, during an Australian tour, the Dalai Lama made public appearances in Perth, Bendigo, Melbourne, Geelong, Sydney, Canberra and Brisbane. On 6 December 2008, Nicolas Sarkozy, President of France and current Chairman of the European Union met the Dalai Lama in Poland and appeased the situation after China postponed a China-EU summit.

After suffering abdominal pain in the October 2008, the Dalai Lama was hospitalized in New Delhi. He had routine surgery on 10 October to remove a gallstone. Four marks on the Dalai Lama's right arm are the consequence of a childhood smallpox vaccination and do not have any special significance. His right arm is uncovered in accordance with Buddhist tradition.

In May 2007, Chhime Rigzing, a senior spokesman for the Tibetan spiritual leader's office, stated that the Dalai Lama wants to reduce his political burden as he moves into "retirement". However, in 2008 the Dalai Lama himself ruled out such a move, saying "There is no point, or question of retirement." Rigzing stated "The political leadership will be transferred over a period of time but he will inevitably continue to be the spiritual leader because as the Dalai Lama, the issue of relinquishing the post does not arise".

The Dalai Lama announced he would like the elected Tibetan Parliament in Exile to have more responsibility over administration. On 1 September 2007, China issued new rules controlling the selection of the next Dalai Lama, declaring that any reincarnation must bear the seal of approval by China's cabinet. These regulations could potentially result in one Dalai Lama approved by the Chinese government, and another chosen outside of Tibet. This would be similar to the present situation with the Panchen Lamas and Karmapas. In November 2007, Tashi Wangdi said the new rules mean nothing. "It will have no effect" said Wangdi. "You can't impose a Pope. You can't impose an imam, an archbishop, saints, any religion... you can't politically impose these things on people. It has to be a decision of the followers of that tradition. The Chinese can use their political power: force. Again, it's meaningless".

During the 2008 unrest in Tibet, the Dalai Lama called for calm and concurrently condemned Chinese violence. His call was met with Tibetan frustration at his methodology and goals and Chinese allegations that he himself incited the violence in order to ruin the 2008 Summer Olympics. In response to the continued violence perpetrated by Chinese as well as Tibetans, on 18 March 2008, the Dalai Lama threatened to step down, a move unprecedented in the history of the office of the Dalai Lama.

Aides later clarified that this threat was predicated on a further escalation of violence, and that he did not presently have the intention of leaving his political or spiritual offices. Many Tibetan exiles expressed their support for the Dalai Lama, and the People's Republic of China intensified their campaign of attacks against him.

In the ensuing months, he held meetings aimed at discussing the future institution of the Dalai Lama, including:

A conclave, like in the Catholic Church, a woman as my successor, no Dalai Lama anymore, or perhaps even two, since the Communist Party has, astonishingly enough, given itself the right to be responsible for reincarnations.

He has clarified that his goal is to relinquish all temporal power and to no longer play a "pronounced spiritual role" and have a simpler monastic life.

3

Beginning of Buddhism in Tibet

Tibetan Buddhism is the body of Buddhist religious doctrine and institutions characteristic of Tibet and certain regions of the Himalayas, including northern Nepal, Bhutan, and India (Arunachal Pradesh, Ladakh and Sikkim). It is also practiced in Mongolia and parts of Russia (Kalmykia, Buryatia, and Tuva) and Northeast China. Tibetan Buddhism comprises many distinct schools, but is primarily divided into four main traditions: Nyingma, Kagyu, Gelug, and Sakya.

All schools categorize their teachings into three "vehicles": Hinayana, Mahayana, and Vajrayana, although some schools, the Gelug for example, consider Vajrayana a part of Mahayana. The Nyingma tradition classifies the corpus of Buddhist teachings into Nine Yanas, among the highest of which is known as Atiyoga or Dzogchen (Great Perfection). In the wake of the 1959 Tibetan uprising, a Tibetan diaspora has made Tibetan Buddhism more widely accessible to the rest of the world. Tibetan Buddhism has since spread to many Western countries, where the tradition has gained popularity.

THE TIBETAN BUDDHA IDEAL

The ideal goal of spiritual development in Tibetan Buddhism, a Mahayana tradition, is to achieve the enlightenment (Buddhahood) in order to most efficiently help all other sentient beings attain this state. Buddhahood is sometimes partially defined as a state of omniscience. "Omniscience" relates to the

Buddhist principle that all things are created by mind. When, in Buddhahood, one is freed from all mental obscurations, one is said to attain a state of continuous bliss mixed with a simultaneous cognition of emptiness, the true nature of reality.

In this state, all limitations on one's ability to help other living beings are removed. It is said that there are countless beings that have attained Buddhahood. Buddhas spontaneously, naturally and continuously perform activities to benefit all sentient beings. However it is believed that sentient beings' karmas limit the ability of the Buddhas to help them. Thus, although Buddhas possess no limitation from their side on their ability to help others, sentient beings continues to experience suffering as a result of the limitations of their own former negative actions.

TIBETAN DEFINITIONS OF "BUDDHIST"

Introspection as the mark of a Buddhist is embodied in the Tibetan term for Buddhist: literally, "internalist". More precisely, Tibetans specify two alternative criteria for being Buddhist: a) formal: having taken refuge and b) in belief: acceptance of the three (sometimes four) marks of existence.

GENERAL METHODS OF PRACTICE

TRANSMISSION AND REALISATION (LUNGTOK, LUNG-RTOGS)

An emphasis on oral transmission as more important than the printed word derives from the earliest period of Indian Buddhism, when it allowed teachings to be kept from those who should not hear them. Hearing a teaching (transmission) readies the hearer for realisation based on it. The person from whom one hears the teaching should have heard it as one link in a succession of listeners going back to the original speaker: the Buddha in the case of a sutra or the author in the case of a book. Then the hearing constitutes an authentic lineage of transmission. Authenticity of the oral lineage is a prerequisite for realisation, hence the importance of lineages.

Merely reading about a teaching is helpful but no substitute for receiving a transmission on it. Having a text recited aloud by someone who holds the lineage for transmission of that text makes oneself also a holder of that lineage and the more ready for realization of the teaching in it. Oral transmissions by lineage holders traditionally can take place in small groups or mass gatherings of listeners and may last for seconds (in the case of a mantra, for example) or months (as in the case of a section of the canon). A transmission can even occur without actually hearing, as in Asanga's visions of Maitreya.

ANALYTIC MEDITATION AND FOCUSSED/ FIXATION MEDITATION

Spontaneous realisation on the basis of transmission is possible but rare. Normally an intermediate step is needed in the form of analytic meditation, i.e., thinking about what one has heard. As part of this process, entertaining doubts and engaging in internal debate over them is encouraged in some traditions particularly. Analytic meditation is just one of two general methods of meditation. When analytic meditation achieves the quality of realisation, one is encouraged to switch to "focussed" or "fixation" meditation.

In this the mind is stabilised on that realisation for periods long enough to gradually habituate it to it. A person's capacity for analytic meditation can be trained with logic and that for successful focussed meditation through calm abiding. A meditation routine may involve alternating sessions of analytic meditation to achieve deeper levels of realisation and focussed meditation to consolidate them. The deepest level of realisation is Buddhahood.

SKEPTICISM AND GURU DEVOTION

Of all aspects of Tibetan Buddhism, none more than skepticism and guru devotion have led it into conflict with Chinese socialism and so invited the destruction of the Tibetan intelligentsia under Mao. An attitude of critical skepticism is encouraged to promote abilities in analytic meditation. However, as in other Buddhist traditions, an attitude of reverence for the teacher is also highly prized. In favour of skepticism towards Buddhist doctrines in general, Tibetans are fond of quoting sutra to the effect that one should test the Buddha's words as one would the quality of gold.

On the other hand, at the beginning of a public teaching, a lama will do prostrations to the throne on which he will teach due to its symbolism, or to an image of the Buddha behind that throne, and then students will do prostrations to the lama after he is seated. Merit accrues when one's interactions with the teacher are imbued with such reverence in the form of guru devotion, a code of practices governing them that derives from Indian sources. By such things as avoiding disturbance to the peace of mind of one's teacher and wholeheartedly following his prescriptions, much merit accrues and promotes one's practice.

There is a general sense in which any Tibetan Buddhist teacher is called a lama. A student may have taken teachings from many authorities and revere them all as lamas in this general sense. However, he will typically have one held in special esteem as his own root guru and is encouraged to view the other teachers who are less dear to him, however more exalted their status, as embodied in and subsumed by the root guru.

Often the teacher the student sees as root guru is simply the one who first introduced him to Buddhism, but a student may also change his personal view of which particular teacher is his root guru any number of times. The opposing principles of skepticism and guru devotion are reconciled with the Tibetan injunction to scrutinise a prospective guru thoroughly before finally adopting him as such without reservation. A Buddhist may study with a lama for decades before finally accepting him as his own guru.

THE TIBETAN APPROACH TO VAJRAYANA

Vajrayana is said to be the fastest method for attaining Buddhahood but it carries the caution that for unqualified practitioners it can be dangerous. Even for a qualified advanced practitioner, to engage in Vajrayana without having received the appropriate initiation (also known as an "empowerment") from a lama who is fully qualified to give it is to court controversy. From the time one has resolved to accept a Vajrayana initiation, skepticism towards the person giving that initiation as guru is suspended and the utmost sustained effort in guru devotion towards them is essential.

Just as Sutrayana preceded Vajrayana historically in India, so sutra practices constitute those that are preliminary to tantric ones. Preliminary practices include all Sutrayana activities that yield merit like hearing teachings, prostrations, offerings, prayers and acts of kindness and compassion, but chief among the preliminary practices are realizations through meditation on the three principle stages of the path: renunciation, the altruistic bodhicitta will for enlightenment and the wisdom realizing emptiness.

For a person without the basis of these three in particular to practice Vajrayana can be like a small child trying to ride an unbroken horse. While the practices of Vajrayana are not known in Sutrayana, all Sutrayana practices are common to Vajrayana. Without training in the preliminary practices, the ubiquity of allusions to them in Vajrayana is meaningless and even successful Vajrayana initiation becomes impossible.

The merit acquired in the preliminary practices facilitates progress in Vajrayana. While many Buddhists may spend a lifetime exclusively on sutra practices, however, an amalgam of the two to some degree is common. For, example, in order to train in calm abiding, one might use a tantric visualisation as the meditation object.

ESOTERICISM

In Vajrayana particularly, Tibetan Buddhists subscribe to a voluntary code of self-censorship, whereby the uninitiated do not seek and are not provided with information about it. This self-censorship may be applied more or less strictly depending on circumstances such as the material involved. A depiction of a mandala may be less public than that of a deity. That of a higher tantric deity may be less public than that of a lower. The degree to which information on Vajrayana is now public in western languages is controversial among Tibetan Buddhists.

Buddhism has always had a taste for esotericism since its earliest period in India. Tibetans today maintain greater or lesser degrees of confidentiality also with information on the Vinaya and emptiness specifically. In Buddhist teachings generally, too, there is caution about revealing information to people who may be unready for it. Esoteric values in Buddhism have made it at odds with the values of Christian missionary activity, for example in contemporary Mongolia.

NATIVE TIBETAN DEVELOPMENTS

Some commentators have emphasised Tibetan innovations such as the system of incarnate lamas, but such genuine innovations have been few. True to its roots in the Pala system of North India, however, Tibetan Buddhism carried on a tradition of eclectic accumulation and systematisation of diverse Buddhist elements, and pursued their synthesis. Prominent among these achievements are the Stages of the Path *(lamrim, lam-rim)* and motivational training *(lojong, blo-sbyong)*.

Schools

Tibetan Buddhism has four main traditions:

- Nyingma (pa), *The Ancient Ones*. This is the oldest, the original order founded by Padmasambhava.
- Kagyu (pa), *Lineage of the (Buddha's) Word*. This contains one major subsect and one minor subsect. The first, the Dagpo Kagyu, encompasses those Kagyu schools that trace back to Gampopa. In turn, the Dagpo Kagyu consists of four major sub-sects: the Karma Kagyu, headed by a Karmapa, the Tsalpa Kagyu, the Barom Kagyu, and Pagtru Kagyu. There are further eight minor sub-sects, all of which trace their root to Pagtru Kagyu. Among the eight sub-sects the most notable of are the Drikung Kagyu and the Drukpa Kagyu. The once-obscure Shangpa Kagyu,

which was famously represented by the 20th century teacher Kalu Rinpoche, traces its history back to the Indian master Niguma, sister of Kagyu lineage holder Naropa. This is an oral tradition which is very much concerned with the experiential dimension of meditation. Its most famous exponent was Milarepa, and eleventh century mystic.

- Sakya (pa), *Grey Earth,* headed by the Sakya Trizin, founded by Khon Konchog Gyalpo, a disciple of the great translator Drokmi Lotsawa. Sakya Pandita 1182–1251CE was the great grandson of Khon Konchog Gyalpo. This school very much represents the scholarly tradition.
- Gelug (pa), *Way of Virtue,* whose spiritual head is the Ganden Tripa and whose temporal head is the Dalai Lama. Successive Dalai Lamas ruled Tibet from the mid-17th to mid-20th centuries. This order was founded in the 14th to 15th century by Je Tsongkhapa, based on the foundations of the Kadampa tradition. Tsongkhapa was renowned for both his scholasticism and his virtue. The Dalai Lama belongs to the Gelugpa School, and is regarded as the embodiment of the Bodhisattva of Compassion.

Texts recognized as scripture and commentaries are fixed by the Tibetan Buddhist canon. These major schools are sometimes classified into Nyingma ("Old Translation") and Sarma ("New Translation") traditions according to translations and lineages of various Tantric texts. Besides these major schools, there are a number of minor ones like Jonang. The Jonangpa were suppressed by the rival Gelugpa in the 1600s and were once thought extinct, but are now known to survive in Eastern Tibet. There is also an ecumenical movement known as Rimé.

STUDY OF TENET SYSTEMS IN TIBETAN BUDDHISM

Tibetan Buddhists practise one or more understandings of the true nature of reality, the emptiness of inherent existence of all things. Emptiness is propounded according to four classical Indian schools of philosophical tenets. Two belong to the older Hinayana path (Skt. for *Lesser Vehicle,* Tib. theg dman). (Hinayana is sometimes referred to as Úravakayâna (Skt. *Vehicle of Hearers*) because "lesser" may be considered derogatory):

- Vaibhashika (Tib. *bye-brag smra-ba*)
- Sautrantika (Tib. *mdo-sde-pa*)

The primary source for the former is the Abhidharmakosha by Vasubandhu and commentaries. The Abhidharmakosha is also an important source for the Sautrantikas. Dignaga and Dharmakirti are the most prominent exponents.

The other two are Mahayana (Skt. *Greater Vehicle*) (Tib. *theg-chen*):

- Yogacara, also called Cittamatra (Tib. *sems-tsam-pa*), *Mind-Only*
- Madhyamaka (Tib. *dbu-ma-pa*)

Yogacarin base their views on texts from Maitreya, Asanga and Vasubandhu, Madhyamikas on Nagarjuna and Aryadeva. There is a further classification of Madhyamaka into Svatantrika-Madhyamaka and Prasangika-Madhyamaka. The former stems from Bhavaviveka, Santaraksita and Kamalashila, and the latter from Buddhapalita and Chandrakirti. The tenet system is used in the monasteries and colleges to teach Buddhist philosophy in a systematic and progressive fashion, each philosophical view being more subtle than its predecessor.

Therefore the four schools can be seen as a gradual path from a rather easy-to-grasp, "realistic" philosophical point of view, to more and more complex and subtle views on the ultimate nature of reality that is on emptiness and dependent arising, culminating in the philosophy of the Madhyamikas, which is widely believed to present the most sophisticated point of view.

MONASTICISM

Although there were many householder-yogis in Tibet, monasticism was the foundation of Buddhism in Tibet. There were over 6,000 monasteries in Tibet, and nearly all were ransacked and destroyed by the Chinese communists (many of them young ethnic Tibetan Red Guards), mainly during the Cultural Revolution. Most of the major ones have been at least partially re-established but many still remain in ruins. In Mongolia during the 1920s, approximately one third of the male population was monks, though many lived outside monasteries.

By the beginning of the 20th century about 750 monasteries were functioning in Mongolia. These monasteries were largely dismantled during Communist rule, but many have been reestablished during the Buddhist revival in Mongolia which followed the fall of Communism. Monasteries generally adhere to one particular school. Some of the major centers in each tradition are as follows:

Nyingma

The Nyingma lineage is said to have "six mother monasteries," although the composition of the six has changed over time:

- Dorje Drak
- Dzogchen Monastery
- Kathok
- Mindroling
- Palyul
- Shechen

Also of note is

- Samye - the first monastery in Tibet, established by Padmasambhava and Shantarakshita

Kagyu

Many Kagyu monasteries are in Kham, eastern Tibet. Tsurphu, one of the most important, is in central Tibet, as is Ralung.

- Palpung Monastery - the seat of the Tai Situpa and Jamgon Kongtrul

- Ralung Monastery-the seat of the Gyalwang Drukpa
- Surmang Monastery - the seat of the Trungpa tülkus
- Tsurphu Monastery - the seat of H.H. the Gyalwa Karmapa

Sakya

- Sakya Monastery - the seat of H.H. the Sakya Trizin

Gelug

The three most important centers of the Gelugpa lineage are Ganden, Sera and Drepung Monasteries, near Lhasa:

- Ganden Monastery - the seat of the Ganden Tripa
- Drepung Monastery - the home monastery of the Dalai Lama
- Sera Monastery

Three other monasteries have particularly important regional influence:

- Tashilhunpo Monastery in Shigatse - founded by the first Dalai Lama, this monastery is now the seat of the Panchen Lama
- Labrang Monastery in eastern Amdo
- Kumbum Jampaling in central Amdo

Great spiritual and historical importance is also placed on:

- Jokhang Temple in Lhasa - said to have been built by King Songtsen Gampo in 647 AD, a major pilgrimage site

According to a Tibetan legendary tradition, Buddhist scriptures (among them the Karandavyuha Sutra) and relics (among them the Cintamani) arrived in southern Tibet during the reign of Lha Thothori Nyantsen, the 28th king of Tibet (fifth century). The tale is miraculous (the objects fell from the sky on the roof of the king's palace), but it may have a historical background (the arrival of Buddhist missionaries). The earliest well-documented influence of Buddhism in Tibet dates from the reign of King Songtsän Gampo, who died in 650.

He married a Chinese Tang Dynasty Buddhist princess, Wencheng, who came to Tibet with a statue of Shakyamuni

Buddha. According to a Tibetan legendary tradition, Songtsän Gampo also married a Nepalese Buddhist princess, Bhrikuti; but Bhrikuti, who bears the name of a goddess, is not mentioned in reliable sources. Songtsän Gampo founded the first Buddhist temples. By the second half of the 8th century he was already regarded as an embodiment of the bodhisattva Avalokiteshvara. The successors of Songtsän Gampo seem to have been less enthusiastic about the propagation of Buddhism. But in the 8th century, King Trisong Detsen (755-797) established Buddhism as the official religion of the state.

He invited Indian Buddhist scholars to his court. In his age the famous tantric mystic Padmasambhava arrived in Tibet according to the Tibetan tradition. In addition to writing a number of important scriptures (some of which he hid for future *tertons* to find), Padmasambhava established the Nyingma school ("the old school"). Tibetan Buddhism exerted a strong influence from the 11th century CE among the peoples of Central Asia, especially in Mongolia and Manchuria. It was adopted as an official state religion by the Mongol Yuan dynasty and the Manchu Qing dynasty that ruled China.

TRANSMISSION OF CHAN TO THE NYINGMAPA

According to A. W. Barber of the University of Calgary, Chan Buddhism was introduced to the Nyingmapa in three principal streams: the teachings of Master Kim, Kim Ho-shang, (Chin ho shang) transmitted by *Sang Shi* in ca. 750 CE ; the lineage of Master Wu Chu of the Pao T'ang School was transmitted within Tibet by *Ye shes dbang po*; and the teaching from Mo Ho Yen, (Tibetan: *Hwa shang Mahayana*) that were a synthesis of the Northern School of Chan and the Pao T'ang School.

Tibetan king *Khri srong lde btsan* (742–797) invited the Ch'an master Mo-ho-yen (whose name consists of the same Chinese characters used to transliterate "Mahayana") to transmit the Dharma at Samye Monastery. Mo-ho-yen had been disseminating Dharma in the Tun-huang locale, but, according to Tibetan sources, lost an important philosophical debate on the nature of emptiness with the Indian master Kamalashila, and the king declared Kamalashila's philosophy should form the basis for Tibetan Buddhism. However, a Chinese source says their side won, and some scholars conclude that the entire episode is fictitious. According to some scholars, Hwashang's ideas of the Chan School are preserved by the Nyingmapas in the form of dzogchen teachings. Whichever may be the case; Tibetan Buddhists today trace their spiritual roots from Indian masters such as Padmasambhava, Atisha, Tilopa, Naropa and their later Tibetan students.

TIBETAN BUDDHISM IN THE CONTEMPORARY WORLD

Today, Tibetan Buddhism is adhered to widely in the Tibetan Plateau, Nepal, Bhutan, Mongolia, Kalmykia (on the north-west shore of the Caspian), Siberia (central Russia, specifically Buryatia and Chita Oblast), and the Russian Far East (concentrated in Tyva). The Indian regions of Sikkim and Ladakh, both formerly independent kingdoms, are also home to significant Tibetan Buddhist populations. In the wake of the Tibetan diaspora, Tibetan Buddhism has gained adherents in the West and throughout the world; there are estimated to be tens of thousands of practitioners in Europe and the Americas. Celebrity Tibetan Buddhism practitioners include Richard Gere, Adam Yauch, Jet Li, Sharon Stone, Allen Ginsberg, Philip Glass, and Steven Seagal (who has been proclaimed the reincarnation of the tulku Chungdrag Dorje).

Probably Buddhism was first introduced to Tibet in 173 CE during the reign of the 28th Yarlung king Lha Thothori Nyantsen, but had apparently no impact. The first official historic introduction of a Buddhist scripture into Tibet happened during reign of King Hlato Ri Nyentsen (28th king of Tibet - around 500 CE), however, the book was not translated at the time. The 33rd King of Tibet, Song Tsen Gampo (born 617) had the book translated and married two Buddhist princesses. With this, one can say that Buddhism was first really introduced to Tibet as a practice.

The 37th King of Tibet, Trisong Detsen invited Indian Pandit Shantarakshita and Kamalasila, who suggested inviting

Padmasambhava (or Guru-Rinpoche) to Tibet, who arrived in 817. An ordained spiritual community was established in the first Buddhist monastery; Samye, which was built by Padmasambhava. In this period, translation of scriptures genuinely began. As of this time, one can say that Buddhism was firmly established in Tibet, as the presence of Sangha is considered essential. In 792, after a great philosophical debate, King Trisong Detsen officially declared Indian Buddhism and not Chinese Buddhism to be the religion of Tibet.

DECLINE AND REVIVAL

Buddhism almost disappeared after 842 when King Lang Dharma violently persecuted Buddhism. After this, for a long time there were no ordinations and no central religious authority in Tibet. Instead, the original Bon religion prevailed. In 978, with the introduction of several Indian Pandits and Tibetan monks studying in India, Buddhism revived, with the help of King Yeshe O. A real revival occurred after 1042, when Atisha-di-Pankhara (or Lama Atisha) put Tibetans "back on the right track".

He presented the Buddhist philosophy in a very clear and condensed manner, which became the basis for philosophical teachings in most Tibetan traditions. After Atisha, the influence from Indian teachers was limited. Atisha's main disciple was the layman Dromtönpa, who founded the Kadam-tradition. This tradition does not exist in that form anymore, but strongly influenced the later schools of Kargyu, Sakya and especially Gelug. Note that Tibetan teachers like His Holiness the Dalai Lama insist that Tibetan Buddhism these days still carefully reflects the Buddhism as was present in India around the 11th century. He also rejects the term Lamaism, as it suggests as if the Tibetan teachers have developed their own form of Buddhism.

NYINGMA

The Nyingma School is more or less a continuation of the initially introduced Buddhism by the Indian Pandit Padmasambhava. Historic information of Padmasambhava is generally shrouded in myths, (he is said to have lived for 3,600 in India prior to coming to Tibet), but he came to Tibet in 817 at the invitation of King Trisong Detsen.

Initially, the study of logic and philosophy was limited, but much emphasis was put on tantric practice. It must be noted however, that also within the Nyingma school considerable reformation has taken place over the ages. Some typical aspects for the Nyingma tradition: the practice of *Dzogchen* (seeking to examine the fundamental nature of mind directly, without relying on visualizations and images) and the presence of hidden scriptures or "*terma*" from Padmasambhava, which are discovered by later Masters.

KADAM

Not existing as such anymore, but it was the main reformation school after revival of Buddhism in the 11th century by Atisha di Pankara from India (c. 982-1052) and Dromtonpa as his Tibetan disciple. Atisha combined two lineages: from Manjushri via Nagarjuna (emphasising emptiness) and from Maitreya via Asangha (emphasising compassion). Atisha's brief text 'A lamp for the path to full awakening' formed the basis of the later Gelug presentation of *Lamrim*.

KARGYU

This tradition started with the Tibetans Marpa Chökyi and Khyungpo Nyaljor, in the 11th century, who had Tilopa (988-1069) and his disciple Naropa (1016 - 1100) as Indian masters. Probably the most famous practitioner and master in the lineage is Milarepa (1040-1123), who attained Buddhahood in one life time by an incredible display of perseverance (image on the right). Milarepa was a disciple of Marpa (image on the left) who in turn was a pupil of Naropa. The Kargyu tradition is both a meditation lineage and philosophy training lineage.

Typical aspects of the Kargyu tradition are the practice of *Mahamudra* (not unlike Dzogchen of the Nyingma) and the *Six Yogas of Naropa*. It should be noted that currently several suborders of the Kargyu lineage exist, like the Karma Kargyu (with as leader the Karmapa), the Drikung Kargyu and the Drukpa Kargyu schools.

SAKYA

The Sakya tradition has its origins with the translator Drogmi, who transferred the lineage of the Indian master Virupa to Khon Konchog Gyalpo. On this occasion, Khon Konchog Gyalpo built the Sakya monastery (meaning grey earth) and founded the Sakya tradition. In 1247, the Mongolian prince Godan Khan conquered Tibet and gave temporal authority over Tibet to Lama Kunga Gyaltsen (better known as Sakya Pandita), who was one of the earliest major figures in this lineage.

In 1254 Mongol emperor Kublai Khan invited Chögyal Phagpa for teachings. Also Kublai Khan made Buddhism state religion in Mongolia and made Chogyal Phagpa the first religious and secular leader over Tibet. Sakya masters ruled Tibet more than 100 yrs, before the Gelug took over secular power with the Dalai Lamas. A typical aspect of the Sakya tradition is called *Lamdrey* (leading to state of Hevajra), a concise presentation of the Buddhist philosophy. The Sakyas were much influenced by the Kadam lineage. In 1354, the rule over Tibet was given to the monk Changchub Gyaltsen, who was not a Sakya. After this, the tradition declined in importance.

GELUG

The Gelugs (yellow hats) tradition was founded by Tibetan teacher Je Tsongkhapa (1357-1419). The basis is formed by the old Kadam lineage, but it in fact includes all other Tibetan traditions. For example; Tsongkhapa's main teacher was the Sakya teacher Rendawa. Sonam Gyatso (1543-1588), received the title 'Dalai Lama' (Ocean of Wisdom) from the Mongol ruler Althan Khan in 1578. In 1642, the 5th Dalai Lama became temporal and spiritual leader of Tibet by order of the Mongol ruler Gushri Khan.

Although trained in all four schools, basically all Dalai Lamas were Gelug; one of the reasons that Gelug tradition is most widespread in Tibet. Note that the posthumously declared "First Dalai Lama" named Gedun Truppa (born 1391) was a disciple of Je Tsongkhapa. Unlike what many people think, the Dalai Lamas are not the spiritual heads of the Gelugpa School; this is always the Gaden Tripa. Some typical aspects of the Gelug tradition: emphasis on ethics and sound scholarship. Main Buddhist teachings are collected in the *Lamrim* presentation (not unlike the Lamdrey teachings of the Sakya). The Gelug introduced a scholarly title, *Geshe*, for a fully qualified and authoritative spiritual master.

WORDS OF TRUTH

Honoring and Invoking the Great Compassion of the Three Jewels; the Buddha, the Teachings, and the Spiritual Community:

O Buddhas, Bodhisattvas, and disciples of the past, present, and future:

Having remarkable qualities immeasurably vast as the ocean,

Who regard all helpless sentient beings as your only child;

Please consider the truth of my anguished pleas.

Buddha's full teachings dispel the pain of worldly existence and self-oriented peace;

May they flourish, spreading prosperity and happiness throughout this spacious world.

O holders of the Dharma: scholars and realized practitioners;

May your ten fold virtuous practice prevail.

Humble sentient beings, tormented by sufferings without cease,

Completely suppressed by seemingly endless and terribly intense, negative deeds,

May all their fears from unbearable war, famine, and disease be pacified,

To freely breathe an ocean of happiness and well-being.

And particularly the pious people of the Land of Snows who, through various means,

Are mercilessly destroyed by barbaric hordes on the side of darkness,

Kindly let the power of your compassion arise,

To quickly stem the flow of blood and tears.

Those unrelentingly cruel ones, objects of compassion,

Maddened by delusion's evils, wantonly destroy themselves and others;

May they achieve the eye of wisdom, knowing what must be done and undone,

And abide in the glory of friendship and love.

May this heartfelt wish of total freedom for all Tibet,

Which has been awaited for a long time, be spontaneously fulfilled;

Please grant soon the good fortune to enjoy

The happy celebration of spiritual with temporal rule.

O protector Chenrezig, compassionately care

For those who have undergone myriad hardships,

Completely sacrificing their most cherished lives, bodies, and wealth,

For the sake of the teachings, practitioners, people, and nation.

Thus, the protector Chenrezig made vast prayers

Before the Buddhas and Bodhisattvas

To fully embrace the Land of Snows;

May the good results of these prayers now quickly appear.

By the profound interdependence of emptiness and relative forms,

Together with the force of great compassion in the Three Jewels and their Words of Truth,

And through the power of the infallible law of actions and their fruits,

May this truthful prayer be unhindered and quickly fulfilled.

This prayer, Words of Truth, was composed by His Holiness Tenzin Gyatso, the Fourteenth Dalai Lama of Tibet, on 29 September 1960 at his temporary headquarters in the Swarg Ashram at Dharamsala, Kangra District, and Himachal State, India. This prayer for restoring peace, the Buddhist teachings, and the culture and self-determination of the Tibetan people in their homeland was written after repeated requests by Tibetan government officials along with the unanimous consensus of the monastic and lay communities.

OPINION OF THE CURRENT SITUATION IN TIBET

"They were conquerors, and for that you want only brute force - nothing to boast of, when you have it, since your strength is just an accident arising from the weakness of others. They grabbed what they could get for the sake of what was to be got. It was just a robbery with violence, aggravated murder on a great scale, and men going at it blind - as is very proper for those who tackle darkness. The conquest of the earth, which mostly means the taking it away from those who have a different complexion or slightly flatter noses than ourselves, is not a pretty thing when you look into it too much."

Heart of Darkness by Joseph Conrad Tibetan Buddhism derives from the confluence of Buddhism and yoga which started to arrive in Tibet from India briefly around the late eighth century and then more steadily from the thirteenth century onwards. Indian Buddhism around that time had incorporated both Hindu yogic and tantric practices along with the classical teachings of the historical Buddha who lived around 500 BC. It acknowledged that there were two paths to enlightenment (complete transcendence of identification with the personal ego). One path was that taught in the sutras according to the historical teachings.

The heart of sutra practice was based on morality,

concentration, and wisdom (not identifying with the personal ego). The other path, which has become the cornerstone of Tibetan variations, was tantric. This practice blended the sutra teachings with techniques adapted from Hindu systems of yoga and tantra. Tantric systems transform the basic human passions of desire and aversion for the purpose of spiritual development. Rather than denying such primal urges, tantra purifies them into wholesome and helpful forces. It is very much like trying to deal with a wild horse charging towards you. One way is denial: put up your hands and shout out, "stop, stop!" Probably you will be bowled over by the animal.

Another, cleverer, approach is to step aside and then jump on its back as it charges past you. In such a case, you have a chance to start coaxing it to move in certain directions, and over time you may be able to direct it into a stable. Truthfully, one needs some skill in both self-control and acceptance if one is to be successful with tantric work. Tibetan Tantra (also known as the Vajrayana) incorporates the major aspects of both the Hinayana and Mahayana Buddhist teachings. It is basically an esoteric extension on these themes.

Hinayana and Mahayana are two schools of Buddhist practice that have basically similar goals and techniques but somewhat differing philosophies. For instance, Theravadin Buddhism (known for its Vipassana meditation) is a Hinayana teaching and Zen Buddhism is a Mahayana teaching. Tantra itself has various schools which can be grouped by the relative emphasis they place on working with exoteric and esoteric practices.

TANTRA

The tantric path includes the following steps:

Lamrim (literally, stages of the path)-These are indispensable topics for reflection and contemplation and also the meditations and activities that should naturally follow on from them. The Lamrim embodies the necessary prerequisites for tantra. It is set out as a progressive set of steps.

- Relying Upon a Spiritual Guide (learning from someone already on the path).

- The Preciousness of Human Life (the importance of using life for something valuable).
- Death and Impermanence (uncertainty of death and the unsatisfactory nature of this world).
- The Danger of being Reborn in a Lower Realm.
- Taking Refuge from Samsara (the cycle of endless grasping and eventual disappointment).
- Karma (the law of cause and effect which works in this world as well as at esoteric levels).
- Developing Renunciation for Samsara (integrating spiritual understanding and values).
- Developing Equanimity (accepting, and seeing past, both good and bad experience).
- Recognizing that all Beings are as Precious as our Mothers (the beginnings of bodhichitta).
- Remembering the Kindness of Others.
- Equalizing Self and Others (realising that we all want, and deserve, to be happy).
- The Disadvantage of Self-Cherishing.
- The Advantage of Cherishing Others (loosening the hold of ego through caring).
- Exchanging Self with Others (this is the core practice for developing bodhichitta-it involves developing the wish to voluntarily take on others' problems and freely give them one's own happiness in exchange. A sketch of the technique is as follows: breathe in others' woes as black smoke-let it settle into the heart, then breathe out all one's own happiness as white light-let it expand to fill all the cosmos. A practitioner should imagine and rejoice at the effect of both the in- and out-breath. For, on the in-breath, the reality and weight of all the problems in this world sink into the heart and help to dissolve the ego. Likewise, the out-breath brings relief and joy to all others).
- Developing Great Compassion.
- Taking Responsibility to Relieve Others' Burdens ("exchanging self with others" in action).
- Sharing One's Own Good Fortune with Others.

- Bodhichitta (the desire to attain full enlightenment for the sake of all beings).
- Tranquil Abiding (developing advanced stages of concentration).
- Superior Seeing (developing emptiness-that is, non-identification with the personal ego).

COMMON PRELIMINARY TANTRIC PRACTICES

These are the beginning activities that are unique to the Vajrayana path.

- Prostrations (physical prostration, visualisation and prayer for taking refuge).
- Vajrasattva Meditation (visualisation and mantra recitation for purification).
- Mandala Offering (visualisation and prayer for developing surrender and gaining merit).
- Guru Yoga (visualisation, mantra recitation and prayer for developing devotion and receiving blessings).

GENERATION STAGE OF TANTRA

These are preparatory practices that utilise imagination and much visualisation. They prepare the psychological and psychic groundwork for the spiritual energy that will be developed and harnessed in the following completion stage practices.

- Beginning Meditation (visualisation of oneself as a deity in the centre of a mandala full of other deities).
- Subtle Meditation (visualisation of a body mandala which corresponds to points on the subtle nervous system).

COMPLETION STAGE OF TANTRA

These are very advanced meditations that primarily utilise subtle energies known as winds (prana and chi are some other names for this energy). These winds normally circulate throughout the psychic nervous system. When they are collected into a central place they provide great stability and clarity for the meditator. The normal collection point is commonly known as a chakra. It corresponds to a node or plexus in the psychic nervous system and acts as a link between the psychic, or astral, level of existence and our normal level of experience.

Tibetan yoga employs a simplified version of the metaphysical structure that is used in Hindu yoga. According to the Tibetan scheme there are three realms to consider in spiritual practice. These correspond to the Emanation Body (this world), the Enjoyment Body (the astral dimension), and the Truth Body (a dimension that is much deeper-that is, much more subtle-than the astral).

- Isolated Body, Speech, and Mind (progressive isolation of consciousness from this level of reality).
- Illusory Body (development of an astral body. Consciousness now is based in the astral not the physical).
- Clear Light (development of a very subtle consciousness at the Truth Body level).
- Union or Full Enlightenment (linking the Truth Body consciousness to the Enjoyment, or astral, Body).

Meditation on emptiness is integral throughout this practice. A simple way to understand emptiness is as follows. In the physical world, the personal ego has a relative span and will cease when the body does. So relative to it, the soul, or Enjoyment Body, is much more important since it will continue on after death.

Thus saying the ego or self is empty means it is better to ground awareness in the soul and experience the ego as a garment, rather than only experiencing the ego and having no real connection with the soul. Thus emptiness is a statement about priority-we should consider the bigger context of our experience in order to live more wisely and wholesomely.

The same principle of emptiness applies as progressively higher levels of reality are experienced. Hence, when the Enjoyment Body, or soul, becomes a living reality for the meditator, she or he continues to take it as relatively real and keeps grounding awareness in the encircling context. The context, or deeper level, for the soul is the Truth Body (which is just a more subtle version of the soul). So as a meditator realises the Truth Body, the Enjoyment Body becomes the new object for meditation on emptiness.

To recapitulate the entire process: at the beginning we have a body and mind (the personal ego or self). Next an astral body (Enjoyment Body) is developed and it is as if the physical body and personal ego have become the "body" and the astral body has become the "mind". Next a very subtle body (Truth Body) is developed and the final result is that the astral body becomes the "body" and the Truth Body becomes the "mind". At each stage of this sequence, the "body" is subjectively experienced as being empty by the "mind".

What is the experience of emptiness like? At the beginning level of physical body and mind, emptiness means that one does not identify with any experience whatsoever. Any sight, sound, or other sense is recognised and honoured for what it is, but it is not clung to. Similarly, all thoughts and feelings are also taken in this way-as being real and valuable, but not as being in one's possession so that one does not cling to the experience of them. It is as if all experiences, whether external (in the world "out there") or internal (inner thoughts, hopes, feelings, and desires), are viewed as clouds passing by.

The reality is the sky which the clouds float by in. And if the sky is noticed, it too is taken as just another cloud wafting by. The result of this amazing relation to one's experience is an enormous sense of relief, peace, and clarity. At first it seems that one will die if one doesn't cling to experience, but after awhile it becomes apparent that one continues to live on anyway. We are more than just the experiences that we engage in.

The same process applies at progressively more subtle levels of experience. The contents of experience become more and more amazing and wonderful (to our normal way of thinking) but the most skilful way of relating to them still remains the practice of mindfulness (emptiness meditation). So once a yogi creates an astral body and can experience reality at that level, he or she works at non-identification with the astral body. And similarly, once a Truth Body exists, meditation on its emptiness continues as well.

DZOGCHEN

This is also a very advanced teaching whose end result is the same as for the tantric path. Its techniques and emphasis are a bit different. Primarily, Dzogchen underscores direct perception of the fundamental nature of reality. So instead of working to create higher energy bodies such as the astral body, it seeks to ground awareness directly back into the Truth Body. And as mentioned above, this Body reaches the limits of human experience and expression so that its subjective experience is one of all-encompassing emptiness. That is, there is nothing more to be said about this level with the common tools of human experience-words and emotions.

The main practice is similar to Zen meditation and consists of holding a constant perceptual openness to all experience. For such practice to lead to more subtle insight, however, a Dzogchen practitioner needs to receive empowerments (transmission of spiritual energy) from a qualified teacher. These act somewhat as a self-correcting guidance system to help a meditator to gradually open to the deeper dimensions of reality. Some Dzogchen meditations are similar to tantric visualisation and energetic practices. The basic prerequisites for Dzogchen are similar to Tantra.

TIBETAN BUDDHISM IN RELATION TO OTHER BUDDHIST TRADITIONS

The three yanas (vehicles or schools) of Buddhism teach a similar approach to enlightenment. It consists of morality, concentration, and wisdom. They differ in the emphasis placed on these areas and also on the level of reality that is primarily worked with. The main goal and result of each school is moving beyond identification with the personal ego. The resulting wisdom, or enlightenment, is experienced at various levels of reality-from the physical-astral interface for Vipassana and Zen, to the astral-very deep interface for Tantra and Dzogchen.

The Sutra and Vajrayana teachings place great emphasis on building a proper moral basis upon which to build the insights of emptiness. In contrast, both Zen and Dzogchen place most of their focus upon directly working to develop the wisdom of emptiness. In practice, both the Gradual and Fast Paths have strengths and weaknesses. The gradual approach guarantees a steady mind and heart when one begins to experience very deep states of meditation.

This is extremely useful as the power of the subconscious mind that can be unleashed in such states is enormous and can lead to psychological imbalance if one is not basically well-rounded by such a stage of practice. The drawback, of course, is that it takes a long time to really begin to purify one's mind and heart. Many great masters have spent their entire lives with the purification and transformation of mind and heart as their chief practice.

The fast approach provides the quickest means to experience awareness beyond that normally associated with the ego. Its drawback is the potential fragility of the ego to withstand such rapid and deep-reaching change-the very thing gradual paths strive to guard against. An analogous situation holds for the exoteric and esoteric schools. Exoteric traditions are more solid and balanced since they mostly work with the perceptions and energies of the physical plane. So even though it is not uncommon to be visited with various astral experiences during advanced stages of Zen or Vipassana meditation, the emphasis of such schools is to continue grounding back to this earth-to the sights, sounds, tastes and thoughts that comprise ordinary experience.

The drawback is that the primal energies that underpin the physical world are only indirectly addressed. Esoteric traditions, on the other hand, determine to apply themselves directly to the forces that underlie ordinary existence. They reach for the essential nature of the experience of living which manifests as subtle energy and consciousness. The drawback is that similar to reaching too far, too fast, into the psyche as for the fast traditions, esoteric work can reach too far, too fast into subtler fields of energy.

This can manifest variously as, for instance, unwanted communication with other beings, energetic imbalances of the body and mind, and uncontrolled effects on the environment and other beings. The confluence of Buddhism and other mystical teachings in the West is resulting in a blending of these various approaches to spirituality. It is likely that, along with the aforementioned paths, a blending of them which puts emphasis somewhere in between along both axes will develop as a useful approach for those who wish to remain in a regular lifestyle.

4

Introduction of Tantras in Tibet

Vajrayâna Buddhism is also known as Tantric Buddhism, Tantrayâna, Mantrayâna, Secret Mantra, Esoteric Buddhism and the Diamond Vehicle. The period of Vajrayana Buddhism has been classified as the fifth or final period of Indian Buddhism. Vajrayana is a complex and multifaceted system which evolved over several centuries and reveals much inconsistency and a variety of opinions. Vajrayana probably came into existence in the 6th or 7th century CE, while the term Vajrayana first came into evidence in the 8th century CE. Its scriptures are called the Tantras.

The distinctive feature of Vajrayana Buddhism is ritual, which is used as a substitute or alternative for the earlier abstract meditations. Vajrayana scriptures refers to one of three routes to enlightenment, the other two being Hinayana and Mahayana. Buddhist Tantra, or Vajrayana, according to its own history, originates with Shakyamuni Buddha. It is not an invention of Himalayan practitioners or Tibetan ones, even according to conventional western scholarship. The first instance of its transmission came when teaching was requested by King Indrabuthi, who wished to practice dharma but was unwilling to give up his kingdom and queens, as was normally expected of the Buddha's monks.

Clearly, it should be noted, the Buddha saw special spiritual qualities in the king or would not have conferred such unusual teachings. Sending away his less accomplished monks, the Buddha taught the Guhyasamaja Tantra. Among the Buddha's disciples, the bodhisattvas Vajrapani, Manjusri, and Avalokiteshvara were entrusted with the tantric teachings. These teachings were then passed down in secrecy, teacher to disciple, for many centuries. They began to surface in a more public way in India in roughly 500 A.D. This was the era of what are called the "84 Mahasiddhas," or "84 Great Realized Ones." They came from all aspects of Indian society: kings, scholars, monks, laborers, prostitutes, and so on.

What they seemed to have in common was an ability to apply the tantric teachings to the very concrete details of their lives to achieve enlightenment. In a representative tale, a man employed breaking rock with a sledge hammer-and deeply unhappy with his lot-is stopped by a passing yogi who teaches him, in a poetic stanza, to penetrate the nature of rock using the sledge of his mind, and this instruction becomes the seed of his eventual realization, accomplished via the very labor that was oppressing him. In another story, a yogi with a fondness for liquor attains enlightenment by-miraculously-imbibing 72 gallons of liquor. One of these mahasiddhas, Padmasambhava-a master of the Maha Ati teachings- traveled to Tibet 12 centuries ago, establishing Vajrayana as the state religion and initiating the first tantric lineage in Tibet, called in Tibetan the "Nyingma."

About three centuries later a Tibetan known as Marpa the Translator arrived in India and received transmission from another mahasiddha called Naropa, a Mahamudra master, and brought it back to Tibet, starting the Kagyu lineage. The Sakya lineage began as well by bringing teachings from India, while the Gelug, the Dalai Lama's lineage, originated later on in Tibet itself. Vajrayana eventually spread through central Asia, into Mongolia and China, and as far as Japan.

HINAYANA AND MAHAYANA

Vajrayana is grounded in the Hinayana and Mahayana teachings. For the purpose of this chapter, I will only discuss them in the context of how Vajrayana understands its own system. This is not a comment on other forms of Buddhism but only on the internal principles by which Vajrayana understands itself. Vajrayana sees the path as having three stages. In a traditional image, Hinayana establishes the foundation, Mahayana erects the walls, and Vajrayana is the golden roof of the temple. As we can see from this analogy, there would be no building at all if there were only Vajrayana. Hence the absolute necessity in developing the first two stages of the path before embarking on the third.

The Hinayana ("Narrow Vehicle") teachings introduce the notion of individual salvation. We are in samsara, the wheel of birth, death, suffering, and confusion. By applying ourselves to mindfulness and awareness or shamatha and vipashyana, we calm our minds through meditation practice and develop insight into their functioning. A great many of the Hinayana teachings are concerned with the development of ego and how it perpetuates itself. The teaching of the five skandhas looks at the ego as a series of transient mind moments: we project a basic sense of duality, followed by primitive feelings and conceptualization, and arrive at an experience of consciousness, adorned with thought and emotion. This is seen then as an illusion we grasp and try to make real, believing in a self and on that basis engendering suffering. But this self has no solid, unalterable basis.

We have merely solidified a series of momentary mental tendencies. Unraveling this process through meditation leads us to see our own essential egolessness. So through renunciation of samsara, the realm of ego-based suffering, we begin the path to nirvana, the egoless realm of cessation of suffering. Along the way, as our awareness and personal discipline develops, so does our sensitivity to the suffering of people around us. The gentleness and selflessness we've developed in our practice begins to extend to the world. The Mahayana ("Great Vehicle") teaches that compassionate action for the sake of others is the path. Not only are we egoless, but we have bodhicitta ("awakened heart"), the very nature of the Buddha inside us.

If we look for this nature, we can find no thing in itself, but in our daily activity it expresses itself in terms of our empathy for others and an intuitive understanding of how to act skillfully in situations. By developing our compassion and prajna ("discriminating awareness wisdom"), we extend our egolessness and dissolve the boundary between ourselves and others. The fruition is the recognition of emptiness. The fundamental statement of the Mahayana view of reality is in the Prajnaparamita Sutra, which says "form is emptiness, emptiness is form," and goes on to list as empty all the basic teachings of Hinayana: the rest of the five skandhas, the nidanas, the four noble truths and so forth. Because there is no self, there is no other as well.

Form itself, or the basic duality of self and other, is built on a fiction. Once the world has separated into self and other, then we assign names and solid, unchanging qualities to the forms we perceive. If we see that neither self nor other has any intrinsic, permanent, and unchanging form-a table exists by our naming it a table, but is only a collection of impermanent parts-and that our whole perception of the solidity of form changes when we remove the veil of duality, we can see the truth of "form is emptiness." Samsara, the world of birth and death, is Nirvana, the transcendental world free of time and suffering. But "emptiness is form." The world hasn't disappeared into nothingness. Form itself does arise from emptiness, indivisible from it. Samsara endlessly displays its forms, all of which are empty. Nirvana is samsara. Sentient beings misapprehend samsara as a self and another, while the bodhisattva, the Mahayana practitioner, seeks out of compassion to help them, even as he recognizes what sentient beings don't see: sentient beings are Buddhas and samsara is nirvana.

THE FIVE SKANDHAS AS THE FIVE BUDDHAS

Vajrayana ("Indestructible Vehicle") is called the "Path of Fruition" because it sees the path from the point of view of the already accomplished Buddhas. Until now we've been seeing the path as sentient beings see it: I'm stuck in samsara but want to arrive in nirvana, in heaven, somewhere up above, on the mountain top. Vajrayana reverses these terms, playing out the implications of the Mahayana. We are, and always have been, awakened Buddhas. Our ignorance has obscured this but can't destroy it.

If, in fact, form is emptiness and emptiness is form, we can safely say that the forms arising from the absolute (nirvana) and indivisible from it, are themselves relative expressions of the absolute. To say it another way, if emptiness is the absolute, awake nature of the Buddha's mind, then the energy which arises from it-which we normally call samsara-is displaying the forms of that mind. Hence the skandhas, if seen from an enlightened view point, are naturally arising expressions of Buddha wisdom. The skandhas are by nature indivisible from the absolute, awake mind. So Vajrayana teaches that the five skandhas are the five Buddhas. Vairochana Buddha, in the center, corresponds to the skandha of consciousness, as well as to the klesha of ignorance and the wisdom of all-encompassing space. Akshobya Buddha in the east corresponds to the skandha of form, the klesha of anger, mirror-like wisdom, to the element of water and the season of winter.

Ratnasambhava Buddha in the south is related to the skandha of feeling, the klesha of pride, the wisdom of equanimity, to the earth and the autumn. Amitabha Buddha in the west is connected to the skandha of perception, the klesha of passion, discriminating awareness wisdom, fire and spring. Amogasiddhi Buddha is related to the skandha of formation, the klesha of jealousy, the wisdom of all-accomplishing action, to wind and summer. Each Buddha has a female Buddha consort representing one of the elements; hence the internal perceiver of the skandhas is in union with the external world of the elements. Subject and object, sense and sense field, are non-dual, imbued with unconditional bliss called "mahasukha." The point here-so that we don't get lost in the technicalities-is to see ourselves and our world as a pure expression of awakened mind. All aspects of the universe-its elements, seasons, directions-and all constituents of our being-our senses, concepts, and emotions-arise as non-dual energy, the mandala of the Buddhas.

ENTERING THE VAJRAYANA

The formal entrance into the Vajrayana begins with what are called the "ordinary and extraordinary preliminaries." The "ordinary preliminaries" is to practice reflection upon "the four thoughts which turn the mind": the difficulty of obtaining a precious human birth, impermanence, karma and its retribution, and the futility and suffering of samsara. These encourage our renunciation of samsara (in the ordinary sense) and fire up our enthusiasm to practice. The "extraordinary preliminaries" include a 100,000 prostrations and repetitions of the refuge formula to establish commitment. This is followed by a 100,000 repetitions of the Vajrasattva ("indestructible being") mantra intended to purify "neurotic crimes and subtle obscurations." Then there are 100,000 mandala offerings, in which the practitioner imagines he is offering the universe-and his personal enlightenment-to the lineage figures.

Finally, having established devotional commitment, practiced purification, and offered his wealth, the practitioner invites the lineage blessing through a million repetitions of the guru yoga mantra. In this way he prepares himself for formal empowerment. We are brought into the vajra mandala or vajra world through what's called abhisheka. Abhisheka literally means "sprinkling" or "anointing." Through ritual means, the vajra guru blesses our body, speech, and mind, connecting us to the sacred world of the deity and its mandala. The teacher generates an atmosphere of blessing or power. He represents a kind of outlet that the student plugs into. It is not that the teacher has all the energy and the pupil has none, but that the student's energy is blocked.

It's not connecting properly. So by creating the energy bank of an abhisheka, the student is re-connected to the wisdom of his own basic nature. This is taught to be indispensable for doing the meditation practice the student then receives. Otherwise it would be like trying to drive a car without fuel, or run a machine without electricity. This is the formal way practices are often transmitted. But we can understand abhisheka as "meeting the guru's mind." This can come in myriad informal ways in the interaction of teacher and student. Naropa, for example, received the final transmission of enlightenment from his teacher Tilopa when Tilopa turned suddenly, as they climbed a path, and struck Naropa across the face with his sandal.

VAJRAYANA MEDITATION PRACTICES

When we receive a formal abhisheka, we are empowered to practice a sadhana. Sadhanas are liturgies based around a particular kind of deity. They always include the refuge and bodhisattva vows, a visualization of the deity, a mantra, the practice of formless meditation, and a dedication of merit. With body, we keep erect posture, and practice mudras, or ritual hand gestures. With speech, we chant liturgy and mantra. With mind we visualize the deity and its mandala. This corresponds to the practice of shamatha, and is called uttpatikrama, or "the development stage."

If the practice of following our breath in shamatha is challenging, consider the myriad of details in visualization practice, including costumes, multiple arms, subsidiary deities, details of the mandala palace, and so on. The visualization is always practiced as being indivisible from emptiness. When we finish the visualization, it is dissolved back into space, and we rest in formless meditation practice. This is called sampannakrama, or "fruition stage," and is connected to vipashyana. The effectiveness of this kind of practice relates in part to its ability to develop shamatha and vipashyana in us, and magnetize the qualities and wisdom of the deity we are practicing.

It also offers the possibility of transforming the energy of our thoughts and emotions into the deity's egoless wisdom. The practices provide tremendously effective skillful means for penetrating the nature of mind and liberating its energy. Vajrayana is known as the "Vehicle of Skillful Means." There are a very great many kinds of sadhanas. There is, additionally, a whole order of practices called "The Six Yogas of Naropa" (there are other similar sets of practices with other names), which include the practices of inner heat, illusory body, dream transformation, luminosity, bardo, and the transference of consciousness. These are yogic means that work with the subtle energy and chakras (centers of energy) in our mental bodies. There's a vast set of teachings on Mahamudra that develop stages of formless meditation There's a set of practices developing the final stages of enlightenment called Maha Ati, and many other practices too numerous to list.

THE ICONOGRAPHY OF DEITIES AND MANDALAS

The Tibetan word for mandala is "kyilkor," which means "center and fringe." Therefore we're talking about a circle, a center and circumference, which establish a complete world. At the center of the mandala is always a central deity. This deity is the Buddha principle, i.e., it stands for nothing, the emptiness that pervades the mandala. It says, in effect, nothing is at the center, and this then is the central gateway into the absolute Buddha mind. At the four gates and sometimes intermediate points, you will find subsidiary deities which express the different aspects and elements of the central deity's world. And possibly too, lesser figures who function as protectors of the mandala, guarding it against the demons of ego-clinging.

There are peaceful, semi-wrathful, and wrathful deities. They have different colors, bodily forms, and costumes, and correspond to different Buddha families, which we discussed above. There's a palace the deity occupies and sanctified grounds the palace is on. The important thing here is that every aspect of this iconography corresponds to some principle of awake mind. In essence, all deities, male or female, have the exact same nature: enlightenment. Relatively, they magnetize different energies of enlightened mind for the practitioner to work with. For example, white, peaceful Avalokiteshvara, bodhisattva of compassion in princely costume, develops a calm, compassionate energy which cools the furious rage of conflicting emotions. Wrathful, blue Vajrakilaya, with fangs, multiple heads, and multiple arms holding fire and weapons, cuts through the obstacles to awakened mind and enlightened action.

The shocking features of some deities symbolize enlightened mind transmuting demons into Buddhas, and the deities' wild appearance is a vigorous call to us to wake up from our dream of conventional appearances. Each aspect of a deity has its own symbolism. For example, Vajrayogini, a red semi-naked dancing goddess related to the Prajnaparamita and known as the "Mother of all the Buddhas," has three bloodshot eyes symbolizing her ability to know the past, present, and future. Her crown of five skulls symbolizes transmuting the five kleshas into the five wisdoms. The 51 severed heads in a garland around her neck show that she has conquered the 51 samskaras (ego-centered concepts). Her fangs terrify the maras, or the demons of ego-clinging. The flames she stands in are the flames of wisdom, and so on.

SAMAYA, GURU, AND DEVOTION

But why, we may ask, is all of this elaborate methodology necessary? Why aren't Hinayana and Mahayana sufficient? The answer is two-fold. The first is that in the Mahayana method there is still a subtle obscuration that's encouraged. The practitioner is still striving heroically upwards, trying to leave samsara for nirvana and bringing sentient beings with him. What's in the way here is a subtle quality of heroic ego. The noble aspiration of the bodhisattva path becomes an obstacle in itself. The practitioner is still subtly trying to accomplish something, and in the process separating himself from the awakened state. The Mahayana view of emptiness itself, while clearing away samsara, still encourages a subtle bias toward nirvana. So the practitioner needs to open up fully to the energies of the world outwardly, and to the energies of his own wisdom inwardly, and let go completely of strategies for becoming a purer, greater being.

The Vajrayana confirms the intrinsic spontaneity of awakened mind, and gives the yogi tools with which to dance with its energies, rather than strive to overcome them. The second reason we must go beyond the Hinayana and Mahayana methods can be told in three words: They're too slow. By giving us means to work directly with samsaric energy and transmute it into enlightened energy, we've been set on what's called "the quick path." Hinayana and Mahayana take countless lives to perfect; Vajrayana can potentially be accomplished in one. But for this very reason-its swiftness, its access to the power of enlightened mind-it presents real dangers to the practitioner. Specifically, the practitioner's ego can seek to use the power it acquires for its own selfish ends, growing inflated and poisonous in its dealings with others. The karmic retribution for this misuse of tantra is called vajra ("indestructible") hell, which offers little or no chance of escape.

Hence the necessity of developing the egolessness and compassion of the lower yanas and the nature of the tantric Samaya vow. The Hinayana refuge vow commits us to the Buddha, Dharma, and Sangha. The Mahayana Bodhisattva vow binds us to the path of compassionate activity as long as samsara lasts. The Samaya vow of Vajrayana, in the strictest sense, binds us to the Buddha mind itself. We are vowing never to stray from our own awake nature and the view of sacred outlook, which sees the world as the pure, non-dual Buddha field. It is a vow of non-duality. The teacher who gives us the vow is known as the guru, or vajra master.

We are bound to our own awakened mind, to the deity of our practice, and to the vajra master and his sangha. The vajra master is of utmost importance in tantric Buddhism. Through him-and the power of his realization-we are able to connect our body, speech, and mind to that of the lineage, and be guided in our understanding and practice of the teaching authoritatively. At the Hinayana level, the teacher functions as an elder giving us a good advice, guiding our progress. At the Mahayana level, he's a kalyanamitra, "spiritual friend," who has a much more intimate and personal relationship with us, critical and encouraging, demanding and inspiring. In the Vajrayana, the vajra master is seen as the Buddha himself, in the flesh. He holds lightning in his hand, and represents for us in a personal and direct way the power and inscrutability of the cosmos itself. Because he can point out the nature of mind to us, we can recognize it in ourselves.

More than someone who instructs us in the correct ways

to view dharma and to practice, he's the animating principle of the deities and their mandalas, and therefore the awakened energy of our body, speech, and mind, and our world itself. The guru is the ultimate gate into enlightenment. Therefore devotion to the guru is the key practice of vajrayana, in which the other issues are contained. Devotion we can define as a quality of longing and openness. We are longing for the awakened state of mind and open to our perception. In this way we are empty, pure vessels for the blessings of the lineage. The awakened heart of compassion and desire for enlightenment we've cultivated on the path becomes our connecting point with the vajra master's world.

The teacher, a living breathing, human being, introduces us to this world through his words, his skillful actions, and the intensity of his presence. We are brought to recognize our potential for living in the world he lives in: a sacred world where samsara and nirvana are indivisible, and the vajra master dances in effortless spontaneity and razor precision with phenomena. Devotion then becomes a matter of discipline altogether; to practice any teaching of the dharma is to express devotion, and to recognize the nature of our minds is to fulfill it. I would like to note here that the term "lamaism" is misapplied to tantra and inappropriate.

"Lama" is a Tibetan word and means guru. And while it's certainly the case that the lama or guru is of central importance in Vajrayana, Lamaism is a misleading term. It originates with early western explorers of Asia and implies that Vajrayana is based on personality cults and not the Buddha's teaching. The equivalent would be if we called Catholics "Popists," and Catholicism "Popism." While the Pope is obviously very important to Catholicism, it would not be accurate to centralize him at the expense of all else. Lamaism is an out-dated term, and was dropped from scholarly usage in Buddhist studies in the west long ago.

MAHAMUDRA AND MAHA ATI

The original tantric teachings to enter Tibet came first through Padmasambava, who taught the higher tantras called Maha Ati. Marpa the Translator brought the teachings of the lower tantras to Tibet, called Mahamudra. Together these teachings present a complete path of Vajrayana. The fruition of Mahamudra ("Great Symbol") is to dissolve our conceptualization of the universe completely into "non-meditation." Every aspect of phenomena is seen with direct and penetrating precision, unclouded by duality.

The displays of our thoughts and senses articulate the wisdoms of the five Buddhas. Chogyam Trungpa Rinpoche uses the example of a rock: "If we hold a piece of rock in our hands with that clarity of perception which is the direct contact of naked insight, we not only feel the solidity of that one rock; we experience it as an absolute expression of the solidity and majesty of the earth. I do not mean this in a physical sense alone; but I am speaking of solidity in the spiritual sense, the solidity of peace and energy, indestructible energy...the Wisdom of Equanimity. Everything [the yogi] sees is an expression of spiritual discovery. There is a vast understanding of symbolism and a vast understanding of energy. Whatever the situation, he no longer has to force results."

In Maha Ati we finally exhaust the ego-centered goal of attaining enlightenment. We wear out any bias toward samsara or nirvana and relinquish even the subtlest spiritual reference points to an ego, realizing what's called in Tibetan kadak or "alpha pure" being liberated entirely from conditions.

The term "vajra" denoted the thunderbolt, a legendary weapon and divine attribute that was made from an adamantine, or indestructible, substance and which could therefore pierce and penetrate any obstacle or obfuscation. As a secondary meaning, "vajra" refers to this indestructible substance, and so is sometimes translated as "adamantine" or "diamond". So the Vajrayana is sometimes rendered in English as "The Adamantine Vehicle" or "The Diamond Vehicle".

A vajra is also a scepter-like ritual object, which has a sphere (and sometimes a gankyil) at its centre, and a variable number of spokes (depending on the sadhana), enfolding either end of the rod. The vajra is often traditionally employed in tantric rituals in combination with the bell or ghanta; symbolically, the vajra may represent method and the bell stands for wisdom.

Serious academic study of Vajrayana is still in its early stages, because of a number of problems that make research difficult:

1. Although a large number of Tantric scriptures are extant, they have not been put into any kind of order.
2. Because Vajrayana was influenced by Hinduism, further research into Hinduism is necessary.
3. Ritual as well as doctrine needs to be investigated.

CLASSIFYING VAJRAYANA

VAJRAYANA AS A NEWLY COMPOSED TEACHING

The literature of Vajrayana is absent from the oldest Buddhist literature of the Pali Canon and the Agamas. Vajrayana claims that its teachings were first expounded by the Buddha 16 years after his enlightenment, but scholars have called this claim 'patently absurd'. Scholars have said that an early stage of Mantrayana began in the 4th century CE. Only from 7th or the beginning of the 8th century CE, tantric techniques and approaches increasingly dominated Buddhist practice in India. The first tantric (Vajrayana Buddhist) texts appeared in the 3rd century CE, and continued to appear until the 12th century CE.

VAJRAYANA AS EVOLVED FROM THE LOCAL CONDITIONS OF MEDIEVAL INDIA

Although the Vajrayana claims to be as ancient and authentic as any other Buddhist school, it evidently grew up gradually in an environment with previously existing texts such as the mahasannipata and the ratnaketudharani. The basic position of Vajrayana is still the same as the early Buddhist position of not-self: there is nothing which is eternal. The changes that took place agreed with the changing society of medieval India: the presentation has changed, the techniques of the way to enlightenment have changed, the outward appearance of Buddhism came to be dominated by ritualism and the array of Buddhas and Bodhisattvas and gods and godesses.

Classification based on Vajrayana scriptures and commentaries

The tantric scriptures and its commentaries provide three strategies to discuss the theoretical nature of Vajrayana Buddhism:

1. Vajrayana as a subset of Mahayana Buddhism
2. Vajrayana as a fruitional or advanced vehicle (where Mahayana is a prelude to Vajrayana)
3. Vajrayana as the sorcerer's discipline (vidyadharasamvara)

VAJRAYANA AS A SUBSET OF MAHAYANA BUDDHISM

According to this schematism, Indian Mahayana revealed two ways (naya): the method of the perfections (paramitanaya) and the method of mantra (mantranaya). The Paramitanaya consists of the six or ten paramitas, of which the scriptures say that it takes 3 incalculable aeons to lead one to Buddhahood. The tantra literature, however, claims that the method of the mantra leads one to Buddhahood in one single life. According to the literature, the mantra is an easy path without the difficulties inherent to the paramitanaya. Mantranaya is sometimes portrayed as a method for those of inferior abilities. However the practitioner of the mantra still has to adhere to the vows of the Bodhisattva.

When viewed as a subset of Mahayana, it is one of two practice paths: the *Sutrayana* method of perfecting good qualities and the *Vajrayâna* method of taking the intended outcome of Buddhahood as the path. Vajrayana requires mystical experience in order to experience Buddha-nature prior to full enlightenment. In order to transmit these experiences, a body of esoteric knowledge has been accumulated by Buddhist tantric yogis and is passed via lineages of transmission. In order to access this knowledge, the practitioner requires initiation from a skilled spiritual teacher or guru.

VAJRAYANA AS FRUITIONAL VEHICLE

According to the Vajrayana theory, Vajrayana refers to one of the three routes to enlightenment, the other two being

Hinayana and Mahayana. According to this view, there were three "turnings of the wheel of dharma":

1. In the first turning Shakyamuni Buddha taught the Four Noble Truths at Varanasi in the 5th century BC, which led to the founding of Buddhism and the later early Buddhist schools. Details of the first turning are described in the Dhammacakkapavattana Sutta. The oldest scriptures do not mention any further turnings other than this first turning.
2. The Mahayana tradition claims there was a second turning in which the Perfection of Wisdom sutras were taught at Vulture's Peak, which led to the Mahayana schools. Generally, scholars conclude that the Mahayana scriptures (including the Perfection of Wisdom Sutras) were composed from the first century CE onwards,
3. According to the Vajrayana tradition, there was a third turning which took place at Dhanyakataka sixteen years after Buddha's enlightenment. Scholars have strongly denied that Vajrayana appeared at that time, and placed it at a much later time. The first tantric (Vajrayana Buddhist) texts appeared in the 3rd century CE, and they continued to appear until the 12th century CE.

VAJRAYANA AS THE SORCERER'S DISCIPLINE

Vajrayana teaches that in order to access esoteric knowledge, the practitioner requires initiation from a skilled spiritual teacher or guru.

DISTINGUISHING FEATURES OF VAJRAYANA

The distinction between traditions is not always rigid. For example, the tantra sections of the Tibetan Buddhist canon of texts sometimes include material not usually thought of as tantric outside the Tibetan Buddhist tradition, such as the Heart Sutra and even versions of material found in the Pali Canon.

RITUAL

The distinctive feature of Vajrayana Buddhism is ritual, which is used as a substitute or alternative for the earlier abstract meditations.

GOAL AND MOTIVATION

The goal of spiritual practice within the Mahayana and Vajrayana traditions is to become a Buddha by following the bodhisattva path, whereas the alternative goal for Theravada practice is the ending of suffering. As with the Mahayana, motivation is a vital component of Vajrayana practice, and Vajrayana teaches that all practices are to be undertaken with the motivation to achieve Buddhahood for the benefit of all sentient beings.

UPAYA

The Vajrayana is based on the concept of "skillful means" (Sanskrit: upaya) as formulated in Mahayana Buddhism. It is a system of lineages, whereby those who succesfully receive an initiation (permission to practice) are seen to share in the mindstream of the realisation of a particular skillful means of the vajra Master. In the Vajrayana these skillful means mainly relate to tantric, Mahamudra or Dzogchen practices. Vajrayana teaches that the Vajrayana techniques provide an accelerated path to enlightenment.

TWO TRUTHS DOCTRINE

Vajrayana subscribes to the two truths doctrine of conventional and ultimate truths, which is present in all Buddhist tenet systems. The Two truths doctrine is a central concept in the Vajrayana practice path and is the philosophical basis for its methods. The Two Truths identifies "conventional" and "ultimate" truths. Conventional truth is the truth of consensus reality, common sense notions of what does and does not exist. Ultimate truth is reality as viewed by an awakened or enlightened mind.

In the Sutrayana practice, a path of Mahayana, the "path of the cause" is taken, whereby a practitioner starts with his or her potential Buddha-nature and nurtures it to produce the fruit of Buddhahood. In the Vajrayana the "path of the fruit" is taken whereby the practitioner takes his or her innate Buddha-nature as the means of practice. The premise is that since we innately have an enlightened mind, practicing seeing the world in terms of ultimate truth can help us to attain our full Buddha-nature.

Experiencing ultimate truth is said to be the purpose of all the various tantric techniques practiced in the Vajrayana. Apart from the advanced meditation practices such as Dzogchen and Mahamudra, which aim to experience the empty nature of the enlightened mind that can see ultimate truth, all practices are aimed in some way at purifying the impure perception of the practitioner to allow ultimate truth to be seen. These may be ngondro, or preliminary practices, or the more advanced techniques of the tantric sadhana.

VOWS AND BEHAVIOUR

In general, practitioners of the Vajrayana need to abide by a various tantric vows or samaya of behaviour. These are extensions of the rules of the Pratimoksha vows and Bodhisattva vows for the lower levels of tantras and are taken during iniations into the empowerment for a particular Anuttarayoga tantra. The special tantric vows vary depending on the specific mandala practice for which the iniation is received and also depending on the level of iniation. A tantric guru, or teacher, is expected to keep his or her samaya vows in the same way as his students. Proper conduct is considered especially necessary for a qualified Vajrayana guru. For example, the *Ornament for the Essence* of Manjushrikirti states:

Distance yourself from Vajra Masters who are not keeping the three vows who keep on with a root downfall, who are miserly with the Dharma, and who engage in actions that should be forsaken. Those who worship them go to hell and so on as a result.

The Ngagpa Yogis from the Nyingma School keep a special lay ordination.

ESOTERIC TRANSMISSION

Vajrayana Buddhism is esoteric, in the sense that the transmission of certain teachings only occurs directly from teacher to student during an initiation or empowerment and cannot be simply learned from a book. Many techniques are also commonly said to be secret, but some Vajrayana teachers have responded that secrecy itself is not important and only a side-effect of the reality that the techniques have no validity outside the teacher-student lineage. In order to engage in Vajrayana practice, a student should have received such an initiation or permission.

Reginald Ray writes that "If these techniques are not practiced properly, practitioners may harm themselves physically and mentally. In order to avoid these dangers, the practice is kept "secret" outside the teacher/student relationship. Secrecy and the commitment of the student to the vajra guru are aspects of the samaya (Tib. *damtsig*), or "sacred bond", that protects both the practitioner and the integrity of the teachings."

The teachings may also be considered "self-secret" meaning that even if they were to be told directly to a person, that person would not necessarily understand the teachings without proper context. In this way the teachings are "secret" to the minds of those who are not following the path with more than a curious investigation. The esoteric transmission framework can take varying forms. The Nyingma school of Tibetan Buddhism uses a method called Dzogchen. The Tibetan Kagyu School and the Shingon School in Japan use an alternative method called Mahamudra.

SUB-SCHOOLS

Although there is historical evidence for Vajrayana Buddhism in Southeast Asia and elsewhere today the Vajrayana exists primarily in the form of two major sub-schools, with one minor subschool.

TIBETAN BUDDHISM

The Tibetan Buddhist schools, based on the lineages and textual traditions of the Kangyur and Tengyur of Tibet, are found in Tibet, Bhutan, northern India, Nepal, southwestern and northern China, Mongolia and various constituent republics of Russia that are adjacent to the area, such as Amur Oblast, Buryatia, Chita Oblast, the Tuva Republic and Khabarovsk Krai. Tibetan Buddhism is also the main religion in Kalmykia. Vajrayana Buddhism was established in Tibet in the 8th Century when Úântarakcita was brought to Tibet from India at the instigation of the Dharma King Trisong Detsen, some time before 767 CE. He established the Nyingma School as a Tantric Mahasiddha Padmasambhava's contribution ensured that Tibetan Buddhism became part of the Vajrayana tradition.

While Vajrayana Buddhism is a part of Tibetan Buddhism in that it forms a core part of every major Tibetan Buddhist school, it is not identical with it. Buddhist scholar Alexander Berzin refers to "the Mahayana and Vajrayana traditions of Tibetan Buddhism". Training in the "common paths" of Sutra (including Lamrim) are said to be the foundation for the "uncommon path" of Vajrayana. The Vajrayana techniques which add 'skillful means' to the general Mahayana teachings for advanced students. The 'skillful means' of the Vajrayana in Tibetan Buddhism refers to tantra techniques, Dzogchen (Tibetan: *maha-ati*) and Mahamudra (Tibetan: *Chagchen*).

SHINGON BUDDHISM

The Shingon School is found in Japan and includes practices, known in Japan as Mikkyo, which are similar in concept to those in Tibetan Vajrayana Buddhism. The lineage for Shingon Buddhism differs from that of Tibetan Vajrayana, having emerged from India and Central Asia (via China) and is based on earlier versions of the Indian texts than the Tibetan lineage. Shingon shares material with Tibetan Buddhism - such as the esoteric sutras (called Tantras in Tibetan Buddhism) and mandalas - but the actual practices are not related. The primary texts of Shingon Buddhism are the Mahavairocana Sutra and Vajrasekhara sutra.

The founder of Shingon Buddhism was Kukai, a Japanese monk who studied in China in the 9th century during the Tang Dynasty and brought back Vajrayana scriptures, techniques and mandalas then popular in China. The school mostly died out or was merged into other schools in China towards the end of the Tang Dynasty but flourished in Japan. Shingon is one of the few remaining branches of Buddhism in the world that continues to use the siddham script of the Sanskrit language.

Although the Tendai School in China and Japan does employ some esoteric practices, they are peripheral and therefore Tendai is not seen as a truly esoteric school. The esoteric rituals came to be considered of equal importance with the exoteric teachings of the Lotus Sutra. By chanting mantras, maintaining mudras, or practicing certain forms of meditation, one is able to understand sense experiences as taught by the Buddha, have faith that one is innately an enlightened being, and that one can attain enlightenment within the current lifetime.

NEWAR BUDDHISM

Newar Buddhism is practiced by Newars in Nepal. This is the only form of Vajrayana Buddhism in which the scriptures are written in Sanskrit. Its priests do not follow celibacy and are called Vajracharyas.

TANTRA TECHNIQUES

According to the Vajrayana tradition, at certain times the bodymind is in a very subtle state which can be used by advanced practitioners to transform the mindstream. Such liminal times are known in Tibetan Buddhism as Bardo states and include such transitional states as during meditation, dreaming, sex and death.

DEITY YOGA

Deity yoga (Tibetan: *lha'i rnal 'byor;* Sanskrit: *Devata-yoga*) is the fundamental Vajrayana practice, often involving a sadhana liturgy and form, in which practitioners visualize themselves as the meditation Buddha or yidam. The purpose of Deity yoga is to bring the meditator to the realization that the deity and the practitioner are in essence the same, non-dual.

By visualizing oneself and environment entirely as a projection of mind, it helps the practitioner become familiar with the mind's ability and habit of projecting conceptual layers over all experience. This experience undermines a habitual belief that views of reality and self are solid and fixed. Deity yoga enables the practitioner to release, or 'purify' him or herself from spiritual obscurations (Sanskrit: klesha) and to practice compassion and wisdom simultaneously.

Beer (2004: p.142) states:

Deity Yoga employs highly refined techniques of creative imagination, visualisation, and photism in order to self-identify with the divine form and qualities of a particular deity as the union of method or skilful means and wisdom. As His Holiness the Dalai Lama says, "In brief, the body of a Buddha is attained through meditating on it".

The realization of Deity yoga is attained as a result of pure concentration on bringing the three bodies into the path, in which the practitioner mentally generates themselves as a Tantric Deity (Skt. Yidam) and their surroundings as the Deity's mandala. The purpose of doing this is to overcome ordinary appearances and conceptions which, according to Vajrayana, are the obstructions to nirvana and omniscience. Recent studies indicate that Deity yoga yields quantifiable improvements in the practitioner's ability to process visuospatial information, specifically those involved in working visuospatial memory.

FOUR COMPLETE PURITIES

Four Purities (Tibetan: *yongs su dag pa bzhi; yongs dag bzhi*) In defining Vajrayana, Yuthok *et al.* identify the "Four Purities" which define the principal Tantric methodology of Deity Yoga that distinguishes it from the rest of Buddhism:

Vajrayana...is a subdivision of Mahayana, which may be divided into Sutrayana and Vajrayana (or Tantrayana). Vajrayana is regarded as a swifter path and is considered superior to Sutrayana. Whereas Sutrayana focuses on the causal method, Vajrayana teaches the Resultant method [sic] because it includes the 'four purities': (1) purity of environment (2) purity of body (3) purity of resources and (4) purity of deeds.

Geshe Kelsang Gyatso explains:

Tantra is defined as an inner realization that functions to prevent ordinary appearances and conceptions and to accomplish the four complete purities... The four complete purities are the pure environment, body, enjoyments and activities of a Buddha.

Kalachakranet identifies and defines the "Four Purities" in a complementary though different fashion:

The main tantric practices can be summarised in the "Four Purities":

1. Seeing one's body as the body of the deity.
2. Seeing one's environment as the pure land or mandala of the deity.
3. Perceiving one's enjoyments as bliss of the deity, free from attachment.
4. Performing one's actions only for the benefit of others (bodhichitta motivation, altruism).

Imagery and ritual in deity yoga: representations of the deity, such as statues (murti), paintings (thangka), or mandala, are often employed as an aid to visualization, in Deity yoga. Mandalas are sacred enclosures, sacred architecture that house and contain the uncontainable essence of a yidam. In the book *The World of Tibetan Buddhism*, the Dalai Lama describes mandalas thus: "This is the celestial mansion, the pure residence of the deity."

In the same context, all ritual in Vajrayana practice can be seen as aiding in this process of visualization and identification. The practitioner can use various hand implements such as a vajra, bell, hand-drum (damaru) or a ritual dagger (phurba), but also ritual hand gestures (mudras) can be made, special chanting techniques can be used, and in elaborate offering rituals or initiations, many more ritual implements and tools are used, each with an elaborate symbolic meaning to create a special environment for practice. Vajrayana has thus become a major inspiration in traditional Tibetan art.

GURU YOGA

Guru yoga (or teacher practice) (Tibetan: *bla ma'i rnal 'byor*) is a practice that has many variations, but may be understood as a tantric devotional process where the practitioners unite their mindstream with the mindstream of the guru. The guru is engaged as yidam, as a nirmanakaya manifestation of a Buddha. The process of guru yoga might entail visualization of an entire lineage of masters (refuge tree) as an invocation of the lineage. It usually involves visualization of the guru above or in front of the practitioner. Guru yoga may entail a liturgy or mantra such as the *Prayer in Seven Lines* (Tibetan: *tshig bdun gsol 'debs*), an evocation and invocation of Padmasambhava, though this is neither necessary nor mandatory.

The Guru or spiritual teacher is essential as a guide during tantric practice, without their example, blessings and grace, genuine progress is held to be impossible for all but the most keen and gifted. Many tantric texts qualify the Three Jewels of Buddha, Dharma and Sangha thus: "Guru is Buddha, Guru is Dharma and Guru is Sangha" to reflect their importance for the disciple. The guru is considered even more compassionate and more potent than the Buddha because we can have a direct relationship with the guru. The guru therefore appears with the yidam and dakini in the Three Roots refuge formulation of the three factors essential for tantric attainments.

DEATH YOGA

Death yoga (or "bringing the three bodies into the path of death, intermediate state (bardo) and rebirth") is another important aspect of Tantra techniques. Although it is sometimes called death yoga, it is mainly practiced during life, during meditation. It can be practiced first according to generation stage and then according to completion stage. The accumulation of meditative practice helps to prepare the practitioner for what they need to do at the time of death. At the time of death the mind is in a subtle state (clear light) that can open the mind to enlightenment if it is skilfully used to meditate on emptiness (shunyata). During completion stage meditation it is possible to manifest a similar clear light mind and use it to meditate on emptiness.

This meditation causes dualistic appearances to subside into emptiness and enables the practitioner to destroy their ignorance and the imprints of ignorance that are the obstructions to omniscience. It is said that masters like Lama Tsong Khapa used these techniques to achieve enlightenment during the death process. Actually, there are three stages at which it is possible to do this; at the end of the death process, during the bardo (or 'in between period') and during the process of rebirth. During these stages, the mind is in a very subtle state, and an advanced practitioner can use these natural states to make significant progress on the spiritual path.

The Tibetan Book of the Dead is an important commentary for this kind of traditional practice. This Death yoga should not be confused with the non-Tantric meditation on impermanence and death, which is a common practice within Buddhist traditions used to overcome desirous attachment.

GENERATION AND COMPLETION STAGE PRACTICE IN THE ANNUTARAYOGA TANTRAS

In the highest class of tantra, two stages of practice are distinguished. In the first stage of generation, one practices oneself in the identification with the meditational Buddha (yidam), generally until one can meditate single-pointedly on 'being' the deity. In the next stage of completion, one engages in practices with the subtle energy system of the body (chakras and energy channels etc.) to actualize the physical and mental transformation into the meditation Buddha. (Similar practices are also found in Hindu tantra and yoga.)

In some Buddhist tantras, both stages can be practiced simultaneously, whereas in others, one first actualizes the generation stage before continuing with the completion stage practices. Details of these practices are normally only explained to practitioners by their teachers after receiving an initiation or 'permission to practice'.

CLASSIFICATIONS OF TANTRA

BY SCHOLARS

The scholar J.M. Kitagawa says that Tantrayana may be divided into three main types of tantra:

1. Vajrayana - established the symbolic terminology and the liturgy that would characterize all forms of the tradition.
2. Sahajayana - was dominated by long-haired, wandering siddhas who openly challenged and ridiculed the Buddhist establishment.
3. Kalachakra Tantra - is farthest removed from the earlier Buddhist traditions, and incorporates concepts of messianism and astrology not present elsewhere in Buddhist literature.

BY THE NEW TRANSLATION SCHOOLS

The Sarma or New Translation schools of Tibetan Buddhism (Gelug, Sakya, and Kagyu) divide the Tantras into four hierarchical categories, namely,

- Kriyayoga (action tantra)
- Charyayoga (performance tantra)
- Yogatantra (yoga tantra)
- Anuttarayogatantra (highest yoga tantra)
  - Further divided into "mother", "father" and "non-dual" tantras.

BY THE ANCIENT TRANSLATION SCHOOL

A different division is used by the Nyingma or Ancient school:

a. Three Outer Tantras:

- Kriyayoga
- Charyayoga
- Yogatantra

b. Three Inner Tantras, which correspond to the Anuttarayogatantra:

- Mahayoga
- Anuyoga
- Atiyoga (Tib. *Dzogchen*)
  - The practice of Atiyoga is further divided into three classes: Mental SemDe, Spatial LongDe, and Esoteric Instructional MenNgagDe.

HISTORY OF VAJRAYANA

INDIA

There are differing views as to where in the Indian subcontinent Vajrayana began. Some believe it originated in Bengal, now divided between the Republic of India and Bangladesh, with others claiming it began in Uddiyana, located by some scholars in the modern day Swat Valley in Pakistan, or in South India. In the Tibetan Buddhist tradition, it is claimed that the historical Shakyamuni Buddha taught tantra, but that since these are 'secret' teachings, confined to the guru/disciple relationship, they were generally written down long after the Buddha's other teachings, the Pali Canon and the Mahayana sutras.

The earliest texts appeared around the early 4th century. Nalanda University in northern India became a center for the development of Vajrayana theory, although it is likely that the university followed, rather than led, the early Tantric movement. India would continue as the source of leading-edge Vajrayana practices up until the 11th century producing many renowned Mahasiddha. (Vajrayana) Buddhism had mostly died out in India by the 13th century, and tantric religions of Buddhism and Hinduism were also experiencing pressure from invading Islamic armies.

By that time, the vast majority of the practices were also available in Tibet, where they were preserved until recently. In the second half of the 20th century a sizable number of Tibetan exiles fled the oppressive, anti-religious rule of the Communist Chinese to establish Tibetan Buddhist communities in northern India, particularly around

Dharamsala. They remain the primary practitioners of Tantric Buddhism in India and the entire world.

CHINA

Vajrayana followed the same route into northern China as Buddhism itself, arriving from India via the Silk Road some time during the first half of the 7th century. It arrived just as Buddhism was reaching its zenith in China, receiving sanction from the emperors of the Tang Dynasty. The Tang capital at Chang'an (modern-day Xi'an) became an important center for Buddhist studies, and Vajrayana ideas no doubt received great attention as pilgrim monks returned from India with the latest texts and methods.

TIBET AND OTHER HIMALAYAN KINGDOMS

In 747 the Indian master Padmasambhava traveled from Afghanistan to bring Vajrayana Buddhism to Tibet and Bhutan, at the request of the king of Tibet. This was the original transmission which anchors the lineage of the Nyingma School. During the 11th century and early 12th century a second important transmission occurred with the lineages of Atisa, Marpa and Brogmi, giving rise to the other schools of Tibetan Buddhism, namely Kadam, Kagyu, Sakya, and Geluk (the school of the Dalai Lama).

JAPAN

In 804, Emperor Kammu sent the intrepid monk Kûkai to the Tang Dynasty capital at Chang'an (present-day Xi'an) to retrieve the latest Buddhist knowledge. Kûkai absorbed the Vajrayana thinking and synthesized a version which he took back with him to Japan, where he founded the Shingon school of Buddhism, a school which continues to this day.

INDONESIAN ARCHIPELAGO

The empire of Srivijaya in southeast Sumatra was already a center of Vajrayana learning when the monk I-Tsing resided there for six months in 671 CE, long before Padmasambhava brought the method to Tibet. In the 11th century CE, Atisha studied in Srivijaya under Serlingpa, an eminent Buddhist scholar and a prince of the Srivijayan ruling house.

Through early economic relationships with the Srivijaya Empire, the Philippines came under the influence of Vajrayana. Vajrayana Buddhism also influenced the construction of Borobudur, a three-dimensional mandala, in central Java circa 800 CE.

MONGOLIA

In the 13th century, long after the original wave of Vajrayana Buddhism had died out in China itself, two eminent Tibetan Sakyapa teachers, Sakya Pandita Kunga Gyaltsen and Chogyal Phagpa, visited the Mongolian royal court. In a competition among Christians, Muslims, and Buddhists held before the royal court, Prince Godan found Tibetan Buddhism to be the most satisfactory and adopted it as his personal religion, although not requiring it of his subjects. As Kublai Khan had just conquered China (establishing the Yuan Dynasty), his adoption of Vajrayana led to the renewal of Tantric practices in China as the ruling class found it useful to emulate their leader.

Vajrayana practice declined in China and Mongolia with the fall of the Yuan Dynasty, to be replaced by resurgent Daoism, Confuianism, and Pure Land Buddhism. However, Mongolia saw another revival of Vajrayana in the 17th century, with the establishment of ties between the Dalai Lama in Tibet and the Mongolian princedoms. This revived the historic pattern of the spiritual leaders of Tibet acting as priests to the rulers of the Mongol empire. Tibetan Buddhism is still practiced as a folk religion in Mongolia today despite more than 65 years of state-sponsored communism.

TANTRA TECHNIQUES (VAJRAYANA)

Tantra techniques in Vajrayana Buddhism are techniques used to attain Buddhahood. Vajrayana partially relies on various tantric techniques rooted in scriptures such as tantras and various tantric commentaries and treatises. The most important aspect of the tantric path is to 'use the result as the Path'; which means that rather than placing full enlightenment as a goal far away in the future, one identifies with the indivisible three vajras that is, the enlightened body, speech and mind of a Buddha. The practitioner focusses on and identifies with the resultant Buddha-form or 'meditation deity', the *yidam* (Tibetan) or (Sanskrit) 'ishtadevata'.

In order to achieve this self-identification with the yidam, much symbolism, ritual and visualization is used in Buddhist tantric techniques. Tantra is defined as an inner realization that functions to prevent ordinary appearances and conceptions and to accomplish the four complete purities of a Buddha (environment, body, enjoyments and deeds). Secrecy is a cornerstone of tantric Buddhism, simply to avoid harming oneself and others by practicing without proper guidance.

It is not even allowed to explain the full symbolism and psychology of the practice to the uninitiated, which can easily lead to misunderstanding and dismissal by the uninitiated. Tantric techniques may initially appear to consist of ritualistic nonsense; however, it should only be practiced on the basis of a thorough understanding of Buddhist philosophy and strictly following the traditions.

Tenzin Gyatso, the 14th Dalai Lama says:

Tantra is limited to persons whose compassion is so great that they cannot bear to spend unnecessary time in attaining Buddhahood, as they want to be a supreme source of help and happiness for others quickly.

PRACTICES

Tantric techniques include:

- Repetition of special ritual phrases (mantras).
- Use of various yoga techniques such as Trul Khor, including breath control (Pranayama), yantra and the use of special hand positions (mudras).
- *Ganachakra* feasts with ritual consumption of meat and alcohol.

- Paramita sadhana.
- Lojong.
- Use of an extensive vocabulary of visual aids, such as cosmic mandala diagrams which teach and map pathways to spiritual enlightenment. Seed syllables in Tibetan and Lendza are also used.
- The use of ritual objects such as the vajra and bell (ghanta), phurba, hand drum (damaru), and many other symbolic tools and musical instruments.
- Use of specialized rituals rooted in Vajrayana cosmology and beliefs.
- Importance of a guru-disciple relationship, for example by ritual 'empowerments' or 'initiations' wherein the student obtains permission to practise a particular tantra.
- Of high importance are the oral transmissions given by a tantric master. These teachings are only given personally from teacher to student and are secret, because they demand a certain maturity of the student. Otherwise they might have a negative effect. Such teachings describe certain aspects of the mind and how to attain them, realize them by certain practices that can be dangerous to one's health if not prepared thoroughly; as such states of mind are normally experienced at the time of death. A mature yogi 'dies' in the meditation and comes back again, experiencing all the levels of mind.

DEITY YOGA

Deity yoga (Tibetan: *lha'i rnal 'byor;* Sanskrit: *Devata-yoga*) is the fundamental Vajrayana practice, generally involving a sadhana practice in which the practitioner visualizes themselves as the meditation Buddha or yidam of the sadhana. The purpose of Deity yoga is to bring the meditator to the realization that the deity and the practitioner are in essence the same, non-dual.

The yidam generally appears in a mandala and the practitioner visualizes themself and their environment as the yidam and mandala of their Deity Yoga practice. This visualization method undermines a habitual belief that views of reality and self are solid and fixed, enabling the practitioner to purify spiritual obscurations (Sanskrit: *klesha*) and to practice compassion and wisdom simultaneously. Robert Beer describes the process:

Deity Yoga employs highly refined techniques of creative imagination, visualisation, and photism in order to self-identify with the divine form and qualities of a particular deity as the union of method or skilful means and wisdom. As His Holiness the Dalai Lama says, "In brief, the body of a Buddha is attained through meditating on it".

VISUALISATION IN DEITY YOGA

Representations of the deity, such as a statues, paintings (Tibetan: *thangka*), or mandalas, are often employed as an aid to visualization in both the Generation Stage (Tibetan: *Kye-rim*) and the Completion Stage (Tibetan: *Dzog-rim*) of Anuttarayoga Tantra. The mandalas are symbolic representations of sacred enclosures, sacred architecture that house and contain the uncontainable essence of a yidam. In the book, *The World of Tibetan Buddhism*, the Dalai Lama describes a mandala: "This is the celestial mansion, the pure residence of the deity."

GURU YOGA

The Guru or spiritual teacher, in Tibetan Buddhism generally the lama, is essential as a guide during tantric practice. Without the guru's example, blessings and grace, genuine progress is held to be impossible for all but the most keen and gifted. Many tantric texts qualify the Three Jewels of refuge thus: "Guru is Buddha, Guru is Dharma and Guru is Sangha" to reflect their importance for the disciple. In the Vajrayana the guru is considered even more compassionate and more potent than the Buddha because a direct relationship can be had with the guru.

The Guru also appears in the 'Inner' refuge formulation of the Three Roots, the three foundations of tantric practice.

Guru yoga (or 'teacher practice') (Tibetan: *bla ma'i rnal 'byor*) is a practice that has many variations, but may be understood as a tantric devotional process where the practitioner unites their mindstream with the mindstream of the guru's Three Vajras. Guru yoga is akin to Deity yoga since the guru is engaged as the yidam, or meditational deity, a nirmanakaya manifestation of a Buddha.

The process of guru yoga generally entails visualization of a refuge tree as an invocation of the lineage, with the root guru channelling the blessings of the refuge tree (and thus the entire lineage) to the practitioner. It might involve visualization of the guru above or in front of the practitioner. Guru yoga may also entail a liturgy or mantra such as the *Prayer in Seven Lines* (Tibetan: *tshig bdun gsol 'debs*), an evocation and invocation of Padmasambhava, though this is neither necessary nor mandatory.

CLEAR LIGHT YOGA

The yoga of Clear Light focusses on accessing the luminosity of the mindstream that is seen to be its essential nature. Practices often include aspects of dream yoga, including lucid dreaming. It is one of the six yogas of Naropa.

BARDO PRACTICES

According to the Vajrayana tradition, at certain times when a person's mind is in a transitional state, or 'bardo', the various Vajrayana techniques can be particularly effective. Some of this states include during sex, death, meditation and dreaming and at other liminal states, the bodymind is in a very subtle state which can be used by advanced practitioners to transform the mindstream. According to the Vajrayana tradition it is possible to attain enlightenment in a single lifetime by practicing certain techniques.

Death yoga (or 'death practice') is another important aspect of Tantra techniques. Although it is called Death yoga, most of the practice actually happens during life. It is the accumulation of meditative practice that helps to prepare the practitioner for what they need to do at the time of death. At the time of death the mind is in a state (clear light) that can open the mind to enlightenment, when used very skillfully. It is said that masters like Lama Tsong Khapa used these techniques to achieve enlightenment during the death process.

Actually, there are three stages at which it is possible to do this; at the end of the death process, during the bardo (or 'in between period') and during the process of rebirth. During these stages, the mind is in a very subtle state, and an advanced practitioner can use these natural states to make significant progress on the spiritual path. The Tibetan Book of the Dead is an important commentary for this kind of traditional practice. This Death yoga should not be confused with normal meditation on death, which is a common practice within Buddhist traditions. In most non-tantra traditions it is done to reduce attachment and desire, and not to use the death process itself as a means to practice.

TANTRIC SADHANA

Tantric sadhana may include:

- Six Lokas
- Chöd
- Zhitro
- Dark retreat

There is an aspect of sex in Highest Yoga Tantra practice which is both symbolic as well as descriptive of the practice of using sexual intercourse to transform one's sexual potential into a blissful consciousness directed towards achieving enlightenment. The purpose is to refrain from ejaculating and this is the most important part, as one should be able to control the winds and energies of one's body.

It is also important for the consort to be as equally realised a practitioner as oneself. This practice is not a necessity to practise Vajrayana, as it is well known that Lama Tsong Khapa gained enlightenment without this practice. It is important to remember that sexual practices in the Vajrayana context are very different from ordinary sexual activity. This is an extremely advanced practice and should only be performed once realisations of the path have been achieved.

Some of the realisations include renunciation and bodhicitta, or the enlightened mind that is committed to attaining enlightenment for the sake of others. This is very different from ordinary sexual activity. Sexual symbolism is common in Vajrayana iconography, where it basically represents the union of wisdom and compassion or wisdom and method. This is of utmost importance as this shows that enlightenment can only be achieved through practising both wisdom and compassion.

According to some Tibetan authorities, the physical practice of sexual yoga is necessary at the highest level for the attainment of Buddhahood. The use of sexual yoga is highly regulated. It is only permitted after years of training. The physical practice of sexual yoga is extremely rare, and has been historically. A great majority of Tibetans believe that the only proper practice of tantric texts is metaphorically, not physically, in rituals and during meditative visualizations. The dominant Gelug sect of Tibetan Buddhism holds that sexual yoga as an actual physical practice is the only way to attain Buddhahood in one lifetime.

The founder of the sect Tsongkhapa did not, according to tradition, engage in this practice, but instead attained complete enlightenment at the moment of death, that being according to this school the nearest possible without sexual yoga. The school also taught that they are only appropriate for the most elite practitioners, who had directly realized emptiness and who had unusually strong compassion. The next largest school in Tibet, the Nyingma, holds that this is not necessary to achieve Buddhahood in one lifetime. The current de facto leader of the Gelug sect, the fourteenth Dalai Lama, holds that the practice should only be done as visualization. Shingon, along with all non-tantric forms of Buddhism, does not recognize sexual yoga.

5

Sacred Vajrayana Commitments

Over the half century or so that Vajrayana has been known in the West and the world at large, it has been liable to a great deal of misinterpretation and misunderstanding. The element that has probably been the cause of the greatest misunderstanding is the institution of initiation. Many have objected to initiation being a component of a path in the Buddhist tradition. There is nothing formally different in the Vajrayana initiation that sets it apart from other rites of passage which play an important role in the Buddhist tradition.

It is hard to understand why people can accept the refuge ceremony and the rite of monastic ordination but have difficulty with the idea of a Vajrayana initiation. I hope that, by indicating the contents of Vajrayana initiation and its role and function within the tradition, some of the misinterpretation and misunderstanding will be dispelled. Let us first look at the meaning of the Sanskrit term abhishekha, which has been translated as 'initiation,' 'consecration,' and even 'empowerment.' None of these is a literal translation of the original term, which in fact means 'sprinkling' or 'watering'- specifically, sprinkling water on an area of earth, such as a field.

We can begin to learn something about the nature of Vajrayana initiation if we consider why the term abhisheka was chosen for this ritual. The answer is that we have here a ceremony the purpose of which is to enliven or quicken the disciple's progress toward enlightenment. Just as we might sprinkle water on a field in which seeds have been sown, and by that sprinkling enliven and quicken the growth of the seeds, so in the Vajrayana initiation we enliven and quicken the growth of the seed of the disciple's spiritual potential.

We have here references to ideas that are already well developed in the Mahayana tradition-namely, the notion of the Buddha nature, or the potential for enlightenment, that all living beings possess. The process of growth and fruition of this spiritual potential is quickened by abhisheka, or 'sprinkling'-a clear indication of the function of that sprinkling, or initiation. Although it is inconvenient to translate abhisheka as 'watering' or 'sprinkling,' it is important to remember that the term refers to a process rather different in its purpose and intention from what we might think if we took it at face value, regarding it as a sort of initiation into a secret society or the like.

Let me try to expand on this very fundamental and linguistic definition of initiation in the Vajrayana tradition. Vajrayana initiation means introducing the disciple into the mandala- the sacred or magic circle of one of the tutelary deities of the Vajrayana pantheon-deities who are special esoteric forms of the Buddha, meditation on whom can bring about enlightenment. We saw that the mandala is a symbolic representation of the universe. In the context of an initiation, it represents not the universe as we know it, from an unenlightened point of view, but the sacred or pure universe that we achieve on the level of enlightenment, when our vision is purified of unwholesome tendencies.

Buddhas is applicable to this notion of the purified or transformed universe. Therefore, when we say that the Vajrayana initiation introduces a disciple into the mandala of one of the tantric tutelary deities, what we mean is that it introduces him or her to the purified universe of one of these deities. The Vajrayana tutelary deities can be divided into four classes of ascending power or efficacy in bringing about the transformation from an unenlightened mode of existence to an enlightened and sacred mode of existence: (1) the kriya class, (2) the charya class, (3) the yoga class, and (4) the anuttarayoga class. Initiation is the introduction of a disciple into the sacred universe of the tutelary deity of one of these classes of tantra.

The kriya class refers to a group of tutelary deities and practices primarily concerned with externalized rituals and practices. Kriya means 'action,' 'ritual,' 'ceremony.' The tutelary deities who belong to this class are associated with practices that are, by and large, external and ritualistic. Practices associated with the kriya class of tantra often involve vegetarianism, regular and even ritual bathing, and ritual offering.

In contrast, the tutelary deities of the charya class of tantra are associated with practices that have to do primarily with the internal attitudes, intentions, and conceptions of the practitioner. Whereas kriya tantra practices are external, the practices associated with the charya tantra class are usually internal, to the exclusion of the external practices. Practitioners of the charya class often present a much less sociable appearance than those of the kriya class of tantra. The third class, the yoga class of tutelary deities, is associated with a combination of practices belonging to the kriya and charya classes. Practices associated with the yoga class seek to arrive at a balance between the external and internal practices.

This balance, or union, between the internal and external practices is reflected in the term yoga, which means 'combination' or 'union.' In the case of the anuttarayoga tutelary deities, we have a transcendence or dissolution of the barriers that define the first three classes of practice (external, internal, and the combination of the two). Anuttara means 'transcendence,' in this case, a transcendence of external and internal practice alike. Thus the anuttara class of tutelary deities and practices is the most highly developed within the Vajrayana tradition.

It is at this level that we achieve, in its fullest sense, complete integration of experience into the Vajrayana path, integration that leads spontaneously to the transformation of being. This is the ideal referred, when discussing the purpose of the methodology of the Vajrayana-namely, complete integration of experience into the path. Initiation itself can be of three varieties. The first of these is the major initiation, which has a kind of comprehensive, all-encompassing function.

To use a rather prosaic analogy, a major initiation might be likened to a license empowering you to drive all kinds of motor vehicles, or to the broad powers that a government might give a special envoy to take up all decisions regarding a particular set of questions. A major initiation is a kind of complete empowerment that usually requires two days. The first day is given over to preparatory practices, which in general have to do with the purification of the disciple.

The second day is reserved for actually introducing the disciple into the mandala of the particular deity involved. The second kind of initiation is the subsidiary initiation, which might be likened to a license that empowers you to handle a rare, specialized class of practices, which are nonetheless important and highly efficacious. The third class is even more limited in scope, consisting of rather simple initiations, often very brief in terms of the time required to bestow them, that enable one to engage in relatively simple practices associated with subsidiary deities belonging to a larger family to whom one has already been introduced by means of the appropriate initiation.

These are sometimes termed 'subsequent initiations,' because they are traditionally given subsequent to major or subsidiary ones. Vajrayana deities are also divided into families (not related to the four classes of tutelary deities mentioned a moment ago) that are associated with the Buddhas of the Five Families-Vairochana, Ratnasambhava, Amitabha, Amoghasiddhi, and Akshobhya. For example, the tutelary deity Hevajra is associated with the Vajra family headed by Akshobhya, while *Chakrasamvara* is associated with the Buddha family of Vairochana.

A major initiation can be likened to the purchase of a season ticket for a whole series of events. The season ticket entitles you to participate in any or all of the events, although whenever you do you will naturally have to produce your ticket and perhaps have it stamped. Similarly, a major initiation entitles you to receive a whole series of subsidiary and lesser initiations, although, when receiving each initiation, you will still have to participate in the appropriate ritual. Traditionally, it is the major initiation that provides the disciple with access to the whole range of Vajrayana deities and practices.

In recent years, however, because of the growing demand for tantric initiations, Vajrayana masters sometimes choose to give one of the lesser, subsequent initiations first, since the practices associated with them are simpler. This has sometimes been found to be useful, in that it serves as a kind of trial exposure to Vajrayana practice, just as one might be given a license to drive a motor scooter before obtaining a license to drive all kinds of motor vehicles. All these initiations must be given by a qualified Vajrayana preceptor.

There are two types of qualification the preceptor may have. In the first case the preceptor, having achieved a very high level of mental development, receives direct empowerment from the deity concerned. This type of qualification is typified by the cases of the men of great attainment, or Mahasiddhas, in India, and also, less commonly, in Tibet. The second type of qualification is much more common. In this case the preceptor receives the empowerment of the deity from a qualified master.

He or she must also perform the required meditational practices-the retreats and so forth-stipulated by the tradition, so as to secure a sufficiently intimate association with the deity to function as a go-between with the power to introduce others to the mandala of the deity concerned. It is important that the Vajrayana initiation be received from a preceptor who has at least the second type of qualification. In the course of the Vajrayana initiation, the disciple regards the preceptor as identical with the tutelary deity into whose sacred circle he is being introduced.

Similarly, he regards the environment, the situation of the initiation, as identical with the sacred universe of that tutelary deity. In the course of the initiation, he is introduced to and identifies both with that tutelary deity (in the form of the preceptor in the initiation) and with the sacred universe, which is symbolized by the situation of the initiation itself. This process of introduction and identification takes place through the use of symbols. These symbols are both specific and general. The specific symbols are best represented by a variety of ritual objects.

These ritual objects are associated with, and stand for, the elements or actors who participate in this sacred drama, who inhabit this sacred universe. In our discussions of the symbols of the Vajrayana and of the five archetypal Buddhas of the Five Families, we spoke of a number of symbols that have particular meanings. We spoke of the five Buddha families being represented by symbols such as the vajra, the crown, the bell, and so forth.

In the Vajrayana initiation, these objects function as specific symbols by means of which the disciple can be introduced to the sacred universe and then identify himself with that sacred universe, that pure experience of an enlightened mode of being. In the course of the initiation, the disciple is given a vajra and bell to hold, a crown to wear, and so forth. These symbolic actions function to bring about (a) the introduction of the disciple to the sacred universe, and (b) an identification of the disciple with that sacred universe.

In addition to these specific symbolic objects, there are also the more general and dynamic symbols of identification. These are the symbols of light and water, which we also encountered in our discussion of Vajrayana symbolism. In the course of the initiation, light and water are used as a way of identifying the disciple with the tutelary deity and with the sacred universe. Light is used as a medium for identifying the disciple with the preceptor, who, in the context of the initiation, is identical with the tutelary deity.

Similarly, water is used as a symbol for identifying the disciple with the various levels of understanding of the sacred universe. In the initiation, both light and water form a kind of bridge by means of which the two initially different modes of being-namely, the distinction between the disciple and the preceptor in the form of the tutelary deity, and that between the experience of the disciple and the experience of the sacred universe-are identified and made one. The disciple is asked to participate in the process by visualizing light and water as media of identification with the purified universe portrayed in the Vajrayana initiation.

The initiation is a vehicle for transformation or, to put it more crudely, for rebirth, or regeneration. This is indicated by the fact that in a major initiation the disciple is given a new name, just as a new name is given when one becomes a Buddhist in the ceremony of the taking of refuge, or when one is ordained. The bestowal of the new name stands for the regeneration of the disciple in a new form, by virtue of his introduction to and identification with both the form of the tutelary deity and the experience of the sacred universe.

The initiation is important not only because it is itself an introduction to and identification with the sacred universe, but also because it supplies the disciple with the methods, or keys, with which he can later reintroduce, re-identify, and reintegrate himself with the sacred universe first encountered during the initiation. These methods or keys are (i) the vision with which he is supplied in the context of the initiation, when he sees for the first time, in symbolic form, the sacred and purified universe; and (ii) the mantra appropriate to the tutelary deity that he is given in the course of the initiation.

By means of this vision and this mantra, the disciple can recreate the sacred vision, reintroduce himself to the sacred experience, and re-identify himself with the sacred universe. This will occur subsequent to the initiation, in the practice of the meditation appropriate to the particular tutelary deity whose initiation the disciple has received. In the context of this meditation, he will use the keys received during the initiation-the vision and the mantra-to recreate, reintroduce, and re-identify him with the sacred experience on his own. He will then no longer need the support, the external environment, of the initiation.

Rather, he will be able to recreate, reintroduce, and re-identify himself with the pure experience represented by the initiation by means of the elements he received there. This is the primary role and function of the Vajrayana initiation. Like other initiations, the Vajrayana initiation brings with it certain commitments that must be respected and preserved by the disciple. Prosaic cases, such as licensing to drive motor vehicles or to practice medicine, also bring with them a commitment to respect certain codes or rules of action and intention. Similarly, in the Buddhist tradition as a whole, rites such as taking refuge and ordination into the monastic order bring with them certain commitments the disciple is expected to fulfill.

In very general terms, there are three sets of commitments in the Buddhist tradition-those appropriate for individual liberation (the pratimoksha vows), those appropriate for the resolve to liberate all living beings (the Bodhisattva vows), and those appropriate to Vajrayana practice (the Vajrayana vows). In brief, the essential quality of the commitments appropriate for individual liberation is the avoidance of injury to others; the essential quality of the commitments of the Bodhisattva is to benefit others; and the essential quality of the Vajrayana commitments is to regard all living beings as part of the pure vision, as deities of the sacred universe which the disciple has appropriated through the Vajrayana initiation.

It is important to bear in mind that consistency is not something that is given 100% attention to in Vajrayana. By this I mean that depending on different texts, sources, lineages and teachers, you will get slightly different classifications of things. For example, generally it is said that there are five Buddha-families but occasionally you will get references to a sixth family with Vajrasattva as the lord (in the five family classification, Vajrasattva belongs to the Vajra family with Aksobhya as the lord).

Apparently, this six family scheme is rather popular among the Vajrayana lineages in Nepal. Anyway, back to the original point. Therefore, what I write here might not totally agree with what some others might have heard or read. But basically, I think the idea should be the same - that is assuming I am on the right track. In a particular tradition that I am familiar with, it is said that there are three kinds of protectors. They are dharmapalas, lokapalas and ksetrapalas. Respectively they translate to "dharma-protectors," "world(ly)-protectors" and "field-protectors." Dharma-protectors are those who are highly advanced on the Path.

From Vajrayana's point of view, these beings are actually manifestations of the activities of the Buddhas. Some of these beings are considered Buddhas while some are on different levels of the Bodhisattva path. For example, Mahakala and Ekazati are both considered fully enlightened beings while someone like Dorje Lekpa is considered a tenth stage bodhisattva. The worldly-protectors refer to beings who have pledged to protect the teachings and practitioners.

These include powerful worldly gods, local spirits, energies and other beings. It is said that sometimes these beings do not even fully accept the teachings of the Buddha. They are in other words as deluded as we are some of them more, others less. Field protectors are usually associated with very specific places or buildings. In Tibet, families live in the same place and house for hundred of years. As time passes, it is believed that there are certain protectors especially connected with that particular house, clan or family. Spiritually both the worldly and field protectors are much lower than the Dharma-protectors. Both the worldly and field protectors are not particularly related to Dharma in the same way as Dhama-protectors are.

How should we relate to the protectors? I remember reading His Holiness the Dalai Lama's response to a similar question. His Holiness advised that it is actually sufficient to regard the Triple Gem (Buddha, Dharma and Sangha) as protectors. In his opinion, if one truly takes refuge in the Triple Gem they will be the best protectors one can have. He further explained that protectors are related to Vajrayana practice and only those who are deeply involved with Vajrayana practices should be concerned with the protectors. I suspect that His Holiness' response in this case is spoken for the general audience and in no way indicates that he is not in favor of protector practices. Other teachers also agree that if one really relies on the Triple Gem, protection is guaranteed.

Very briefly, according to Vajrayana, protectors should never be seen as something separate from oneself. Protectors actually have two levels which we can relate with. On the relative level, there are protectors like Mahakala, Palden Lhamo, Dorje Lekpa or Ekazati. There are numerous sadhanas (practices) associated with these protectors. But ultimately, it is our own rigpa (the natural mind which is empty, spacious and open) that is the protector.

The sadhanas usually have a structure where the meditator visualizes him or herself as a particular protector. The meditator is reminded again and again that his or her nature is never separate from the protectors'. Some teachers further explain that in a way, these protectors are simply our own awareness and mindfulness. Because we are beings with both body and mind, it is easier in the beginning for us to focus on some being with a form - the various protectors.

By meditating on their enlightened form - the various attributes and ornaments (these are related to different enlightened qualities and activities), one is to actualize these same enlightened qualities in oneself. In a sense, we can say that the protectors are our own awareness and mindfulness appearing in enlightened forms. With right awareness and mindfulness, we will be able to relate to things as they truly are (the wisdom aspect) and carry out the bodhisattva activities (the compassionate aspect).

Therefore, the effectiveness of these protectors is directly related to our own level of awareness and mindfulness. I have also heard another teacher explaining that the law of karma is the real protector. Here, he means that if one were to truly understand cause and effect, one will then abstain from performing any negative actions but instead only cultivate good. Perhaps on a more advance level, the Dharma-protectors are related to different forms and levels of energies. These energies are said to be latent in us.

By relating to a particular protector, one learns how to channel up a particular energy and to deal with it in an enlightened way. Because energy is simply energy (with negative and positive potentials), there is always a chance of not knowing how to deal with a certain energy that has been aroused through practice. Or perhaps the means of arousing that energy is misused. This is when it is believed that negative effects will occur. This effect might not only affect the practitioner himself but might include other as well.

Therefore, some teachers are extremely cautious when it comes to protector practices. In traditional language, protector's practice is something that one does only if one is certain that one can fulfill all the commitments (samaya or damtshig) related to that practice. Unlike practices like Chenrezig meditation or Tara, it is said that when the protector practice is done wrongly or is not done consistently, the protectors will get extremely "wrathful." These protectors are guardians of the different practices. It is also said that protectors are there to make sure that the purity of the lineage is protected.

And to do that, they guard the practices of the practitioners. It is not uncommon to hear people saying that when they became lazy in their practice or got distracted, something mysterious or supernatural happened that pulled them back into the Path again! And devout Tibetans will straightaway acknowledge the protectors for fulfilling their duties. There are also stories of protectors who guard term as - hidden "treasures" (teachings, ritual objects etc, that have supposedly been hidden by masters like Padmasambhava to be retrieved in latter days to benefit people).

Some of these protectors are even believed to fiecely guard these termas so that if the wrong people get these termas, they might be destroyed or the termas will simply vanish. These protectors are usually not Dharma-protectors but some worldly protectors. Therefore, on the relative level, these protectors are treated like independent beings who have pledged to protect the Dharma (but since the ultimate and relative can never be taken as distinct, one is always reminded of the ultimate protector - one's own natural mind).

Different lineages, teachers and practices have different special protectors. For example, Palden Lhamo and Dharmaraja is particularly associated with the Gelugpas. For the Kagyupas, Mahakala is especially significant. Different aspects of Mahakala (two-armed, four-armed, six-armed, female aspects) are practised by the Sakyas, Gelugs, Kagyus and Nyingmas. In the Drikung-Kagyu (one of the major sects in the Kagyu school), Achi Chokyi Drolma is a protector intimately related to members of this lineage. Milarepa himself is related to the five protector goddesses of Tibet - known as the Tseringmas.

Among the Nyingmapas, Ekazati, Rahula and Dorje Lekpa are protectors very closely related to Dzog-chen. The famous deity of the Nechung oracle is the personal protector of the Dalai Lamas. Various elaborate rituals and sadhanas are performed to these protectors in the lives of practitioners. There are certain monasteries that have protector practices carried out 24 hours a day for 365 days a year. If I am not mistaken, there are a group of monks specially charged with the task of performing protector practices for the welfare of His Holiness the Dalai Lama in particular, and the live of the Dharma in general.

So, if I have not totally confused my readers, I hope some of you will at least get a faint idea of what protectors are. If there is anyone out there that have further knowledge and experience that can be shared, do contribute! Call me a conservative, but part of the problem with trying to explain protector practice is that I am not sure what I should write and what I shouldn't. IMHO, protectors can be easily misunderstood. They can be easily seen as spiritual policeman that are out there to get you if you misbehave.

And lots of superstitions can come up from this kind of understanding - this is the last thing that I am trying to do. If I have to summarize the significance of protectors very briefly, in say one or two sentences, the following will be it: "Protectors, like other Buddhas and dieties related to one's practice, should never be seen as separate from one's natural mind, one's rigpa.

And to be mindful at all times of cause and effect is perhaps the most direct protector one can get."

DESCRIPTION OF THE PATH

The path begins and continues with meditation. Students are introduced to Buddhist and Shambhala teachings in the context of an ongoing meditation practice. Shambhala Meditation Centers around the world offer a broad and carefully thought-out range of classes, meditation programs and community activities. At our residential practice and retreat centers, students can deepen their meditation through longer programs, and engage in periods of intensive study.

The path consists of a series of programs designed to stabilize and strengthen a student's meditation practice, and to clarify their understanding of the teachings. Our courses offer entry into the classical teachings of the Kagyu and Nyingma lineages of Tibetan Buddhism, as well as the Shambhala wisdom presented by Chögyam Trungpa Rinpoche and Sakyong Mipham Rinpoche. Shambhala Training and the Shambhala Schools of Buddhist Studies both serve as graduated paths of instruction in the profound vision of the lineage.

In order to provide an environment in which Buddhism can flourish in the West, Chögyam Trungpa Rinpoche presented the spiritual journey in the cultural context of Shambhala-a personal and social vision of awakening that is accessible to everyone, all the time, even in the midst of busy daily life. The name and outlook for his approach comes from the legendary kingdom of Shambhala. This land has for centuries been seen throughout central Asia as a source of individual and cultural virtue: a place in which inhabitants led meditative lives of bravery, gentleness and intelligence, where they acted with responsibility and delight in caring for one another.

THE WAY OF SHAMBHALA

The Way of Shambhala is a complete introduction to the foundations of Shambhala Buddhism. This series of workshops and classes is an experiential overview of meditation practices, wisdom teachings, contemplative arts, and physical disciplines rooted in the ancient traditions of Shambhala and Tibetan Vajrayana Buddhism.

SHAMBHALA TRAINING: HEART OF WARRIORSHIP

The Shambhala Training Heart of Warriorship program introduces teachings on "warriorship" that cultivate genuineness, confidence, humor, and dignity in daily life. This course of study prepares students who wish to develop their practice and study further for Sutrayana Seminary and the Shambhala Sacred Path program.

SHAMBHALA SCHOOL OF BUDDHIST STUDIES

The Shambhala School of Buddhist Studies consists of a series of weekly classes and weekend intensives for anyone interested in learning about Buddhism. In the Shambhala School of Buddhist Studies, students delve into foundational Buddhist topics, such as karma, egolessness, and compassion with time for discussion and contemplation.

CONTEMPLATIVE ARTS AND PRACTICE

Inspired by Nalanda, an eleventh-century Indian university that welcomed teachings and disciplines from many different traditions- a number of arts, disciplines and activities have developed within Shambhala. The arts and other contemplative disciplines, including flower arranging, photography, tea ceremony, and kyudo, are a vehicle for integrating mindfulness and awareness into everyday life. Each represents a genuine contemplative path that further enriches our day-to-day experience.

SACRED PATH

The Sacred Path program introduces further practices to develop warriorship and extend the student's training in meditation. These practices are based on a societal vision and aspiration to help the world.

WARRIOR ASSEMBLY

Warrior Assembly, the culmination of the Sacred Path program, is a living teaching in creating enlightened society.

This training cultivates one's dignity and natural gifts in order to widen one's sphere of compassionate and practical influence.

DATHUN

Dathun (Tibetan for "month session") is a one-month group meditation retreat led by a senior teacher. It is a powerful introduction and deepening of mindfulness-awareness meditation, open to anyone. The program includes sitting and walking meditation, talks, study, and a short work period.

Silence and functional talking are observed and meals are served in the shrine room oryoki-style. Oryoki is a practice of mindful eating borrowed from the Zen tradition. After attending a dathun, students may choose to do a solitary retreat, and a number of Shambhala practice centres have facilities for individual retreats. Dathun is a prerequisite for attending Shambhala Seminary.

ENLIGHTENED WORLD

This new program taught by Sakyong Mipham Rinpoche provides an introduction and exploration of the basic principles of Buddhism. The teachings take the student through the three yanas (vehicles), from the foundation teachings of the Hinayana to the advanced teachings of tantra (vajrayana), giving an idea of the breadth of the Buddhist teachings as well as the unique path of Shambhala. Held at residential practice centres, this retreat includes meditation instruction, study, and contemplation and will provide an opportunity to meet the Sakyong and practice under his guidance.

REFUGE VOW

The refuge vow marks the decision to commit oneself wholeheartedly to the Buddhist path and to further one's practice and training. It is the formal commitment to being a Buddhist, following the example of the Buddha Shakyamuni, his teachings (the dharma) and joining the community (sangha) of fellow practitioners.

SHAMBHALA SUTRAYANA SEMINARY

Sutrayana Seminary deepens and expands a student's practice and study in a two week residential program alternating periods of intensive meditation practice with classes in Buddhist and Shambhala view. The program is led by a Shambhala acharya, assisted by other senior teachers.

BODHISATTVA VOW

The bodhisattva vow is further commitment to put others before oneself and to work wholeheartedly for their benefit. The basis of this vow is the aspiration to develop friendliness, compassion, and genuine insight through the practice of the six paramitas and to undertake the view and practice of the Mahayana.

SHAMBHALA VAJRAYANA SEMINARY

The Shambhala Vajrayana Seminary is the gateway for entering the Shambhala lineage and engaging in vajrayana Buddhist practices. These practices are based on the Kagyu and Nyingma traditions of Tibetan Buddhism and the Shambhala teachings, transmitted through Chögyam Trungpa and his lineage heir, Sakyong Mipham. The vajrayana path offers powerful methods for cultivating one's innate compassion and wisdom and is based on a strong teacher-student connection.

VAJRAYANA PRACTICE

At Shambhala Vajrayana Seminary, students receive vajrayana transmission from Sakyong Mipham and instructions to begin the special preliminary practices (ngöndro) of the vajrayana path. The vajrayana path of practice and study includes ngöndro practices, abhishekas (empowerments), the various sadhanas associated with them, and mahamudra and dzogchen practices. Vajrayana practice and study programs are held at both urban and residential Shambhala Meditation Centres to support a student's practice with teachings, group practice and guidance from acharyas and the Sakyong.

MONKS AND YOGIS

THE WAY OF THE FAKIR

The way of the fakir is the way of struggle with the physical body, the way of work on the first room. This is a long, difficult, and uncertain way. The fakir strives to develop physical will, power over the body. This is attained by means of terrible sufferings, by torturing the body. The whole way of the fakir consists of various incredibly difficult physical exercises. The fakir either stands motionless in the same position for hours, days, months, or years; or sits with outstretched arms on a bare stone in sun, rain, and snow; or tortures himself with fire, puts his legs into an ant-heap, and so on.

If he does not fall ill and die before physical will is developed in him, then he attains the fourth room or the possibility of forming the fourth body. But his other functions - emotional, intellectual, and so forth - remain undeveloped. He has acquired will but he has nothing to which he can apply it; he cannot make use of it for gaining knowledge or for self-perfection. And, as a rule, he is too old to begin new work.

But where there are schools of fakirs there are also schools of yogis. Yogis generally keep an eye on fakirs. If a fakir attains what he has aspired to before he is too old, they take him to a yogi school where they heal him, restore his power of movement, and then begin to teach him. A fakir has to learn to walk and to speak like a baby. But he now possesses a will which has already overcome incredible difficulties on his way and this can help him to overcome the difficulties on the second part of the way - the difficulties, namely, of developing the intellectual and emotional functions.

You cannot imagine what hardships fakirs undergo. I do not know whether you have seen real fakirs or not. I have seen many. For instance, I saw one in the inner court of a temple in India and I even slept near him. Day and night for twenty years, he had been standing on the tips of his fingers and toes. He was no longer able to straighten himself. His pupils carried him from one place to another; they took him to the river and washed him like some inanimate object. But this was not attained all at once. Think what he had to overcome, what tortures he must have suffered, in order to get to that stage.

A man becomes a fakir not because he understands the possibilities and the results of this way, and not because of religious feeling. In all Eastern countries where fakirs exist, there is a custom among the common people of promising to give to fakirs a child born after some happy event. Besides this, fakirs often adopt orphans, or simply buy little children from poor parents. These children become their pupils and imitate them, or are made to imitate them - some only outwardly, but some afterwards become fakirs themselves. In addition to these, other people become fakirs simply from being struck by some fakir they have seen.

Near every fakir in the temples, people can be seen who imitate him, who sit or stand in the same posture - not for long, of course, but still occasionally for several hours. And sometimes it happens that a man who went into the temple accidentally on a feast day, and began to imitate some fakir who particularly struck him, does not return home any more but joins the crowd of that fakir's disciples and later, in the course of time, becomes a fakir himself.

You must understand that I take the word 'fakir' in quotation marks. In Persia fakir simply means a beggar; and in India a great many jugglers call themselves fakirs. And Europeans, particularly learned Europeans, very often give the name of fakir to yogis, as well as to monks of various wandering orders. But in reality the way of the fakir, the way of the monk, and the way of the yogi are entirely different. So far I have spoken of fakirs. This is the first way.

THE WAY OF THE MONK

The second way is the way of the monk. This is the way of faith, the way of religious feeling, religious sacrifice. Only a man with very strong religious emotions and a very strong religious imagination can become a 'monk' in the true sense of the word. The way of the monk also is very long and hard. A monk spends years and tens of years struggling with himself, but all his work is concentrated on the second room, on the second body, that is, on feelings. Subjecting all his other emotions to one emotion, that is, to faith, he develops unity in himself, will over the emotions, and in this way reaches the fourth room.

But his physical body and his thinking capacities remain undeveloped. In order to be able to make use of what he has attained, he must develop his body and his capacity to think. This can be achieved only by means of fresh sacrifices, fresh hardships, and fresh renunciations. A monk has to become a yogi and a fakir. Very few get as far as this; even fewer overcome all difficulties. Most of them either die before this or become monks in outward appearance only.

THE WAY OF THE YOGI

The third way is the way of the yogi. This is the way of knowledge, the way of mind. The way of the yogi consists in working on the third room and in striving to enter the fourth room by means of knowledge. The yogi reaches the fourth room by developing his mind; but his body and emotions remain undeveloped and, like the fakir and the monk, he is unable to make use of his attainment. He knows everything but can do nothing. In order to begin to do he must gain the mastery over his body and emotions, that is, over the first and second rooms. To do this he must again set to work and again obtain results by means of prolonged efforts.

In this case, however, he has the advantage of understanding his position, of knowing what he lacks, what he must do, and in what direction he must go. But, as on the way of the *fakir* or the monk, very few on the way of the yogi acquire this understanding, that is, that level in his work on which a man knows where he is going. A great many stop at one particular achievement and go no further.

Teacher and Pupil

The ways also differ from each other by their relation to the teacher or leader. On the way of the fakir a man has no teacher in the true sense of the word. The teacher in this case does not teach but simply serves as an example. The pupil's work consists in imitating the teacher. On the way of the monk a man has a teacher, and a part of his duty, a part of his work, consists in having absolute faith in the teacher - in submitting to him absolutely, in obedience. But the chief thing on the way of the monk is faith in God, in the love of God, in constant efforts to obey and serve God - although, in his understanding of the idea of God and of serving God, there may be much that is subjective and contradictory.

On the way of the yogi a man can do nothing, and must do nothing, without a teacher. In the beginning he must imitate his teacher like the fakir and believe in him like the monk. But, afterwards, a man on the way of the yogi gradually becomes his own teacher. He learns his teacher's methods and gradually learns to apply them to himself. But all the ways, the way of the fakir as well as the way of the monk and the way of the yogi, have one thing in common. They all begin with the most difficult thing, with a complete change of life, with a renunciation of all worldly things.

A man must give up his home and his family if he has one. He must renounce all the pleasures, attachments, and duties of life, and go out into the desert or into a monastery or a yogi school. From the very first day, from the very first step on his way, he must die to the world; only thus can he hope to attain anything on one of these ways.

Difficulty

In order to grasp the essence of this teaching it is necessary clearly to understand the idea that the ways are the only possible methods for the development of man's hidden possibilities. This in turn shows how difficult and rare such development is. The development of these possibilities is not a law. The law for man is existence in the circle of mechanical influences, the state of 'man-machine'. The way of the development of hidden possibilities is a way against nature. This explains the difficulties and the exclusiveness of the ways.

The ways are narrow and strait. But at the same time only by them can anything be attained.

In the general mass of everyday life, especially modern life, the ways are a small, quite imperceptible, phenomenon which, from the point of view of life, need not exist at all. But this small phenomenon contains in itself all that man has for the development of his hidden possibilities. The ways are opposed to everyday life, based upon other principles and subject to other laws. In this consists their power and their significance? In everyday life, even in a life filled with scientific, philosophical, religious, or social interests, there is nothing, and there can be nothing, which could give the possibilities which are contained in the ways.

The ways lead, or should lead, man to immortality. Everyday life, even at its best, leads man to death and can lead to nothing else. The idea of the ways cannot be understood if the possibility of man's evolution without their help is admitted. As a rule it is hard for man to reconcile himself to this thought: it seems to him exaggerated, unjust, and absurd. He has a poor understanding of the meaning of the word 'possibility'. He fancies that if he has any possibilities in himself they must be developed and that there must be means for their development.

From a total refusal to acknowledge in him any possibilities whatever, man generally proceeds forthwith to demand the imperative and inevitable development of these possibilities. It is difficult for him to accept on the one hand the thought that his possibilities may remain altogether undeveloped and disappear; and on the other hand that their development requires of him tremendous effort and endurance. As a matter of fact, if we take all the people who are fakirs, monks, or yogis, and of whom we may say with confidence that they never will be fakirs, monks, or yogis, then we may say with undoubted certainty that their possibilities cannot be developed and will not be developed.

This must be clearly understood in order to grasp all that follows. In the ordinary conditions of cultured life the position of a man - even of an intelligent man who is seeking for knowledge - is hopeless. In the circumstances surrounding him, there is nothing resembling either *fakir* or yogi schools, while the religions of the West have degenerated to such an extent that for a long time there has been nothing alive in them. Various occult and mystical societies and naïve experiments in the nature of spiritualism, and so on, can give no results whatever. The position would indeed be hopeless if the possibility of yet a fourth way did not exist.

A Fourth Way

The fourth way requires no retirement into the desert and does not require a man to give up and renounce everything by which he formerly lived. The fourth way begins much further on than the way of the yogi. This means that a man must be prepared for the fourth way and this preparation must be acquired in ordinary life and be a very serious one, embracing many different sides. Furthermore, a man must be living in conditions favourable for work in the fourth way or, in any case, in conditions which do not render it impossible.

It must be understood that both in the inner and in the external life of a man, there may be conditions which create insuperable barriers to the fourth way. Furthermore, the fourth way has no definite forms like the ways of the fakir, the monk, and the yogi. And, first of all, it has to be found. This is the first test. It is not as well known as the three traditional ways. There are many people who have never heard of the fourth way and there are others who deny its existence or possibility.

COMPARISON WITH OTHER WAYS

At the same time the beginning of the fourth way is easier than the beginning of the ways of the fakir, the monk, and the yogi. On the fourth way it is possible to work and to follow this way while remaining in the usual conditions of life, continuing to do the usual work, preserving former relations with people, and without renouncing or giving up anything. On the contrary, the conditions of life in which a man is placed at the beginning of his work - in which, so to speak, the work finds him - are the best possible for him, at any rate at the beginning of the work.

These conditions are natural for him. These conditions are the man himself, because a man's life and its conditions correspond to what he is. Any conditions different from those created by life would be artificial for a man and in such artificial conditions the work would not be able to touch every side of his being at once. Thanks to this, the fourth way affects simultaneously every side of man's being. It is work on the three rooms at once. The *fakir* works on the first room, the monk on the second, and the yogi on the third.

In reaching the fourth room the fakir, the monk, and the yogi leave behind them many things unfinished, and they cannot make use of what they have attained because they are not masters of all their functions. The *fakir* is master of his body but not of his emotions or his mind; the monk is master of his emotions but not of his body or his mind; the yogi is master of his mind but not of his body or his emotions. Then the fourth way differs from the other ways in that the principal demand made upon a man is the demand for understanding.

A man must do nothing that he does not understand, except as an experiment under the supervision and direction of his teacher. The more a man understands what he is doing, the greater will be the results of his efforts. This is a fundamental principle of the fourth way. The results of work are in proportion to the consciousness of the work. No 'faith' is required on the fourth way; on the contrary, faith of any kind is opposed to the fourth way. On the fourth way a man must satisfy himself of the truth of what he is told. And until he is satisfied he must do nothing.

The method of the fourth way consists in doing something in one room and simultaneously doing something corresponding to it in the other two rooms - that is to say, while working on the physical body to work simultaneously on the mind and the emotions; while working on the mind to work with the physical body and the emotions; while working on the emotions to work on the mind and the physical body. This can be achieved thanks to the fact that on the fourth way it is possible to make use of certain knowledge inaccessible to the ways of the fakir, the monk, and the yogi.

This knowledge makes it possible to work in three directions simultaneously. A whole parallel series of physical, mental, and emotional exercises serves this purpose. In addition, on the fourth way it is possible to individualise the work of each separate person, that is to say, each person can do only what is necessary and not what is useless for him.

This is due to the fact that the fourth way dispenses with a great deal of what is superfluous and is preserved in the other ways simply through tradition. When a man attains will on the fourth way, he can make use of it because he has acquired control of all his bodily, emotional, and intellectual functions. And besides, he has saved a great deal of time by working on the three sides of his being in parallel and simultaneously.

The 'Sly' Man

The fourth way is sometimes called 'the way of the sly man'. The 'sly man' knows some secret which the fakir, monk, and yogi do not know. How the 'sly man' learned this secret is not known. Perhaps he found it in some old books; perhaps he inherited it; perhaps he bought it; perhaps he stole it from someone. It makes no difference. The 'sly man' knows the secret and, with its help, outstrips the fakir, the monk, and the yogi. Of the four, the *fakir* acts in the crudest manner; he knows very little and understands very little.

Let us suppose that by a whole month of intense torture he develops in himself certain energy, a certain substance which produces certain changes in him. He does it absolutely blindly, with his eyes shut, knowing the aim, methods or results, simply in imitation of others. The monk knows what he wants a little better; he is guided by religious feeling, by religious tradition, by a desire for achievement, for salvation; he trusts his teacher who tells him what to do, and he believes that his efforts and sacrifices are 'pleasing to God'.

Let us suppose that a week of fasting, continual prayer, privations, and so on, enable him to attain what the fakir develops in himself by a month of self-torture. The yogi knows considerably more. He knows what he wants, he knows why he wants it, and he knows how it can be acquired. He knows, for instance, that it is necessary for his purpose to produce a certain substance in himself. He knows that this substance can be produced in one day by a certain kind of mental exercises or concentration of consciousness. So he keeps his attention on these exercises for a whole day without allowing himself a single outside thought, and he obtains what he needs.

In this way a yogi spends on the same thing only one day compared with a week spent by the monk and a month spent by the fakir. But on the fourth way knowledge is still more exact and perfect. A man who follows the fourth way knows quite definitely what substances he needs for his aims and he knows that these substances can be produced within the body by a month of physical suffering, by a week of emotional strain, or by a day of mental exercises - and also, that they can be introduced into the organism from without if it is known how to do it.

And so, instead of spending a whole day in exercises like the yogi, a week in prayer like the monk, or a month in self-torture like the fakir, he simply prepares and swallows a little pill which contains all the substances he wants and, in this way, without loss of time, he obtains the required results. It must be noted further that in addition to these proper and legitimate ways, there are artificial ways which give temporary results only, and wrong ways which may even give permanent results, only wrong results. On these ways a man seeks the key to the fourth room and sometimes finds it. But what he finds in the fourth room is not yet known. It also sometimes happens that the door to the fourth room is opened artificially with a skeleton key. In both these cases, the room may prove to be empty.

Western "Culture"

It is, of course, hard for a man of Western culture to accept the idea that an ignorant fakir, a naive monk, or a yogi who has retired from life may be on the way to evolution while an educated European, armed with 'exact knowledge' and all the latest methods of investigation, is moving in a circle from which there is no escape. That is only because people believe in progress and culture. There is no progress whatever. Everything is just the same as it was thousands, and tens of thousands, of years ago.

The outward form changes and the essence do not change. Man remains just the same. 'Civilised' and 'cultured' people live with exactly the same interests as the most ignorant savages. Modern civilisation is based on violence and slavery and fine words. But all these fine words about 'progress' and 'civilisation' are merely words. Gods in Oriental Mythology had a special ability. They could fly. However, ordinary mortals could master the unique art of flying too. For example, Indian Brahmans, yogis, hermits and fakirs could rise and float in the air.

There is a chapter in the Vedas on levitation, a sort of guidelines on how to reach a state required for taking off the ground. Unfortunately, the meaning of many ancient Indic words and concepts has been irretrievably lost over the last few centuries and therefore the invaluable instructions can not be translated into modern languages. As regards the ancient levitators, records at hand say that they were able to rise above the ground up to 90 cm. They did not lift off to impress the onlookers; they simply wanted to assume the most suitable position for performing religious rites.

The art of levitation still exists both in India and Tibet. Many scholars engaged in oriental studies also mention the phenomenon of "flying lamas." Alexandra David-Neel, a British explorer, one day witnessed the flight of a Buddhist monk. The monk flew a few dozen meters over the alpine plateau Cnang Tang. He was bouncing off the ground like a tennis ball to rise in the air again and again. He kept his eyes on some guiding star hanging somewhere in the distance; the monk was the only person who could see the star in broad daylight.

Europeans have long been aware of levitation too. There was one big difference between Eastern and Western medieval levitators. Unlike the Brahmans, yogis and lams, the monks in Europe never took any special training for levitational purposes. They would normally rise in the air after reaching a state of ultimate religious ecstasy. According to trustworthy records, Saint Theresa, a Carmelite nun, was one of the first levitator of the middle Ages. Her flight was seen by 230 catholic priests. The nun wrote about her unusual "gift" in the autobiography dated 1565.

It is quite noteworthy that Saint Theresa herself did not want to fly. She spent long hours praying desperately in an attempt to get rid of her special power. She was asking Lord to relieve her of that grace. One night the Almighty finally heard the nun's praying. She did not fly ever since that night. Josef Desa used to be the most famous "flying man." He was born into a devout family in South Italy. Since he was a boy, Josef was a very religious person prone to inflicting all kinds of torture upon him in order to experience a state of religious ecstasy.

Later he joined the Franciscans. He would get really ecstatic at times and rise in the air. One day he floated right before the Pope's very eyes. Josef arrived in Rome. The Pope Urban VIII granted him an audience. Josef got as excited as one could be. He could not help rising in the air. The head of the Order of St. Francis eventually brought Josef back to earth. Men of science observed more than a hundred cases of levitation of Josef. They put down their comments in the official records. However, the Christians were thought to be embarrassed by Josef's flights. As a result, Josef was sent to a out-of-the-way monastery in 1653.

He was transferred to another monastery three months later, then to another one. The list can go on. Wherever he appeared, the news about the "miracle man" spread like wild fire. People from the neighboring towns and villages stood outside the monastery walls waiting for a miracle. Finally, Josef was transferred to a monastery in Osimo where he died in the fall of 1663. He was canonized four year later. Daniel Douglas Hewm was the most famous levitator of the 19th century. Below is the description of his first flight penned by an editor of an American newspaper.

"All of a sudden Hewm began lifting off and all the people in the room got completely surprised. I could see his legs floating about a foot about the ground. Hewm apparently could not speak as he had a twinge going from top to toe after the clash of fear and rapture in his mind. He went down some time later, and rose up again. He went up to the ceiling during a third ascent."

Hewm learned to levitate of his own free will later on. He showed his outstanding ability to thousands of spectators including such celebrities as William Makepeace Thackeray and Mark Twain, Napoleon III, other politicians, doctors and scientists of note. Hewm has never been accused of hoaxing an audience. There is a lot of controversy regarding a physical nature of levitation. Some researchers say that it is a product of the biogravitational field created by a special kind of mental energy emitted by the human brain. Doctor of Biological Sciences Alexander Dubrov is a supporter of this hypothesis. Dr. Dubnov points out that the biogravitational field is deliberately created by a levitator and therefore the latter can control the field and change the direction of a flight.

Vajrayana's (Tantric yoga) practices and doctrines were in vogue in India when Buddhism flowered there, and were also spread to Tibet, China and Japan long afterwards also. Vajrayana holds as a basic truth that the seeming opposite's nirvana and samsara are much as "two sides of a polarity". *Worth noting:* Kukai (Kobo Daishi -774-835), founded the Buddhist Shingon school in Japan. He taught that:

- 1. In an early stage of human spiritual development, humans are governed by instincts.
- 2. In the second stage they should seek to live morally (and drop detrimental rituals, if any).
- 3. In the third stage individuals strive for enablements.
- 4-5. In the fourth and fifth stages man goes for self-enlightenment.
- 6. The next stages may lead one to compassion.

Kukai's stages of development antedates several educational views in vogue in our days. The acme of spiritual development - fulfilment - is given by the Buddha body beyond, timeless and immutable, yet within many as their

Buddha-nature. Tantrism appears both in Buddhism and in Hinduism. In one form of tantra, Vamacara, (that of "left-handed practises"), the focus is on enjoyment, and halfway ritualising ways to it. Maithuna, sexual coupling, can be good for attaining both enlightenment and bliss in a Vajrayanic process.

Consider the proverb: "Fire is a good servant but a bad master." The subtle Buddha-nature is Enlightenment itself. Becoming aware of Reality thus is truly valuable. And Mahayana emphasises reality-as-such. Besides, proper meditation helps everyday life.

VAJRAYANA (TANTRA YOGA)

In India, Bihar and Bengal remained largely late Mahayana and Tantric Buddhist till the 1200s AD. The Mahayanaic Buddhist tradition of Tibet stems from a conversion between the 600s and 1000s AD. And, "When Tibet was being converted to Buddhism; the most dynamic form of Buddhism in India was Vajrayana." The guru Padmasambhava (Guru Rinpoche) was invited to Tibet in 747 by King Thi-srong-detsan there. His teachings emphasise Tantric ritual, worship, and Yoga. A Tibetan school, Kagyupa (Bka'-brgyud-pa), have guarded the teachings and songs of Milarepa (Mi-la ras-pa) (1040–1123), who is told of as the greatest poet-saint in Tibetan history. The account of his life is fascinating. In the Kagyupa School the supreme goal is named mahamudra ("the Great Seal", "the Great Symbol"). Many lineages have branched out too.

Chief of the celestial bodhisattvas that people got much devoted to, is Avalokitesvara, the Lord of Compassion, and patron saint of Tibet [Ebu "Buddhism"]. From the first century onward celestial bodhisattvas became popular, especially Manjughosa ("Gentle Voice") or Manjusri ("Glorious Gentle One"), the representative of divine wisdom; Avalokitesvara, the "Lord of Compassion"; and Vajrapani, "the one who wields the ritual thunderbolt (vajra)" and who entered the pantheon as a great protector. These three bodhisattvas came to be associated with particular Buddhas.

TANTRAS (TREATISES)

Buddhist tantras (treatises, texts, and works) are written in a highly figurative language, and are individually oriented. They used to be kept secret. In different Buddhist schools [of thinking with their methods and ceremonies], the tantras (texts and treatises) are many. Some deal with ritual, yoga, yoga-sex, and magic. The tantras ("treatises") form a distinctive literature of Esoteric Buddhism. They deal with the existential take of how it is or feels to attain the highest goal. Tantras emphasise the polarities activity, awareness, and their unity.

Handling it

Vajrayana stresses the gaining of enlightenment through a graduated process of contemplation (dhyana and better), directed by an initiated teacher. The Vajrayana practice, which is advancement toward enlightenment, usually requires initiation. It is said to be necessary to get initiation in tantra-yoga (Vajrayana). A proficient guru can direct the pupil's steps so that the pupil learns to control mental and physical processes better. The monastic strives for monasteries and monastic rules; the Highest being for monastic laxity at least.

SYMBOLISM AND ART

Symbols do not help us to recapture inner experiences. Buddhist art contains a wealth of valuable symbols and icons. Hence, tantra yoga is rich in symbols and art. Some ideas and symbols in tantras have in the course of time been explained and commented on. "The Buddha protected by a cobra's hood represents a coalescing of the Buddha myth with the pre-Buddhist cult of snakes as protecting divinities (the naga cult)." Some types of Vajrayana imagery and practice deal with the union of the passive female deity (or wisdom and proper forms), with the dynamic male (virility and demands). A union helps "great bliss" on and up, it is held.

MANTRAYANA (THE WAYS OF MANTRAS)

Mantrayana is associated with the Indian Padmasambhava (Guru Rin-poche), who flourished in the 700s AD and supervised the building of a monastery in Tibet. Esoteric ("Insider") Buddhism played a great role in China earlier. The mantras (syllables, words, sometimes word phrases) in Vajrayana are thought to contain seeds or essences of universal forces. Silent, mental recital of mantras (efficient syllables, words, and phrases) is the essence of mantrayana.

Mantras are either spoken aloud or sounded internally in one's mind. The latter approach is the better one. There is a hint in the Manu Samhita, "An offering, consisting of muttered prayers, is ten times more efficacious than a sacrifice performed according to the rules (of the Veda); a (prayer) which is inaudible (to others) surpasses it a hundred times, and the mental (recitation of sacred texts) a thousand times [2:85]."

The figures Manu employs may be taken to be general or poetic mentions. A transferred idea is that to repeat one's mantra mentally and with skill, tends to be a superior practice. Good mantras are means of entering into contact with a power and prowess encapsuled in a sort of seed form (bija) in the sounds of the mantra. The mantras that embody harmony are far from the only ones that are found. Mantras are said to introduce and infuse great qualities into the mantra yogi.

6

The Four Main Samayas

The samaya is a set of vows or precepts given to initiates of an esoteric Vajrayana Buddhist order as part of the Abhiseka ceremony of empowerment or initiation that creates a bond between the guru and disciple. In one of the most widely followed teachings on samaya, Sakya Pandita, a preeminent 12th century Tibetan Buddhism scholar, outlined fourteen primary points of observance to consider in keeping one's samaya vow "pure." Other outlines however contain three, twenty-eight, or other denominations of points of observance. These may be further divided into *root* and *branch* samayas.

According Keown, *et al.*, *Samaya* may be defined as:

- A particular system of teaching or doctrines;
- The conduct required of a tantric practitioner, often as a set of vows or commitments;
- The realization (*abhisamaya*) of Buddhahood;
- In Tantric Buddhism, union with the Three Vajras, the body, speech and mind of the Buddha.

Jamgon Kongtrul comments on the *Lamrim Yeshe Ningpo* that samaya is established by taking empowerment and is the manner in which practitioners "preserve the life-force of that empowerment within your being".

ROOT AND BRANCH

Khenpo Karthar Rinpoche defines root samayas as any which if violated would remove all the benefit from practicing.

He defines branch samayas as any which if violated would diminish or impair the benefit of practice. He states that the most egregious root samaya to violate is the commitment to one's guru. Foregrounding the mindfullnes observance of the mindstream, whilst intimating the binding reciprocity of samaya, Gyatrul (b.1924) in his commentary to Chagmé, rendered into English by Wallace states:

> If a Lama obstinately refuses to grant instruction to a qualified disciple, this constitutes an infraction of the Lama's samaya. It is proper for the Lama to show some hesitation by not consenting on the first request in order to arouse and examine the disciple. It is not a ploy to see if the amount of offerings can be increased, but rather provides time to examine the student's mind-stream.

In the Nyingma lineage, the three root samayas are categorized as body, speech, and mind. Each requires refraining from non-virtue as well as maintaining sacred view. Maintaining sacred view generally means to view all beings and all phenomenons as 'primordially pure' (Tib: kadak). The samaya of body is to refrain from non-virtue with respect to body, and also to always offer yourself to your guru and to your vajra sangha. The samaya of speech is to avoid non-virtuous speech, and also to never forget one's commitment to practicing mantra. The samaya of mind is to refrain from divulging the secrets and to always maintain the view that one's mind is dharmakaya.

REPAIRING DAMAGED SAMAYA

According to Tulku Urgyen Rinpoche, there are four increasing stages in which one's samaya may be damaged: "infraction, breach, violation, and complete break". Once damaged, samaya may be repaired. But if it is left without repair for more than three years, it is not repairable.

Samaya is easily damaged. Patrul Rinpoche said it is very hard to maintain samaya and used a famous metaphor that maintaining samaya is like keeping a mirror or tile clean that is lifted up into a sand storm; dust settles on it as soon as it is clean and we must continuously clean it. To repair samaya, a practitioner may restore mindfulness and awareness of sacred view; confess the violation to another practitioner that holds samaya; recite the one hundred syllable mantra; or use other methods determined by their guru.

SHINGON BUDDHISM

In the esoteric lineage of Japanese Shingon Buddhism, the Samaya precedes the Abhiseka initiation ceremony proper. The initiate undertakes four precepts:

1. Never to abandon the True Dharma.
2. Never to negate bodhicitta.
3. Never to withhold or be selective of Buddhist teachings toward others.
4. Never to cause any sentient being any harm.

The first recorded taking of the Samaya precepts at Todaiji temple began in 822 when Kukai performed the Abhiseka ritual before the abdicated emperor, Heizei, and helped to establish Shingon Buddhism as a legitimate school in Japan.

THE THREE ROOT SAMAYAS

For Vajrayana practitioners, the entire universe, including the five skandhas, is transformed into the mandala of Buddha's five wisdom families. So the problem of breaking samaya arises when one loses this practice and adheres to the normal concept of 'I and others', or 'this and that'. In Vajrayana, there are three major or root samayas to observe:

- *All forms as deities*
- *All sounds as mantras*
- *All minds as Dharmadhatu*

When one's mind is truly developed to that point, there is no chance of making a mistake. Any mistake or broken samaya is the result of defecting from these three root samayas.

SAMAYA AND GURU

As I mentioned earlier, samaya is connected with the guru. The guru is the key issue in the practice of Vajrayana; therefore we must check the guru before making important connections.

As the Buddha said, "In Buddhist practice, everything must be checked." In Vajrayana, the four initiations are very important; in order to receive the four initiations, you must have a guru and this guru must be chosen by yourself. You cannot rely on your friends who may say, "There is a nice guru who happens to be in town, come and take initiation from him!" People take it so easily, so simply, without even checking on the background of the guru.

Later on they may get headaches and regrets and hear rumors and gossip, so all these negative things happen because they didn't check first. Then there is no one to blame except themselves. Different gurus have different qualities and levels; there is best, good, middling and very little, or sometime having the name as 'guru' but without any qualification. Some of them are even fake and some of them are not. This situation has been occurring throughout history and is not something new that is only happening now. You can see that through various texts and biographies of great masters and discover that many gurus were scolding the monks and practitioners for being careless in selecting gurus.

Therefore, the most important thing is that the masters or gurus must be checked and must be genuine. Many times, people start following gurus with a lot of fantasies and a lot of wrong information and concepts. Most of the time, fantasies come with attachment. Because of the lack of pure motivation, attachment and some forms of fantasies occur on one side and other forms of fantasies occur on the other side, so two mistakes bang together and create a mess. This is the problematic result.

Another problem is that many people don't really know the meaning of root guru. They listen to rumors, read a few pages and get confused with wrong information. For example, some people learn that disciples have to take the guru as a Buddha, so they think, "I must believe my guru is a Buddha." Then they force themselves to believe blindly that this man whom they regard as their guru is the real Buddha. Nothing in the Buddha's teachings or in Vajrayana talks about this. It's a total misunderstanding. The Buddha taught very clearly in his teaching on Vajrayana, he never mentioned that there would be a Buddha appearing between Buddha Shakyamuni and Buddha Maitreya.

What is really taught in Vajrayana is that the master, who teaches us the real meaning of the Buddha's teachings and makes us realize the teachings, is kinder than the Buddha because we do not have the good karma to meet any of the past Buddhas in person. But in this regard, people make mistakes and misunderstand. Patrul Rinpoche, the author of 'The Words of My Perfect Teacher', gave a very clear and simple explanation. He said, "The root guru is respected and treasured as the Buddha not because he is the Buddha, but because his kindness which is beneficial to oneself is even greater than the Buddha's." It's like a poor family supporting you so that you are able to survive and keep your life going, compared with another family who is extremely rich but who doesn't give you even one penny.

So between these two families, who is kinder? Of course the poor family who feeds and supports you is kinder and what you really need is to survive and be alive, not just to know some rich people who do not give you any help and benefits. What we are saying is that the Buddha is great: without Buddha Shakyamuni, there is no way to have any of the teachings. However, without masters who teach, we have no living example, guidance or inspiration. Unless we can see real proof of a living master exemplifying the Buddha's teachings, we cannot be fully trusting or have faith that we can attain realization in one lifetime.

The 'realization' that we talk about here is not fully enlightened Buddhahood. In teachings, we always talk about Drangdon (relative truth) and Nyedon (ultimate truth). Drangdon is for guiding, i.e. to give some idea of the path, to guide people's minds so that they can focus on the main point leading to understanding, which gives hope or inspiration. Nyedon is the ultimate enlightenment or fully enlightened Buddhahood. Sometimes these two are mixed up and this brings about confusion.

OTHER TYPES OF SAMAYAS

There are hundreds of thousands of types of samayas,

such as three samayas, five samayas, 14 samayas and 28 samayas. It all depends on whether you are taking the initiation of Kriya Tantra, Charya Tantra, Yoga Tantra or Anuttara Yoga Tantra such as the Ati Yoga in Dzogchen practice. There is so many of them and it really depends on the level at which one is developing. To condense all of them, there are three root samayas as I have mentioned before. If one keeps these three samayas, there is no chance of breaking any other samaya.

These three are not just samayas, but also Vajrayana practice, just like two sides of one coin that are inseparable. Therefore, if one practices Vajrayana properly and correctly, one would not be able to break any samaya. If one adheres to these three root samayas, one would be able to practice Vajrayana properly. Samaya is found in the four initiations; with vase initiation comes the vase samaya, with secret initiation comes the secret samaya, with wisdom initiation comes the wisdom samaya, and then with recitation initiation comes the recitation samaya.

THE DOWNFALLS OF BREAKING VAJRAYANA SAMAYA

There are 14 root downfalls of breaking samaya. Some of the more significant downfalls are disrespecting the Buddha's teachings, fighting with Vajra brothers or sisters, and abandoning beings from one's mind, which is related to the Mahayana Bodhisattva's vows; this means, "I will not help that person." Even if someone greatly hurts his or her guru or destroys Buddhism entirely, the Buddha never gave the slightest permission to develop hatred; instead he helped this person through different methods. Therefore if you say, "This is a bad person, I will not help him", or even if you have the slightest thought of this, this is breaking samaya.

THE 14 ROOT DOWNFALLS OF BREAKING SAMAYA

1. To physically or verbally harm one's vajra master or to entertain wrong views of him.

2. To oppose the Buddha's teachings and go against the guru's instructions.
3. To develop strong negative and afflictive emotions towards other sentient beings, especially the community of vajra brothers and sisters.
4. To abandon the attitude and practice of loving-kindness towards all sentient beings.
5. To go astray in one's clinging to sexual bliss and to abandon Bodhicitta.
6. To abuse other traditions, lineages or religions with the motivation of gaining more respect for oneself.
7. To reveal Tantric secrets to those who are not spiritually matured, thereby resulting in the misunderstanding of the teachings.
8. To harm one's and others' precious human bodies.
9. To have doubts regarding the Absolute Truth.
10. To refrain from forceful activity when needed so as to overcome destructive influences resulted from negative energies, such as the unwillingness to save or help sentient beings although one has the ability to do so.
11. To have doubts regarding the meaning of suchness.
12. To annoy other sentient beings out of self-concerns.
13. To refrain from certain behavior when appropriate, such as the unwillingness to accept the necessary and appropriate practices (for example, consuming alcohol and meat which are offered in a *Ganachakra* practice) as and when they are required.
14. To abuse women or regard them as inferior.

MENDING OR REPAIRING MISTAKES AND VOWS

In Vajrayana, there are many ways of repairing mistakes and vows. But generally for a Bhikshu or fully ordained monk, once he breaks the four main vows, there is no way he can repair them. In most of the schools, he can still repair. Often in people's minds, if a Bhikshu disrobes and then robes again, they laugh and think he is insane. Some schools allow this and some do not.

THE FOUR FUNDAMENTAL PRECEPTS OF A MONK

1. Not to scold when scolded
2. Not to become angry when provoked
3. Not to reveal another's faults when he reveals one's
4. Not to hit back when being hit

The Buddha's teachings are divided into 18 schools: this was his intentional wish. The Buddha didn't want one large, dominating Buddhist group. Instead, the Buddha made the intentional wish that his disciples and followers would break into 18 entirely different schools. This was said by Buddha Kashyapa, who told his disciple King Kri Kri, when the latter informed him of a dream with 18 men dividing a white sheet of cloth into 18 pieces, "This is the forthcoming Buddha Shakyamuni's intentional wish. He doesn't want a giant school that will control everything as this will result in major corruption. So this will pit all 18 of them against each other, even though each of them follows the path to enlightenment."

In fact, one of these schools is exactly like Hinduism accepting the concept of Atma (meaning divinity, soul or great self in Sanskrit). In Mahayana, once the Bodhisattva vows are broken, you can repair the vows by taking them again. In Vajrayana, there are many different methods of purification, depending on what kind of samaya has been broken. For different types of samaya, the methods of repairing samaya depend on the seriousness, on the period (such as within six months, three years, etc.) and on whether it is with the guru, Sangha or others.

This is one reason why Vajrayana practitioners should develop sincere openness to all others, without discrimination in the context of gender, religion, caste, etc. One should really uproot the discriminating and condescending attitude towards others. There are actually many methods mentioned in the teachings about purification, mending and making good again the samaya or vow that has been broken. In Vajrayana, whether you are a lay person, Bhikshu, a man or a woman, the principles are the same; the only difference is the level of tantra undertaken. For example, the Kriya and the Charya have lesser vows.

If one takes Kriya initiation, it says if you break this or that, then you have to do this or that. If you take Charya initiation and you break this or that, then you do this or that. Once this sort of broken samaya occurs either intentionally or accidentally, the best way to purify is to recite the Vajrasattva hundred-syllable mantra 21 or 108 times a day. It is taught in the teachings that the practice of Vajrasattva purifies any defilement, obscuration or broken samaya at the common level.

SIX BARDOS AND THE SIX DHARMAS OF NAROPA

Mahamudra and Six Yogas are quintessence of Kagyudpa tradition of Tibetan Buddhism. The Six Yogas or Six Dharmas (Chos-drug) are meditation techniques which enhance the practice of Mahamudra (Phyag rgyachen po) at certain points and under special conditions i.e., at that level of practice which is known as the Perfect stage (Sampannakrama, rzdogs-rim) of the Anuttara Yogas such as like Guhyasamaja, He-vajra, *Chakrasamvara* and Kalacakra, etc. Tilopa (988-1069A D.), the first Guru of the Kagyu lineage, received the teaching of the Six Yogas from various Gurus.

He received the teachings of Illusory Body and Transference of Consciousness from Nagar- Lineage of juna and the teachings of Dream and Intermediate Kargyudpa state from Charyapa; the teachings of luminosity from Lawapa (Dombupa) and the teachings of Can- dali (mystic heat) from Yogini Sumati (Sudhagini). As the four oral traditions merged into one) Tilopas lineage came to be known as Kagyu (the oral traditon).

Naropa (1016-1100 A.D.) received the lineage of six Yogas from Tilopa and he along with his sister Nigunia expounded the teachings so much so that the teachings became known as the Six Yogas of Naropa and Six Yogas of Niguma, both of which are still preserved in Kagyu teachings. Marpa, the translator (1012-1097 A.D.), carried them to Tibet and through his noted disciple the saint poet Milarepa (1040-1123 A.D.) spread to all sub-sects of Kagyu School.

The teachings have been zealously guarded and secretly transmitted for the last thousand years. They are still preserved in the original form as an oral tradition which is transmitted only after thorough preparation so that they may not be wasted or confused. The Ahapramana-samaya-nama-dakini-upadesa (bka- yong-dak-pa' i-tshed-ma-don-gyi-yige-gsang-ba-mkha'-gro' i-man-ngag) with its commentary by Marpa, forms the principal work of the Six Yogas. Among the 30 odd different kinds of literature on this topic available in India are the earlier and later Kapes (bka'-dpe) written by Tilopa and Naropa respectively.

Tibetan saints and scholars, of course, wrote many commentaries later on. But it should be pointed out here that despite the vast literature available one cannot practise the Six Yogas without the assistance of an experience duGur. Here is riven a general idea of the Six Yogas of Naropa without going into the esoteric aspect of the Teachings-Candali or Tummo means 'fierce' or 'wrathful'. A kind of psychic heat is generated and experienced through certain meditative practices. This heat serves to burr up all types of obstacles and confusion. It is a fierce or wrathful Mystic heat fire.

Although the heat generation is given emphasis (gtum-mo-candali) Candali does not deal with heat generation alone. Another important part of this Yoga is the practice of nadi, piana and bindu. (Tib.rtsa, rlung, thigle) practice helps one to attain realization by synchronising body and mind. The Tantric texts describe prana as the horse, mind-consciousness as the rider, and nadis as the pathway and bindu as mind-nourishment. The prana functions in the left and right channels called Symbolic representation lalana and rasana and therefore our mind conceives of Prana, Mana and the things in duality.

In other words, we lapse Nadi in Tantric text into duality because the prana functions in lalana and rasana. These two channels represent the subjective objective activities and Karmic activities. If the prana functions in the central channels

(Avadhuti) the prana transforms into wisdom-prana. The mind then conceives the non-duality of the things, and realizes all dharmas as unborn. The meditation on prana, nadi and bindu is called inner gtummo. When the inner candali is Mind conceives synchronized with the outer candali which is non-duality of things Mahamudra, prana, nadi and bindu dissolve into sampannakrama non-duality delight.

This is known as the attainment of vajra body, vajra speech and vajra mind. Candali is the root or foundation of all other Yogas. Illusory body or apparition is broadly divided into three categories, viz. the mundane illusory body; the immaculate illus-Illusory Body or body; and the most immaculate illusory body (Sgyu.lus-mayadeha). The universe and its contents are nothing but illusions as they have no substance in their nature. They just appear like illusory bodies, like dreams, like mirror-reflection and the like. To understand this and to meditate upon this helps one to cut off the mundane attachments and to realize the ultimate truth. This practice is known as mundane illusory body. Higher Tantricism makes one realize that the five aggregates, the twelve dhatus and the six sense-organs are divine by nature.

This practice transforms all the mundane thoughts into divine thoughts. The universe becomes a Mandala of divine deities where the forms are gods and goddesses: sounds are mantra; and thoughts are transcendental wisdom. Even this immaculate appearance has no substance and hence is illusory. This practice is, therefore, known as the immaculate illusory body. The immaculate illusory body still has a tinge of artificiality. The most immaculate illusory body, however, is a spontaneous, natural experience, born out of completely pure prana and non-dualistic thought to achieve the last illusory body.

The first stage of dream practice is to recognize dreams during the time of dreaming. The next stage (rmi-lam, svapna) is to use the dream as a means to practise various spiritual exercises including that of illusory body. Dreams are then transformed into the practice of luminosity. A constant practice on dream will have great effect on waking hours. There will be a time when the learner will see no distinction between the dream, waking hours and the death. The Practice of luminosity is believed to be the essence of the path. Luminosity in Tantra Luminosity is the spontaneous, self illuminating enlightened (Hod-gsal, prabhasvara Buddha -nature which could be seen only with the ultimate intuitive perspective or the dtepest meditation.

Though a momentary flash of luminosity appears when dying, fainting, yawning and copulating, it is not recognized, as such the technique here would help to recognize those moments especially in dreams. It is therefore said that a Yogin is meditating even when asleep. Luminosity is regarded as the last stage of Sampannakrama of Anuttarayoga Tantras and its practice leads directly to the experience of Sambhogal and *Dharmakaya*. Intermediate state has been classified into many different ways.

The practice of Baido- yoga is the last stage. The intermediate state after death is calieri 'the ir.inri. 'i his is an important stage as a strong reaction at this period will have an immediate effect in deciding the realm into which the person will be reborn. "In our being we find passion, aversion and bewilderment. Through passion we become spirits, through aversion denizens of hell and through bewilderment brute animals. While through these poisons we bound to wander endlessly in Samsara, by making them a path according to the teaching of Naropa, there will be no birth for us in Samsara.

The three stages of practices are, therefore, recommended for this period. The best of these is to recognize the luminosity when it is experienced at the time of death. The next stage is the practice of illusory body which is practised when the mind-body is separated from the dead physical body. If both of them fail to liberate the subject, the meditative techniques to stop entrance into the six realms of the world are applied. A few of these techniques have been discussed in the Book of Dead. Phoba is also known as the teaching to achieve Buddhahood without meditation. The purpose of these teachings is to be Transference of ready to die and to avoid being reborn in unfavour- Consciousness able situations.

This is also divided into three stages ('Pho-ba, samkranti) of practice as found in Bardo. The first stage is to transform one into luminosity. The second stage is to realize the divine nature and accomplish the illusory body. The last stage is to transfer one's mind-body into the wisdom-mind of the Guru and Yidam or into some Buddha in Sukhavati. These trainings are practised during the life-time and they are used when all the signs of death are manifest. An accomplished person can help another person to a happy departing.

It may be noted here that it is not necessary that all the Six Yogas should always be practised together. But they as a whole make a complete path. The first four are known as the root Yogas and the last two as their parts. It is also not always necessary for the total number to be only six, although the six Yogas of Naropa are the most popular. There are texts which mention eight, ten or varying numbers with the addition of more branch Yogas.

The Six Dharmas of Naropa are the crown jewels of the Kagyu path, and the completion stage practices of both Vajrayogini and *Chakrasamvara*. These profound methods are designed to transform our daily life, sleep, dreams, and death. The Six Dharmas show us how to enter lifetime retreat in the midst of normal life.

BARDO

The Tibetan word Bardo means literally "intermediate state" - also translated as "transitional state" or "in-between state" or "liminal state". In Sanskrit the concept has the name *antarabhâva*. Fremantle (2001) states that there are six traditional bardo states known as the Six Bardos: the Bardo of This Life; the Bardo of Meditation; the Bardo of Dream; the Bardo of Dying; the Bardo of Dharmata; and the Bardo of Existence. Shugchang, *et al.* discuss the Zhitro (Tibetan: Zhi-khro) teachings which subsume the *Bardo Thodol* and mention Karma Lingpa, terma and Padmasambhava and list the Six Bardo:

In the term discovered by Karma Lingpa, Guru Padmasambhava introduces six different bardos. The first bardo begins when we take birth and endures as long as we live. The second is the bardo of dreams. The third is the bardo of concentration or meditation. The fourth occurs at the moment of death. The fifth is known as the bardo of the luminosity of the true nature. The sixth is called the bardo of transmigration or karmic becoming.

Six Bardos:

1. Shinay bardo (Tibetan): is the first bardo of birth and life. This bardo commences from conception until the last breath, when the mindstream withdraws from the body.
2. Milam bardo (Tibetan): is the second bardo of the dream state. The Milam Bardo is a subset of the first Bardo. Dream Yoga develops practices to integrate the dream state into Buddhist sadhana.
3. Samten bardo (Tibetan) is the third bardo of meditation. This bardo is generally only experienced by meditators, though individuals may have spontaneous experience of it. Samten Bardo is a subset of the Shinay Bardo.
4. Chikkhai bardo (Tibetan): is the fourth bardo of the moment of death. According to tradition, this bardo is held to commence when the outer and inner signs presage that the onset of death is nigh, and continues through the dissolution or transmutation of the Mahabhuta until the external and internal breath has completed.
5. Chönyid bardo (Tibetan): is the fifth bardo of the luminosity of the true nature which commences after the final 'inner breath' (Sanskrit: *prana*, vayu; Tibetan: *rlung*). It is within this Bardo that visions and auditory phenomena occur. In the Dzogchen teachings, these are known as the spontaneously manifesting Thödgal (Tibetan: *thod-rgyal*) visions. Concomitant to these visions, there is a welling of profound peace and pristine awareness. Sentient beings who have not practiced during their lived experience and/ or who do not recognize the clear light (Tibetan: *od gsal*) at the moment of death are usually deluded throughout the fifth bardo of luminosity.
6. Sidpai bardo (Tibetan): is the sixth bardo of becoming or

transmigration. This bardo endures until the inner-breath commences in the new transmigrating form determined by the 'karmic seeds' within the storehouse consciousness.

EXEGESIS

Fremantle charts the development of the bardo concept through the Himalayan tradition:

Originally bardo referred only to the period between one life and the next, and this is still its normal meaning when it is mentioned without any qualification. There was considerable dispute over this theory during the early centuries of Buddhism, with one side arguing that rebirth (or conception) follows immediately after death, and the other saying that there must be an interval between the two. With the rise of Mahayana, belief in a transitional period prevailed. Later Buddhism expanded the whole concept to distinguish six or more similar states, covering the whole cycle of life, death, and rebirth. But it can also be interpreted as any transitional experience, any state that lies between two other states.

Its original meaning, the experience of being between death and rebirth, is the prototype of the bardo experience, while the six traditional bardos show how the essential qualities of that experience are also present in other transitional periods. By refining even further the understanding of the essence of bardo, it can then be applied to every moment of existence. The present moment, the now, is a continual bardo, always suspended between the past and the future. Used somewhat loosely, the term "bardo" may refer to the state of existence intermediate between two lives on earth.

According to Tibetan tradition, after death and before one's next birth, when one's consciousness is not connected with a physical body, one experience a variety of phenomena. These usually follow a particular sequence of degeneration from, just after death, the clearest experiences of reality of which one is spiritually capable, to, later on, terrifying hallucinations arising from the impulses of one's previous unskillful actions. For the spiritually advanced the bardo offers a state of great opportunity for liberation, since transcendental insight may arise with the direct experience of reality, while for others it can become a place of danger as the karmically created hallucinations can impel one into a less than desirable rebirth.

In the West, the term *bardo* may also refer to times when our usual way of life becomes suspended, as, for example, when we are on retreat. Such times can prove fruitful for spiritual progress, as external constraints diminish, although they offer challenges because our unskillful impulses can come to the fore, just as in the *sidpa bardo*.

OSHO ON BARDO

Osho has laid great stress on *Bardo* in his lectures and meditation courses. It can be found explained at great length and pain in many of his books. However Osho refers to this term in the sense of a particular Tibetan Buddhist ritual that was used as an attempt to keep a dying man in a total wakeful state while he is on brink of death. In this practice, used only on a monk accustomed to advanced spiritual states, other monks will make loud noises, shout and run about his death-bed to make sure he does not fall into sleep while dying.

Other lamas will repeatedly speak into his ears to stick to wakefullness and not to fall prey to the typical hallucinations that a dying man is commonly subject to. And after passing out of body to take birth only in a better womb and place more agreeable to spirituality. And if possible not to attain a body at all, that is Nirvana (final liberation).

P.D. Ouspensky, the most famous disciple of Gurdjieff is reported to have died in this way. Now, the first bardo, the first aspect of bardo, actually involves life. For example, right now, we are in this state of bardo. From our birth, or since we are conceived, until we die, we follow one main stream of reality. Right now we are human beings of planet Earth of this galaxy. So this is our reality. And we perceive and we interact with everything, mentally, physically, emotionally, based on this reality.

And, until we die, we will be human beings of planet Earth of this galaxy; that's what we will be, and that's what we are.

That changes as soon as we die. So, for that, in this state of bardo, what we have to consider as the practice of bardo is to appreciate and accept the way we are. And any good things that we encounter, we take as opportunity in a positive way, so that those good things will become beneficial for us and for others who are associated with us. Then anything bad and unfavorable that we might encounter in our life, we also have to accept and face and utilize in a way that will be beneficial for us and for others that are associated with us.

And we have to prevent potentially unfavorable circumstances from becoming harmful and negative to ourselves and others that are around us. So that is the first aspect of bardo. The second aspect of bardo is a very short period of bardo, which is dream. As soon as we fall into sleep, we enter into another state of mind, another reality, which is influenced by our human reality, but which goes beyond this human reality's limitations. In dreams what we are experiencing is the subconscious level of our mind, with its emotions and its defilements and all the other things that go with it; so it is the subconscious mind that influences our mind in the sleeping and dreaming state of mind.

So the use of this particular state of consciousness, for a Vajrayana practitioner - and particularly as a practitioner of bardo - is to recognize that the interdependent manifestation of reality is a reality which is nothing more and nothing less than the interdependent manifestation of everything else. And the greatest example and most immediate example of this is the dream state. While dreaming, when we see good things, we feel happy; when we see bad things, we feel upset; when we see something that is fearful, we get afraid; and so on and so forth.

In life, it works the same way; but life is a little bit longer - several tens of thousands of times, maybe several millions times longer - than a dream. I don't know how many times a person dreams in life. In one year a person dreams 365 times, so if a person lives ten years, it should be 3,650 times, isn't it? And if a person lives a hundred years, then their life is 36,500 times longer. That's it. So the only difference is that life is that much longer. But, actually, besides that, life is not anything more or less than quite a long dream. Relatively it is only a long dream. Ultimately it is not long at all.

We start to dream as humans as soon as we are conceived, and that dream ends when we die. In the next life we could be a bird, a nice bird in a Canadian forest, and that dream starts as soon as we are conceived. And then we will be hatched et cetera, et cetera, and then we will be a dead bird. So that will be the end of that dream. And then that process will go on and continue from one life to another. And so that is the second aspect of bardo. Here, in this state of mind, the most important thing is that we appreciate that we are in this world and we are dreaming all of this.

We have friends, families, and so on and so forth, and this is wonderful; we appreciate it and we help each other and we respect each other and do our best to make it as meaningful as possible. But don't hold onto it for more than that, don't expect too much from each other, don't expect too much from anything else. Life is like a dream. But when we are dreaming, we should be able to make the best of it and appreciate those who are in our dream and respect them. They are dreaming us; we are dreaming them. You see? So that's what it is. So that is the second aspect of bardo.

The third aspect of bardo is to realize the ultimate potential, the ultimate nature of everything, the ultimate nature of mind itself. Actually, there is a very particular example used in this aspect of bardo. This is about meditation or contemplation. Here, the mind is understood to be beyond any kind of dualistic identity or dualistic limitation. And the only example that is close to the nature of the mind, used here, is space. And there are some sentences which describe it. So I'd like to share this with you. One can never find the center of space. That means every place in the entirety of space is the center of space.

And, in the same way, one can never find the mind in a dualistic way. So that means that the non-dualistic aspect of clarity and profoundness, completeness, limitlessness is the true nature of mind. Therefore, once a person realizes this limitless mind, the center of the space which is everywhere, once one realizes this, then that person recognizes space, that person recognizes mind. So this is the third aspect of bardo, which is contemplation or meditation. There is nothing that is impossible as a manifestation of mind; there is nothing that cannot manifest out of our mind. Right now, we might think that such and such things are impossible, but there is nothing which is not possible.

Anything is possible. Buddha said that. He said that human beings here have two eyes, two ears, one nose, and one mouth. You see? And we walk on two feet; we work with two hands. But Buddha also said that human beings can exist who are totally opposite to the way we exist. So I don't exactly know exactly what this could mean, but I think your people in the United States, you know, in Los Angeles, down there, they might have figured out several different ways how humans could be! Actually I am fascinated by them, you know; I think it is very, very profound, that medium. So this, the third aspect of bardo, is to realize the ultimate potential, the ultimate nature of everything, the ultimate nature of mind itself. So this is the third bardo.

And the fourth aspect of bardo is the moment before death. Now, this is actually what most people don't want to think about and what people consider inauspicious to think about, which is incorrect, because death is not something terrible. If death is terrible, then birth also has to be terrible, because birth is the other side of death. If we are not born, we are not going to die. We die because we are born. This is very simple. Death begins the moment we are born. From birth it continues [to be the case that at] any moment we can die. After birth, at any moment we can die. We don't have to be afraid of it, we don't have to look at it in a negative way, we don't have to hate it, and we don't have to constantly think of it like some kind of taboo. There is no evil in death. Life, of course, is precious.

This precious human life, which we have right now [is extremely valuable], so we should live as long as we can. We have to do our best to take good care of our health, to take good care of our mind; eat well, live well, do some exercise, breathe well; we should do anything we can to live longer. We should live as long as possible, definitely - but not because death is bad, you see, not because death is bad. Death is only natural. We want to live as long as possible because we know we are human; we have our great privileges as human beings.

We can learn things, we can do things, we can understand things; we have so much opportunity to improve as sentient beings in the form of a human body, in a human environment. Above all, we humans have done pretty well. Right now, we are the dominant rulers of the planet Earth. You see? It is not really fair, but we are. So there is no reason that we shouldn't appreciate it. We should appreciate it, and we should try to live as long as possible, try to be as healthy as possible, but we should never be afraid of dying when death comes. Death is only natural. So that is the fourth aspect of bardo.

And how to deal with it? In the dharma it is taught always that in our minds and in our deeds we have to prepare for this inevitable moment. After death, our death should not become a suffering for many people. So we do our best to make things clear. Don't leave too much unfinished business, because as soon as you die, everybody will fight over your things, you know? And that is not very nice. So take care of everything. Don't be too attached; don't be too suspicious of everybody; learn to trust people, learn to trust someone, learn to respect others, and don't magnify the reality [of death] beyond proportion. Leave reality alone in its place. We have a saying: "Don't hold your thumb against your eye."

This is a very small thing (Rinpoche holds up his thumb), but if I hold it against my eye, it can obscure the whole universe, even the whole of space. But if I just keep it at arm's length - I don't have to learn to do it in some kind of tricky way, I just [simply] keep it at arm's length - then it is just a thumb, insignificant; useful, but insignificant. You know? Without a thumb, I cannot write, so I need it. But, it shouldn't be held close to our eye. So, in the same way we need our ego, we definitely need it; if we don't have ego, we get nowhere. The first step [in dharma study and practice] we have to make with our ego.

The next step is to put a short leash on our ego. The third step is to make ego realize that whether to have that leash on or not is up to him or her. And the fourth step is get rid of that leash. And the fifth step is that ego transforms into limitlessness. These are gradual steps. If we try to get rid of ego before we have anything [in the way of realization], then we get lost; that is the definition of confusion: lost, no confidence, no self-respect. All these things come from that. So ego is always there. And if we don't acknowledge it, it doesn't mean that it is going to go away. I might say something like this: I will say, "I am Buddha." Then you will say, "I don't think so." And I will say, "I am Buddha!" Then you will say, "I don't think so."

Then I will get very mad, and I will say, "If you don't stop, I will call the police. And if you don't believe, I will sue you." So, I mean [by this that] ego can play all kinds of roles. And we have to use the existing self, the ego, to make the first step. So we can't say, "I don't want to be enlightened; I don't want you to think that I want to be enlightened, because that is attachment to enlightenment." That is ridiculous. First we have to have the attachment and desire to be enlightened in order to make the first step. We have to overcome the attachment to serve ourselves in a selfish way. We have to overcome the attachment to fame, fortune, and all those things.

We have to have desire for improvement, for betterment, for enlightenment; that is necessary. Then, once that is established, then we can get rid of that desire. Enlightenment in the end is not possible if there is an attachment to it, but that attachment to enlightenment is where it our path starts. First step is first step. It is as a final result of traversing the path that we overcome those kinds of final and most subtle aspects of defilement e.g., the attachment to enlightenment, the attachment to getting enlightened; but that final result is not a means. The means is using what we already have.

So the fourth aspect of bardo is to deal with reality [in a way] that acknowledges that we will die one day, at any moment, and we prepare for that moment all the time in a most mindful, aware, and wise, and thoughtful way, so that every moment we treat with greatest respect. If I'm going to die today, then I shouldn't feel, "Oh, I thought I would live for some time. I did lots of wrong things. I feel sorry for myself." That [state of mind] shouldn't be there. All of us, when that inevitable moment happens - which can happen at any time - should be ready for it. So that is number four. The fifth and sixth bardo are, I think, what most people talk about when they talk about "the bardo." People talk about bardo as a kind of after death experience, what happens after death. So that is actually the fifth and the sixth bardo, out of six bardos all together. And so I will describe these a little bit.

In this state of mind, as the bardo teachings are transmitted and taught, there are several categories of states of mind, which happen during death, after death and all the way through until you are conceived into the next life. So, during death, after death, and all the way until you are conceived into the next life, into the next physical body is one bardo; this bardo ends there. Now, you have heard about clear light, I think. There are books written on this subject, many, many books, I think. So, when you talk about the clear light, actually two stages of clear light are described. It is described as clear light one and clear light two, the first stage and the second stage. But, when you talk about the bardo of that stage - the "during death and after death" bardo - there are three stages of bardo there.

They're described as first bardo, second bardo, third bardo; and you shouldn't get these three bardos of the fifth bardo mixed up with the three bardos of the sixth bardo. They are totally different. These are the three bardos of the fifth and the sixth bardo. There are two clear lights: first clear light, second clear light. And that is the first clear light of the first bardo, the second clear light of the first bardo so both of them are part of the first bardo, out of three bardos.

Okay, first, second, third bardo: the first bardo has first clear light and second clear light. Very simple. All of that is part, that is, the elaboration of the fifth bardo and sixth bardo, in the sixth bardo. So this is the key for this particular teaching about bardo your first chance at getting enlightened. So that is described as the first clear light of the first bardo. Now, as to the second clear light of the first bardo, after some time, then this unconscious mind wakes up. Now that could be just a moment after falling unconscious, or that could be as long as three days after falling unconscious. So, for this reason, serious Vajrayana people try to leave the deceased person's body alone and not tamper with it for three days. But you can never be sure whether the mind has left the body already, or if it is still there; one cannot be sure.

Great masters, when they pass away - and I myself have seen several masters who passed away in meditation posture - after death continue to sit just like living people, and after two days or after three days sitting like that, then their bodies become like dead bodies; the head falls down, and there are many signs that can happen that indicate that the mind has left the body. And in that way we can tell if the mind is in the body or not. But with an ordinary person, we don't know, because a few hours after death, the person's body becomes cold and there is no sign of life in it. So, in that case, it is hard to tell; but in our tradition, in our culture, we don't take the risk that the mind might not have left the body.

We leave the person uninterrupted for three days just in case the mind is still there in the body. But, of course, one doesn't have to worry too much about all of this. In your culture and your system here, for health considerations and many other reasons, there is some kind of formality or legality concerning the disposition of bodies after death. So you don't have to worry too much. But that is the basic principle, actually, according to the bardo teaching. And now, after this moment after three days, or one day after, then when the mind awakens, the mind has to come out of the body. There is still some karmic connection because of its long association. So there is one thing still left to do, which is that our mind has to come out of the body. That is the last separation; it still has to happen.

After that, then the mind becomes limitless, but until that last separation it is still trapped in the body. Now it is important to understand that, when that last separation happens, the different channels and chakras in the body, such as the crown, eye, ear, and lower chakras, et cetera, represent entryways into the different realms. And now, the first clear light is when our body and mind get separated. They separate inward, not outward. They separate inward. Okay. Now, our body then becomes like a house and our mind becomes like a person who lives in it. So that person goes unconscious, because of the separation. So that is the first clear light.

What happens, is because our body and our mind are connected together through energy, and energy through emotion, emotion through different kinds of energy, energy through different kinds of what we call "air" or "wind." Sanskrit: prana; Tibetan: lung; Chinese: Chi; New Age English: energy: stuffy English, perhaps: psycho-somatic motility. This term is something that keeps our bodies alive; a living body does not rot. But as soon as we die, the body starts to decay. This is so because this energy, the wind, the circulation, stops. So the body starts to rot. That is how the connection between mind and body takes place.

So, when the body is broken or the body is damaged by any kind of disease or anything i.e. by accident or any kind of physical trauma, then the mind and body connection stops. When that happens, then the mind goes back to the center of the body. When we first entered our body, our mind entered at the center of our body. The first thing that developed inside our mother, when we were little, is what you call the embryo. Now, according to Vajrayana teachings, a tube develops in the middle of it, which is filled with "air" or energy. That tube is the central channel and out of that central channel then, the different energies are generated that build the hands, legs, eyes, ears, senses, everything that we are made up of, gradually.

At first we don't have any of that those physical parts. And when we die, we also go back to the same stage; our mind - together with its air, energy, emotions, everything - goes into the center of our body. But it is a tremendous shock, because the body and mind have to be separated. And because of that, we fall into an unconscious state of mind. Now, if you're a great practitioner, if you have realization of the nature of mind, if you are able to maintain the awareness - maintain an awareness of and observe the nature of mind in that state - then you can attain liberation there in that moment of separation of body and mind, because at that point the limitation that the physical body imposes on the mind is gone.

So, in that moment, if you can realize your "nature of mind" the mind's true nature, then that would be the mind of the dead person should be able to leave the body through the higher chakras, hopefully from the crown. That is the highest and most sacred chakra to come out of. So when this happens, then if the person is aware that, "Okay, now I am dead, and now my mind is coming out of my body, I'm going out of my body," then in that time, if you can manage to do the visualization of a deity, and the visualization of the Mandala of a deity, and the practices that you do every day, your sadhana - if you are able to do that - then you will become the embodiment of that deity. So, in that way, we have another great opportunity right there to attain enlightenment. So that is the second clear light.

Now, with that, the first bardo is complete. Now, we will consider the second bardo. At this point we are outside of our body. When we reach that state, then, technically speaking, we are totally free. We are not limited by human kinds of limitations. We are not limited to the planet Earth. We are in the universe. So we can have all kinds of experiences and the ability to affect or be affected by everything, as by the human realm, the animal realm, the gods' realms, asuras, hells, everything. And not only of planet Earth, of the whole universe, so that we have no limitation.

Right now, we only can see certain colors; we only can touch certain physical entities; we can only hear certain sounds. And also we look at things like this (indicating that he sees only what is in front of him and to the sides); I can't see what's behind me, I can't see what's up there. And hearing is also the same thing: I can't hear what's happening outside, I can only hear what's happening in here, my own echo. But in this newly arrived at disembodied state, we don't have this limitation. Instead, we see everything, everywhere; we hear everything, everywhere; and, whatever location we think about, we are instantly there.

You know, you think of something, and you're there; and we don't have to be aerodynamic to get somewhere; we don't have to struggle with gravity to move somewhere. All of these limitations don't exist in this disembodied state. So many texts describe the fear that the mind experiences in this state. And that's so because of this phenomenon. Of course, it would be frightening, you know; there's nothing, everything becomes everything. And, if we don't realize we are dead, then this condition or situation will be very frightening, of course. It is not that somebody tried to frighten us; it isn't like that.

Ultimate freedom is quite frightening. If somebody tells you, in a very limited way, "Okay, you have just become the ruler of planet Earth; you have to do and manage and decide everything." I would be devastated if that happened. But comparing this rather imposing but still limited eventuality to this state of bardo, then being world ruler is nothing. And to be able to have some kind of awareness during that time will be very difficult. I'm not trying to discourage you, but, in reality, it's difficult, as I understand it. It is possible to have awareness at that time. My example for how it might be possible is something like this: I'm taken in an airplane to 35,000 feet high, and then someone puts a paper in my left hand and puts a pen in my right hand, and then throws me out of the airplane with no parachute, and I'm supposed to write the most beautiful poetry before I hit the ground.

It would be possible; it would be possible, but very, very difficult. So, to remember that I am dead and to meditate and to realize or be aware of my "nature of mind," or to have compassion for all sentient beings, or to have devotion to Buddhas and bodhisattvas and the lineage, in that state of mind, will be like that like being thrown out of an airplane and writing poetry on the way down; it will not be easy. But, if we practice now, then it becomes easier. If we get acquainted with these states kinds of meditations and contemplations, and if they become habit, then it will happen that way, because whenever something really terrible happens to somebody or to us - some kind of serious accident or something - we will call our mother or call God or call Buddha's name or the name of our guru.

So, similarly, the same thing can happen after the mind separates from the body. Because this disembodied state after the separation of the mind from the body is the most extreme state of mind, and so one automatically turns to what one believes in most. So, in this way, if we have a strong daily dharma practice, then in this way it will be possible for us to experience proper awareness at that time and to attain enlightenment or a favorable rebirth. But, if we don't cultivate these kinds of virtuous mind states in advance of our death, then whatever we are accustomed or habituated to doing, this might happen.

In Buddhism, we consider saying bad words is no good; thinking bad things is no good. Because, if, in your everyday life, when something happens, you say some very bad words, then when you are reaching this disembodied state of mind that kind of negativity is likely to arise and that would not be so good. Therefore, I think, we have to get habitual with good words and good thoughts instead of bad words and bad thoughts. We have to do our best to practice and establish some sense of devotion and compassion and awareness during our lifetime in order for us to encounter those states of mind during this time in the disembodied state. So that is the second state of bardo.

The third state of bardo (actually, the second and third states go all the way) is starting from our ordinary form, coming out of our body and encountering this limitless freedom, in one way or another, up until we get conceived into the next life. So that is the third bardo. So, during the third bardo, what happens is that a human being of planet Earth (that is us), has a maximum of 49 possible days in the bardo. This is so because of the nature of our body, our mind, the energies involved, the nature of the universe, and the connections and interdependence amongst these. So, we cannot have more than 49 days of bardo. We can have a bardo experience as short as one moment; it could be just a moment. If we attain realization during the first clear light, our bardo experience will be only one moment.

You see? If somebody has really accumulated very, very bad karma - I don't want to mention any names, but there have been quite a few human beings who have done lots of bad things in our history - and what will happen to them, according to the bardo teaching, is that at the very moment they die, they will be born in hell; that very same moment. There will be no bardo. So in the most extremely positive situation, when a person attains realization, there will be no bardo; and in the most extremely negative situations, then there will be no bardo. But, otherwise, there will be different periods of bardo. But a human being of this planet cannot have more than 49 days of bardo. So, during this time, whatever amount of the time of bardo that you experience, it will be divided by stages into two exactly equal halves.

If your bardo experience is going to last two weeks, then one stage will be one week long and the second stage will also be one week long. If your bardo experience is going to be four weeks long, then each stage will last two weeks. If your bardo experience is going to be 49 days long, then each stage will be a little longer than 24 days. During the first part or first stage, the mind will be under the influences of one's past life; one will have the instincts and from time to time occurrences consonant with one's past life. We have been humans, so that kind of thing will happen. And then the last period or the second stage will have the periodic occurrence of what you will be in your future life; you could be a bird, you could be a dog, you could be a tiger, you could be a human, whatever.

So that will happen. And so during the first half, the previous life's influence will fade away, and then during the second half, the future life's influence will become more apparent. And then finally, you will be conceived wherever you will be born, at the end of this bardo period. During this time, of course, there's opportunity to attain liberation at any time. Just as in life there is opportunity to attain liberation at any moment, so in the same way in the bardo there is also opportunity to attain liberation at any moment. Now during this aspect or stage of bardo, you can somehow say you are "in the bardo," what mainstream mentality thinks of as "the bardo," right there. And that bardo will likely go on for quite a long time, as long as 49 days.

And during this time the most obvious way to take advantage of that opportunity will be that you realize that you have died, and that then you try not to be afraid of all the occurrences and try to sincerely supplicate that you want to be born in a family which is positive, where you will have lots of opportunity to be a good human being, and that you will be born into a family not too rich, not too poor, kind of well off, and one with a positive atmosphere (i.e., both parents are happy with each other, they're positive), and that you will be able to learn and develop positively. That would be ideal. You see? And then you might want to supplicate that the place where you will be born be not too cold, not too hot - so you supplicate sincerely for whatever is positive, whatever is your ideal.

Of course, if you can pray for that, that would be wonderful, and the best would be if you can really have the awareness to choose the parents of your conception. That would be the best, but these are only possibilities; it will not be as simple as I speak here. So this is the last part of the bardo, and then after that we will be conceived. But if we don't have the awareness, then our conceiving will be very natural, and very simple, because all of this total exposure to everything else is frightening. And therefore, you're always looking for some way to hide; you're always looking for some kind of refuge.

If we are being chased by 10,000 lions, then we will look for any place to hide, if we can find one. So, in the same way, in the bardo, since we have so much exposure to everything else, then we are constantly looking for a place. So then we find a kind of shadow, a nice place to hide; and when you find that place to hide, that becomes your next rebirth. So that is the natural way in the bardo, if you're not aware. But if you have the awareness, then you can choose with your aspiration, with your prayer; and then some people with their kind of greater realization can even choose intentionally and technically where and to whom to be conceived.

That is a possibility. So this is the third, the last stage of bardo. I share this with you at the request of the lama and the dharma center, and I definitely hope that you will be able to get some benefit out of this conversation, this teaching. I hope for that. One last thing that I want to say is that no matter how much we know about bardo, or no matter how little we know about bardo, whatever karma we have accumulated, whether it is positive or negative, that will determine what will happen to us. We don't have to worry that just because we don't know all the details and ins and outs of the bardo, because we don't realize what's happening, that, therefore, something wrong will happen to us.

We don't have to worry about that. There will be no accidental misfortunate rebirth. There will be no accidental lucky enlightenment. That will never happen. Enlightenment will not happen just because of good luck; and being reborn in the lower realms will not happen simply out of bad luck. This will not happen, so about that eventuality you don't have to worry. The purpose of our practice is realization. Through the realization which you develop through your practice, the negative karmas you have accumulated you can transcend. If we were to have to attain enlightenment by working out every negative karma that we have accumulated, one by one (as you say in your terminology, "an eye for an eye"), there would be no way that anyone would ever get enlightened.

Enlightenment would never happen, because while we would be purifying our past karma, we would be accumulating ten times more karma. You see? So if that were the set-up, then it would be impossible. But because none of those karmas are ultimately bad karma, because ultimately negativity doesn't exist lacks permanent, substantial, singular existence, independent of causes and conditions that give rise to it, then if we realize this directly and experientially in our practice, and if we have realization of our mind's true nature, then all the karma that we have accumulated will be transcended. Enlightenment is only possible through inner liberation, not by "working out" the details of our karma; for example, say we have stolen one penny from somebody, so we imagine that we have to give one penny to them; okay; now my job is done. Okay, now that record is straight.

If we broke somebody's tooth in our past life, and now we say, "Okay, please break my tooth;" it doesn't work like that. One has to attain the inner realization that will transcend. There is an example. If this room is dark and has had no light for 10,000 years, will it take 10,000 years to light this room up? It will not. A light shines in this room; and even if there have been 10,000,000 years of darkness, the darkness will be lit in a moment. So, in the same way, enlightenment, the realization of your mind's true nature transcends everything. And that happens because negativity is not ultimate.

There is also another line of reasoning that demonstrates why we can overcome negativity, because it is not ultimate. If negativity were ultimate, then there would be even negative realization. There would be Buddha on one side, who would be the positive enlightenment, and there would be something else on the other side that would be the negative enlightenment. And both would be equal and fighting with each other. But that is not the case. The ultimate is perfect, the ultimate is limitless, and all the limitations and negativities are relative i.e., they depend up causes and conditions for their existence. Therefore, enlightenment is only possible through inner realization.

So, the thought that I'd like to share with you is that you all do your best to try to develop your inner liberation by doing practices that you receive from profound, pure lineages - not just practices made up by somebody - lineages that come from Buddha, that come from Guru Rinpoche, that come from master to disciple. There are many ways by which lineages come; there is not just one way. There are many ways. But it has to be a pure lineage that you follow. At the same time, also try to be kind to yourself, to others, and try to avoid doing wrong things. You should have some kind of practice that you do, if possible, every day; if not, then periodically. And above all, the most important thing is to have full confidence in the Buddha inside you. Your mind is Buddha.

We Tibetan Buddhists, and Buddhists all over the world, try to build beautiful shrines for Buddha. Why do we put gold up there? Why do we put diamonds up there? Because they are the most valuable things to us. But nothing can substitute for and nothing can be equal to the Buddha that we have inside. So we must believe in it; that is our confidence, which is our hope, which is our potential. So we must always have respect for, appreciation of, and faith in, our ultimate potential, and then we must do our best to uphold and cherish this ultimate potential of ours. If we do this, I think then this human life will be very meaningful, and our bardo definitely will be a beneficial and positive one.

Sometimes, when we talk about bardo, some people get frightened, and that is unnecessary, because you are here; you went through bardo already, in your past life. You're quite okay. So you will be okay in the future, too. Because you're a Buddhist; because of that, this life's bardo will not be terrible. Before you didn't know, so okay; and now you know, it will be terrible? No! You see? We have gone through the bardo countless times. So we're okay, so we will be okay.

7

The Lama, Activity of the Buddhas

The Dalai Lama is a lineage of religious leaders of the Gelug school of Tibetan Buddhism. The Dalai Lamas were also the political leaders of Lhasa-based Tibetan government between the 17th century and 1959. "Lama" is a general term referring to Tibetan Buddhist teachers. The current Dalai Lama is often called "His Holiness" (HH) by Westerners, although this does not translate to a Tibetan title. Tibetans may refer to him by epithets such as *Gyalwa Rinpoche*, meaning "Precious Victor", or *Yishin Norbu*, meaning "Wish-fulfilling Jewel." The Dalai Lama is believed to be the rebirth of a long line of tulkus, who have chosen to be reborn in order to enlighten others. He is also the official leader of the Tibetan government-in-exile, or Central Tibetan Administration (CTA).

Between the 17th century and 1959, the lines of Dalai Lamas were the head of the Tibetan Government, administering a large portion of the area from the capital Lhasa, although the extent of the lineage's political authority and rulership over territory has been contested. Since 1959, the Dalai Lama has presided over the former government of Tibet, now a government in exile. The Dalai Lama is often thought to be the head of the Gelug School, but this position officially belongs to the Ganden Tripa, which is a temporary position appointed by the Dalai Lama (who in practice exerts more influence).

"Dalai" means "Ocean" in Mongolian, and is a translation of the Tibetan name "Gyatso," while "Lama" is the Tibetan equivalent of the Sanskrit word "guru." Putting the terms together, the full title is "Ocean Teacher" meaning a teacher who is spiritually as deep as the ocean. The name is often mistranslated as "Ocean of Wisdom". Before the 20th century, English-speaking sources often referred to the Dalai Lama as the "Grand Lama". For example, in 1795 Benjamin Franklin Bache mocked George Washington by calling him the "Grand Lama of this Country".

In 1252, Kublai Khan granted an audience to Drogön Chögyal Phagpa and Karma Pakshi, the 2nd Karmapa. Karma Pakshi, however, sought the patronage of Möngke Khan. Before his death in 1283, Karma Pakshi wrote a will to protect the established interests of his sect by advising his disciples to locate a boy to inherit the black hat. His instruction was based on the premise that Buddhist ideology is eternal, and a Buddha would send emanations to complete the missions he had initiated. Karma Pakshi's disciples acted in accordance with the will and located the reincarnated boy of their master.

The event marked the introduction of the teacher reincarnation system for the Black-Hat Line of Tibetan Buddhism and during the Ming Dynasty; Emperor Yongle bestowed the title *Great Treasure Prince of Dharma,* the first of the three *Princes of Dharma* upon the Black-Hat Karmapa. Various sects of Tibetan Buddhism responded to the introduction of the teacher reincarnation system by creating similar lineages.

THE ORIGIN OF THE TITLE OF DALAI LAMA

In 1578 the Mongol ruler Altan Khan bestowed what would later become the title *Dalai Lama* on Sonam Gyatso, which was also later retroactively applied to the two predecessors in his reincarnation line, Gendun Drup and Gendun Gyatso. Gendun Gyatso was also Sonam Gyatso's predecessor as abbot of Drepung monastery. However, the 14th Dalai Lama asserts that Altan Khan did not intend to bestow a title as such, and that he intended only to translate the name "Sonam Gyatso" into Mongolian.

As journalist Thomas Laird explains:

> . . . many writers have mistranslated *Dalai Lama* as "Ocean of Wisdom." The full Mongolian title, "the wonderful Vajradhara, good splendid meritorious ocean," given by Altan Khan, is primarily a translation of the Tibetan words *Sonam Gyatso* (*sonam* is "merit").

The 14th Dalai Lama remarks:

> The very name of each Dalai Lama from the Second Dalai Lama onwards had the word Gyatso in it, which means "ocean" in Tibetan. Even now I am Tenzin Gyatso, so the first name is changing but the second part the word "ocean" became like part of each Dalai Lama's name. All of the Dalai Lamas, since the Second, have this name. So I don't really agree that the Mongols actually conferred a title. It was just a translation.

Whatever the intention may have been originally, the Mongolian "Dalai," which has no meaning as a Tibetan term, came to be commonly understood as a title. The name or title *Dalai Lama* in Mongolian may also have originally derived from the title taken by Temüjin or Genghis Khan when he was proclaimed emperor of a united Mongolia in 1206. Temüjin took the name Èingis Qâghan or "oceanic sovereign", the Anglicized version of which is Genghis Khan.

Sonam Gyatso was an Abbot at the Drepung Monastery who was widely considered one of the most eminent lamas of his time. Although Sonam Gyatso became the first lama to hold the title "Dalai Lama" as described above, as he was the third member of his lineage he became known as the "Third Dalai Lama." The previous two titles were conferred posthumously upon his earlier incarnations.

Yonten Gyatso (1589 - 1616), the 4th Dalai Lama and a non-Tibetan, was the grandson of Altan Khan. Verhaegen (2002: p.5-6) states that the tulku tradition of the Dalai Lama has evolved into, and been inaugurated as, an institution and is recognized as a "cornerstone of Tibetan identity and culture":

> The institution of the Dalai Lama has become, over the centuries, a central focus of Tibetan cultural identity; "a symbolic embodiment of the Tibetan national character." Today, the Dalai Lama and the office of the Dalai Lama have become focal points in their struggle towards independence and, more urgently, cultural survival. The Dalai Lama is regarded as the principal incarnation of Chenrezig (referred to as Avalokiteshvara in India), the bodhisattva of compassion and patron deity of Tibet. In that role the Dalai Lama has chosen to use peace and compassion in his treatment of his own people and his oppressors. In this sense the Dalai Lama is the embodiment of an ideal of Tibetan values and a cornerstone of Tibetan identity and culture.

Tibetans address the Dalai Lama as *Gyalwa Rinpoche* ('Precious Victor'), *Kundun* ('Presence') *Yishin Norbu* ('Wishfulfilling Gem'), and so on.

UNIFICATION OF TIBET

The Fifth Dalai Lama, with the support of Gushri Khan (1582-1655), a Mongol ruler of Kokonor, united Tibet:

> After him [Jamphel Gyatso the VIIIth Dalai Lama (1758-1804), the IXth and Xth Dalai Lamas died before attaining their majority: one of them is credibly stated to have been murdered and strong suspicion attaches to the other. The XIth and XIIth were each enthroned but died soon after being invested with power. For 113 years, therefore, supreme authority in Tibet was in the hands of a Lama Regent, except for about two years when a lay noble held office and for short periods of nominal rule by the XIth and XIIth Dalai Lamas.

It has sometimes been suggested that this state of affairs was brought about by the Ambans-the Imperial Residents in Tibet-because it would be easier to control the Tibet through a Regent than when a Dalai Lama, with his absolute power, was at the head of the government. That is not true. The regular ebb and flow of events followed its set course. The Imperial

Residents in Tibet, after the first flush of zeal in 1750, grew less and less interested and efficient. Tibet was, to them, exile from the urbanity and culture of Peking; and so far from dominating the Regents, the Ambans allowed themselves to be dominated. It was the ambition and greed for power of Tibetans that led to five successive Dalai Lamas being subjected to continuous tutelage.

Thubten Jigme Norbu, the elder brother of the present 14th Dalai Lama, describes these unfortunate events as follows:

> It is perhaps more than a coincidence that between the seventh and the thirteenth holders of that office, only one reached his majority. The eighth, Gyampal Gyatso, died when he was in his thirties, Lungtog Gyatso when he was eleven, Tsultrim Gyatso at eighteen, Khadrup Gyatso when he was eighteen also, and Krinla Gyatso at about the same age. The circumstances are such that it is very likely some, if not all, were poisoned, either by loyal Tibetans for being Chinese-appointed impostors, or by the Chinese for not being properly manageable.

Thubten Gyatso, the 13th Dalai Lama, assumed ruling power from the monasteries which previously had great influence in the Regent, in 1895. Due to his two periods of exile in 1904-1909, to escape the British invasion of 1904, and from 1910-1912 to escape a Chinese invasion, he became well aware of the complexities of international politics and was the first Dalai Lama to become aware of the importance of foreign relations. After his return from exile in India and Sikkim in January, 1913 he took control of foreign relations and dealt directly with the Maharaja and the British Political officer in Sikkim and the king of Nepal rather than letting the Kashag or parliament handle it.

Thubten Gyatso issued a Declaration of Independence from China in the summer of 1912, and standardized the Tibetan flag in its present form. He deported all Chinese residents in the country including the Ambans, and instituted many measures to modernise Tibet. The Dalai Lamas continued to rule Tibet until the People's Republic of China invaded the region in 1949 and then took full control in 1959. The 14th Dalai Lama then fled to India and has since ceded temporal power to an elected government-in-exile. The current 14th Dalai Lama seeks greater autonomy for Tibet.

Verhaegen (2002: p.6) frames the trans-polity influence that the Institution of the Dalai Lama has had historically in areas such as western China, Mongolia, Ladakh in addition to the other Himalayan Kingdoms:

> The Dalai Lamas have also functioned as the principal spiritual guide to many Himalayan kingdoms bordering Tibet, as well as western China, Mongolia and Ladakh. The literary works of the Dalai Lamas have, over the centuries, inspired more than fifty million people in these regions. Those writings, reflecting the fusion of Buddhist philosophy embodied in Tibetan Buddhism, have become one of the world's great repositories of spiritual thought.

RESIDENCE

Starting with the 5th Dalai Lama and until the 14th Dalai Lama's flight into exile in 1959, the Dalai Lamas spent the winter at the Potala Palace and the summer at the Norbulingka palace and park. Both are in Lhasa and approximately 3 km apart. In 1959, after the start of the Chinese occupation of Tibet, the 14th Dalai Lama sought refuge in India. The then Indian Prime Minister, Jawaharlal Nehru, was instrumental in granting safe refuge to the Dalai Lama and his fellow Tibetans. The Dalai Lama has since lived in exile in Dharamsala, in the state of Himachal Pradesh in northern India, where the Central Tibetan Administration (the Tibetan government-in-exile) is also established. Tibetan refugees have constructed and opened many schools and Buddhist temples in Dharamsala.

SEARCHING FOR THE REINCARNATION

Palden Lhamo, the female guardian spirit of the sacred lake, Lhamo La-tso, who promised Gendun Drup the 1st Dalai Lama in one of his visions that "she would protect the reincarnation lineage of the Dalai Lamas". In the Himalayan tradition, phowa (Tibetan) is the discipline that transfers the mindstream to the intended body. Upon the death of the Dalai Lama and consultation with the Nechung Oracle, a search for the Lama's reincarnation, or *yangsi* (*yang srid*), is conducted. Traditionally it has been the responsibility of the High Lamas of the Gelugpa Tradition and the Tibetan government to find his reincarnation.

The process can take around two or three years to identify the Dalai Lama, and for the 14th Tenzin Gyatso it was four years before he was found. The search for the Dalai Lama has usually been limited historically to Tibet, although the third tulku was born in Mongolia. Tenzin Gyatso, though, has stated that there is a chance that he will not be reborn although if he is reborn it will not be in a country run by the People's Republic of China. The High Lamas used several ways in which they can increase the chances of finding the reincarnation.

High Lamas often visit the holy lake, called Lhamo La-tso, in central Tibet and watch for a sign from the lake itself. This may be either a vision or some indication of the direction in which to search and this was how Tenzin Gyatso was found. It is said that Palden Lhamo, the female guardian spirit of the sacred lake, Lhamo La-tso, promised Gendun Drup, the 1st Dalai Lama in one of his visions "that she would protect the reincarnation lineage of the Dalai Lamas." Ever since the time of Gendun Gyatso, the 2nd Dalai Lama, who formalised the system, the Regents and other monks have gone to the lake to seek guidance on choosing the next reincarnation through visions while meditating there.

The particular form of Palden Lhamo at Lhamo La-tso is Gyelmo Maksorma, "The Victorious One who Turns Back Enemies". The lake is sometimes referred to as "Pelden Lhamo Kalideva", which indicates that Palden Lhamo is an emanation of the goddess Kali, the Shakti of the Hindu god Siva.

"Lhamo Latso ... is a brilliant azure jewel set in a ring of grey mountains. The elevation and the surrounding peaks combine to give it a highly changeable climate, and the continuous passage of cloud and wind creates a constantly moving pattern on the surface of the waters. On that surface visions appear to those who seek them in the right frame of mind."

It was here that in 1935, the Regent, Reting Rinpoche, received a clear vision of three Tibetan letters and of a monastery with a jade-green and gold roof, and a house with turquoise roof tiles, which led to the discovery of Tenzin Gyatso, the present 14th Dalai Lama.

High Lamas may also have a vision in a dream or if the Dalai Lama was cremated, they will often monitor the direction of the smoke as an indication of the direction of the rebirth.

Once the High Lamas have found the home and the boy they believe to be the reincarnation, the boy undergoes a series of tests to affirm the rebirth. They present a number of artifacts belonging to the previous Dalai Lama and if the boy chooses the items which belonged to the previous Dalai Lama; this is seen as a sign, in conjunction with all of the other indications, that the boy is the reincarnation. If there is only one boy found, the High Lamas will invite Living Buddhas of the three great monasteries together with secular clergy and monk officials, to confirm their findings and will then report to the Central Government through the Minister of Tibet.

Later a group consisting of the three major servants of Dalai Lama, eminent officials and troops will collect the boy and his family and travel to Lhasa, where the boy would be taken, usually to Drepung Monastery to study the Buddhist sutra in preparation for assuming the role of spiritual leader of Tibet. However, if there are several possibilities of the reincarnation, in the past regents and eminent officials and monks at the Jokhang in Lhasa, and the Minister to Tibet would decide on the individual by placing the boys names inside an urn and drawing one lot in public if it was too difficult to judge the reincarnation initially.

FUTURE OF THE POSITION

Verhaegen (2002: p.5) states:

In the mid-1970s Tenzin Gyatso, The Fourteenth Dalai Lama, told a Polish newspaper that he thought he would be the last Dalai Lama. In a later interview published in the

English language press he stated "The Dalai Lama office was an institution created to benefit others. It is possible that it will soon have outlived its usefulness." These statements caused a furor amongst Tibetans in India. Many could not believe that such an option could even be considered. It was further felt that it was not the Dalai Lama's decision to reincarnate. Rather, they felt that since the Dalai Lama is a national institution it was up to the people of Tibet to decide whether or not the Dalai Lama should reincarnate.

Despite its officially secular stance, the government of the People's Republic of China (PRC) has claimed the power to approve the naming of high reincarnations in Tibet, based on the precedent set by the Qianlong Emperor of the Qing Dynasty. The Qianlong Emperor was said to have instituted a system of selecting the Dalai Lama and the Panchen Lama by means of a lottery which utilised a golden urn with names wrapped in barley balls. Controversially, this precedent was called upon by the PRC to name their own Panchen Lama. The Dalai Lama and the Tibetan Buddhists in exile do not regard PRC's Panchen Lama to be the legitimate Panchen Lama. The Dalai Lama has recognized a different child, Gedhun Choekyi Nyima, as the reincarnated Panchen Lama.

This child and his family have been taken into 'protective custody' according to the PRC, although there has been no mention of what or whom the child must be protected from. All attempts by members of the EU parliament and US government to garner guarantees of the family's safety have been denied by the PRC. In September 2007 the Chinese government said all high monks must be approved by the government, which would include the selection of the 15th Dalai Lama after the death of Tenzin Gyatso. The People's Republic of China may attempt to direct the selection of a successor using the authority of their chosen Panchen Lama.

In response to this scenario, Tashi Wangdi, the representative of the 14th Dalai Lama, replied that the Chinese government's selection would be meaningless. "You can't impose an Imam, an Archbishop, saints, any religion...you can't politically impose these things on people," said Wangdi. "It has to be a decision of the followers of that tradition. The Chinese can use their political power: force. Again, it's meaningless. Like their Panchen Lama. And they can't keep their Panchen Lama in Tibet. They tried to bring him to his monastery many times but people would not see him. How can you have a religious leader like that?"

The Dalai Lama said as early as 1969 that it was for the Tibetans to decide whether the institution of the Dalai Lama "should continue or not." He has given reference to a possible vote occurring in the future for all Tibetan Buddhists to decide whether they wish to recognize his rebirth. In response to the possibility that the PRC may attempt to choose his successor, the Dalai Lama has said he will not be reborn in a country controlled by the People's Republic of China, or any other country which is not free. In 2007, two monks from Tashilhunpo monastery of Tibet committed suicide following a campaign of exclusion by Chinese officials. These two monks had recognized the 11th Panchen Lama, Gedhun Choekyi Nyima, and could therefore have been requested to recognize the next Dalai Lama.

On March 10 2009 Dalai Lama criticised China for oppressing his people and misrepresenting his wish for Tibetan autonomy. He warned Tibetans to prepare themselves "in case our struggle goes on for a long time". The Dalai Lama also spoke of his own exile, and that of the 90,000 Tibetans who followed him, as a period of "unimaginable hardship, which is still fresh in the Tibetan memory."

THE DALAI LAMA INTO POPULAR WESTERN CULTURE

Because of the political and geographical isolation of Tibet, there was little mention of the persona of the Dalai Lama or Tibet in mainstream popular Western culture before the Chinese invasion of Tibet in 1950. The earliest New York Times mention of the Dalai Lama was in a July 8, 1853 article entitled "The Fate of Asia", where the Dalai Lama was mentioned once by name in the context of larger nations seeking territory and influence in Asia. A March 3, 1878 *The New York Times* article entitled "Choosing the Dalai Lama" describes the process in 1841 of finding the new Dalai Lama and choosing between 4 child candidates.

In the February 11, 1924 issue of *Time* magazine, in an article entitled "Everest Assault", the Dalai Lama is mentioned as giving permission to British army officers in their attempt to scale Mount Everest. In the early 1940s, the United States Army led an expedition to Tibet, under the Presidency of Franklin D. Roosevelt, to bring gifts to the Dalai Lama, and to strengthen the relationship between the United States and Tibet during the political climate of the Second World War. This expedition was documented on color 16 mm film by the United States Army.

Universal Newsreels, which screened before feature film presentations in American movie theaters through the late 1960s, produced newsreel segments describing the Dalai Lama to American audiences in the 1950s before the 1950 invasion of Tibet by China, as well as reporting on the invasion of Tibet itself. There were also Universal Newsreels reporting on the 1959 fleeing of the 14th Dalai Lama into Northern India. Once in India he told about what he had seen including the destruction of monasteries.

The Dalai Lama was on the cover of *Time* magazine on April 20, 1959, with the headline "The Escape that Rocked the Reds". After the 14th Dalai Lama (Tenzin Gyatso) won the Nobel Peace Prize in 1989, the public awareness of the Dalai Lama became even more prevalent, and the Dalai Lama became the subject of several motion pictures, including *Seven Years in Tibet* starring Brad Pitt, Martin Scorsese's feature film *Kundun*, as well as documentary films like the 2008 theatrically released *Dalai Lama Renaissance*, narrated by Harrison Ford.

By His Holiness the Dalai Lama It is very good to recite the mantra Om mani padme hum, but while you are doing it, you should be thinking on its meaning, for the meaning of the six syllables is great and vast. The first, Om is composed of three letters, A, U, and M. These symbolize the practitioner's impure body, speech, and mind; they also symbolize the pure exalted body, speech, and mind of a Buddha.

Can impure body, speech, and mind be transformed into pure body, speech, and mind, or are they entirely separate? All Buddhas are cases of beings who were like ourselves and then in dependence on the path became enlightened; Buddhism does not assert that there is anyone who from the beginning is free from faults and possesses all good qualities. The development of pure body, speech, and mind comes from gradually leaving the impure states arid their being transformed into the pure.

How is this done? The path is indicated by the next four syllables. Mani, meaning jewel, symbolizes the factors of method-the altruistic intention to become enlightened, compassion, and love. Just as a jewel is capable of removing poverty, so the altruistic mind of enlightenment is capable of removing the poverty, or difficulties, of cyclic existence and of solitary peace. Similarly, just as a jewel fulfills the wishes of sentient beings, so the altruistic intention to become enlightened fulfills the wishes of sentient beings.

The two syllables, padme, meaning lotus, symbolize wisdom. Just as a lotus grows forth from mud but is not sullied by the faults of mud, so wisdom is capable of putting you in a situation of non-contradiction whereas there would be contradiction if you did not have wisdom. There is wisdom realizing impermanence, wisdom realizing that persons are empty, of being self-sufficient or substantially existent, wisdom that realizes the emptiness of duality-that is to say, of difference of entity between subject an object-and wisdom that realizes the emptiness of inherent existence. Though there are many different types of wisdom, the main of all these is the wisdom realizing emptiness.

Purity must be achieved by an indivisible unity of method and wisdom, symbolized by the final syllable hum, which indicates indivisibility. According to the sutra system, this indivisibility of method and wisdom refers to wisdom affected by method and method affected by wisdom. In the mantra, or tantric, vehicle, it refers to one consciousness in which there is the full form of both wisdom and method as one undifferentiable entity. In terms of the seed syllables of the five Conqueror Buddhas, hum is the seed syllable of Akshobhya - the immovable, the unfluctuating, that which cannot be disturbed by anything.

Thus the six syllables, om mani padme hum, mean that in dependence on the practice of a path which is an indivisible union of method and wisdom, you can transform your impure body, speech, and mind into the pure exalted body, speech, and mind of a Buddha. It is said that you should not seek for Buddhahood outside of yourself; the substances for the achievement of Buddhahood are within. As Maitreya says in his Sublime Continuum of the Great Vehicle (Uttaratantra), all beings naturally have the Buddha nature in their own continuum. We have within us the seed of purity, the essence of a One Gone Thus (Tathagatagarbha) that is to be transformed and fully developed into Buddhahood.

MILAREPA AND THE VINAYA

Jetsun Milarepa, (c. 1052-c. 1135 CE) is generally considered one of Tibet's most famous yogis and poets, a student of Marpa Lotsawa, and a major figure in the history of the Kagyu (Bka'-brgyud) school of Tibetan Buddhism. The essence of Milarepa lies in his writings rather than the legends that have grown up around him. The writings, often referred to as the Songs of Milarepa, are canonical Mahayana Buddhist texts and in particular emphasize the temporary nature of the physical body and the need for non-attachment.

In contrast, the legends of Milarepa's life are full of references to magic and lack the same sense of devout non-attachment. They are popularly known from the romanticized biography *Mi-la-rnam-thar* by Gtsang-smyon he-ru-ka rus-pa'i-rgyan-can (1452-1507); although they may be of questionable historic validity, the biographical details given in this chapter are based upon this account or its derivatives. Born in the village of Kya Ngatsa - also known as Tsa - in Gungthang province of western Tibet to a prosperous family he was named Mila

Thöpaga (Thos-pa-dga'), which means "A joy to hear."

The name of his clan was Khyungpo, his family name was Josay. When his father died, Milarepa's uncle and aunt took all of the family's wealth. At his mother's request, Milarepa left home and studied sorcery. While his aunt and uncle were having a party to celebrate the impending marriage of their son, he took his revenge by summoning a giant scorpion to demolish their house, killing 35 people, although the uncle and aunt are supposed to have survived. The villagers were angry and set off to look for Milarepa, but his mother got word to him and he sent a hailstorm to destroy their crops.

Many of Milarepa's deeds took place in Chokyi Dronma's homeland and his life and songs were compiled by Tsangnyon Heruka, sponsored by Chokyi Dronma's brother, the Gungthang king Thri Namgyal De. Milarepa later lamented his evil ways in his older years: "In my youth I committed black deeds. In maturity I practiced innocence. Now, released from both good and evil, I have destroyed the root of karmic action and shall have no reason for action in the future. To say more than this would only cause weeping and laughter. What good would it do to tell you? I am an old man. Leave me in peace."

SUPERNATURAL RUNNING

According to the book *Magic and Mystery in Tibet* by French explorer Alexandra David-Néel, Milarepa boasted of having "crossed in a few days, a distance which, before his training in black magic, had taken him more than a month. He ascribes his gift to the clever control of 'internal air'." David-Néel comments "that at the house of the lama who taught him black magic there lived a trapa [monk who was fleeter than a horse" using the same skill. This esoteric skill, which is known as *Lung-gom-pa* ("Wind Meditation", *lung* = "wind, *gom-pa* = "meditation") in Tibet, allows a practitioner to run at an extraordinary speed for days without stopping. This technique could be compared to that practiced by the *Kaihigyo Monks* of Mt. Hiei in Kyoto, Japan.

TUTELAGE UNDER MARPA

Knowing that his revenge was wrong, Milarepa set out to find a lama and was led to Marpa the translator. Marpa proved a hard task master. Before Marpa would teach Milarepa he had him build and then demolish three towers in turn. When Marpa still refused to teach Milarepa he went to Marpa's wife, who took pity on him. She forged a letter of introduction to another teacher, Lama Ngogdun Chudor, under whose tutelage he began to practice meditation. However when he was making no progress, he confessed the forgery and Ngogdun Chudor said that it was vain to hope for spiritual growth without the guru Marpa's approval. Milarepa returned to Marpa, and after practicing very diligently for twelve years Milarepa attained the state of *Vajradhara* (complete enlightenment).

He is said to be the first to achieve this state within one lifetime. He then became known as Milarepa, which means the "Mila, the cotton clad one" (the suffix "repa" is given to many tantric yogis since they wear white robes) At the age of forty-five, he started to practice at Drakar Taso (White Rock Horse Tooth) cave - 'Milarepa's Cave', as well as becoming a wandering teacher.

Here, he subsisted on nettle tea, leading his skin to turn green, hence the greenish color he is often depicted as having in paintings and sculpture. Pyenzhangling Monastery, also known as Pelgye Ling Gompa, is a small Tibetan Buddhist monastery in a tiny village called Zhonggang, Tibet that is consecrated to Milarepa. It is built around the cave where he once lived. "It was destroyed but has now been rebuilt and decorated by Nepali artisans. This is one of many caves associated with Milarepa between Langtang and Jomolungma."

LINEAGE

Milarepa is famous for many of his songs and poems, in which he expresses the profundity of his realization of the dharma with extraordinary clarity and beauty. He also had many disciples, male and female, which include Rechung Dorje Drakpa (Ras-chung Rdo-rje Grags-pa), Gampopa (Sgam-po-pa) or Dhakpo Lhaje. His female disciples include Rechungma, Padarbum, Sahle Aui and Tseringma. It was Gampopa who became his spiritual successor who continued his lineage and became one of the main lineage masters in Milarepa's tradition.

VINAYA

The Vinaya (a word in Pâli as well as in Sanskrit, with literal meaning 'leading out', 'education', 'discipline') is the regulatory framework for the Buddhist monastic community, or sangha, based in the canonical texts called Vinaya Pitaka. The teachings of the Buddha or Buddhadharma can be divided into two broad categories: 'Dharma' or doctrine, and 'Vinaya', or discipline. Another term for Buddhism is *dharmavinaya*.

At the heart of the Vinaya is a set of rules known as Patimokkha (Pâli), or Pratimoksha (Sanskrit). The Vinaya was orally passed down from the Buddha to his disciples. Eventually, numerous different Vinayas arose in Buddhism, based upon geographical or cultural differences and the different Buddhist schools that developed. Three of these are still in use. The Vinayas are the same in substance and have only minor differences. Buddhists in Burma, Cambodia, Laos, Sri Lanka, and Thailand follow the Theravadin Vinaya, which has 227 rules for the bhikkhus (male monastics) and 311 for the bhikkhunis (female monastics, though the female order died out centuries ago and recent attempts to restore it from the Chinese tradition are controversial).

Buddhists in China, Japan, Korea, Taiwan and Vietnam follow the Dharmaguptaka Vinaya, which has 250 rules for the bhikkhus and 348 rules for the bhikkhunis. Buddhists in Tibet and Mongolia follow the Mûlasarvâstivâda Vinaya, which has 253 rules for the bhikshus and 364 rules for bhikshunis (in theory, though the female order was never introduced in Tibet; it has recently been authorized by the Dalai Lama). In addition to these patimokkha rules there are many supplementary rules.

The Buddha constantly reminds his hearers that it is the spirit that counts. On the other hand, the rules themselves are designed to assure a satisfying life, and provide a perfect springboard for the higher attainments. Monastics are instructed by the Buddha to live as "islands unto themselves". In this sense, living life as the vinaya prescribes it is, as one scholar puts it: "more than merely a means to an end: it is very nearly the end in itself."

Surrounding the rules is a range of texts. Some of these explain the origins of the rules - it is possible to trace the development of the rules from responses to specific situations or actions to a general codification. There are also a number of sutta-like texts which are more general statements about Buddhist doctrine, or which give biographical details of some of the great disciples and their enlightenment. Other sections detail how the rules are to be applied, how breaches are to be dealt with, and how disputes amongst the monks are handled.

It is thought that originally there were no rules and the Buddha and his disciples just lived in harmony when they were together. Most of the time they would have been wandering alone, but every year, during the monsoon season when travelling became impossible; the bhikkhus would come together for a few months. As the sangha became bigger and started accepting people of lesser ability who remained unenlightened, it became necessary to begin having rules. It seems that initially these were quite flexible and were adapted to the situation. By the time of the Buddha's death there would have been a body of rules which bhikkhus were expected to follow.

In the Mahaparinibbana Sutta the Buddha, as part of his last teaching, tells the bhikkhus that they can abandon some minor rules, but that they should stick to the major ones, but there appears to have been some confusion over which was which. It was therefore decided that they would keep all of the rules. Immediately after the Buddha's death there was a council at which all of the teachings were recited, collected and sorted. Legend has it that the huge volume of teachings was recited from memory, with Ananda reciting the dhamma and Upali reciting the Vinaya.

The Vinaya Pitaka, the first division of the Tipitaka, is the textual framework upon which the monastic community (Sangha) is built. It includes not only the rules governing the life of every Theravada bhikkhu (monk) and bhikkhuni (nun), but also a host of procedures and conventions of etiquette that support harmonious relations, both among the monastics themselves, and between the monastics and their lay supporters, upon whom they depend for all their material needs. When the Buddha first established the Sangha, the community initially lived in harmony without any codified rules of conduct.

As the Sangha gradually grew in number and evolved into a more complex society, occasions inevitably arose when a member would act in an unskillful way. Whenever one of these cases was brought to the Buddha's attention, he would lay down a rule establishing a suitable punishment for the offense, as a deterrent to future misconduct. The Buddha's standard reprimand was itself a powerful corrective:

It is not fit, foolish man, it is not becoming, it is not proper, it is unworthy of a recluse, it is not lawful, it ought not to be done. How could you, foolish man, have gone forth under this Dhamma and Discipline which are well-taught, commit such and such offense? It is not, foolish man, for the benefit of un-believers, nor for the increase in the number of believers, but, foolish man, it is to the detriment of both unbelievers and believers, and it causes wavering in some.

The monastic tradition and the rules upon which it is built are sometimes naïvely criticized - particularly here in the West - as irrelevant to the "modern" practice of Buddhism. Some see the Vinaya as a throwback to an archaic patriarchy, based on a hodge-podge of ancient rules and customs - quaint cultural relics that only obscure the essence of "true" Buddhist practice. This misguided view overlooks one crucial fact: it is thanks to the unbroken lineage of monastics that have consistently upheld and protected the rules of the Vinaya for almost 2,600 years that we find ourselves today with the luxury of receiving the priceless teachings of Dhamma. Were it not for the Vinaya, and for those who continue to keep it alive to this day, there would be no Buddhism.

It helps to keep in mind that the name the Buddha gave to the spiritual path he taught was *"Dhamma-vinaya"* - the Doctrine *(Dhamma)* and Discipline *(Vinaya)* - suggesting an integrated body of wisdom and ethical training. The Vinaya is thus an indispensable facet and foundation of all the Buddha's teachings, inseparable from the Dhamma, and worthy of study by all followers - lay and ordained, alike. Lay practitioners will find in the Vinaya Pitaka many valuable lessons concerning human nature, guidance on how to establish and maintain a harmonious community or organization, and many profound teachings of the Dhamma itself. But its greatest value, perhaps, lies in its power to inspire the layperson to consider the extraordinary possibilities presented by a life of true renunciation; a life lived fully in tune with the Dhamma.

The vinaya forms one of the three 'baskets' of the Buddhist scriptures. It is part of the way the Buddha defined the religion he developed - the other part being the teachings, the Dhamma, and the couplet dhamma-vinaya is often encountered in scriptures. It is not possible to cultivate Buddhist practice without both of these being present in some way. For lay people basic vinaya takes the form of the five precepts. "Just as the sea has a single taste, that of salt, so too the Dhamma and Vinaya have a single taste: that of release, nibbana."

The Buddha didn't lay out all the rules at once; they developed over time in response to particular incidents. The vinaya details these incidents along with various 'origin stories' which help in understanding the reasons behind the rules. Some of the stories are classics of Buddhist literature, and show a dry, understated sense of humor together with a perceptive insight into human nature. The number of rules grew and was eventually codified into the 227 rules found in the monks' code of discipline - the patimokkha.

Vinaya= that which is conducive to breaking up or dispelling *[hindrances / rebirth.* It is interesting to note that *vinayako* = spiritual leader, a Buddha.

Patimokkha= thorough bond - *'that which binds the community together'*

Why Rules:

The Buddha, in laying down each rule, gave ten reasons (in 5 pairs) for doing so:

- For the excellence and well being of the Community,
- The control of ill-behaved monks and the comfort of well-behaved monks,
- The restraint of bad habits in this life and the prevention of bad habits in the next,
- The arousing of faith in the faithless and the increase of faith in the faithful,
- The establishment of the Dhamma and support of vinaya.

So the rules are intended to ensure harmony within the sangha and to foster faith. Overall they are to restrain and prevent mental bad habits within individual monks. This encourages mindfulness and reflection in actions of body and speech - both qualities which enhance the training of the mind. Rules in general are usually not very popular; often being seen as an impediment to what 'I' want. They get in *my* way! It is obvious that it would be impossible to have a society without rules - imagine no road rules - but which rules? The monastic standard is set in relation to the patimokkha which provides an objective standard which, allowing it was developed over 2000 years ago and is not subject to change, can't be seen as any particular individual 'laying their trip' on the community.

The paradox of rules is that the more precisely a definition is sought to contain a particular situation the less well it may fit other situations. This is where it is important to consider the principles involved. What was the Buddha pointing to when he outlined *this* rule? For example, the rule about money is literally about 'not handling gold and silver'. So, say the cheeky ones: 'paper money is OK and, credit cards even better'. The spirit of this rule is about giving up the power that money offers. This challenges my desires and wish for independence which directly supports consideration of the second Noble Truth. This is dhamma-vinaya at work.

Even in the Buddha's time situations arose that weren't exactly covered by a rule and he laid out The Four Great Standards which encourages comparison with existing rules. Determining what situation suitably compares with what rule is not the decision of the individual and generally the consent of the resident community would be needed. Although the list of 227 rules can seem a bit daunting, most are refinements of the eight precepts kept by anagarikas (novices) and as one commits to the holy life, through the various levels of ordination, the boundaries of behaviour become more contained and limited; the necessity for cultivating restraint is increased. To the desire mind this sounds crippling - I can't sing or dance, I can't have a girl friend, I can't.... and on, and on.

The mind feels stiffled and without a sound appreciation of the third Noble Truth - letting go of desire - vinaya becomes a formula for disaster. Renunciation is not supression and there is a vast difference between letting go of desire and suppressing desire. Restraint around sexuality may be useful as an example. Because sex is such a major factor in most peoples lives many find it hard to understand celibacy and see it as some kind of repression. I often ask these people what they do when they feel sexually attracted to someone. I mean, do you just jump in there all grabbing and groping? Some do I guess but usually there is some restraint.

This can be through fear but it is possible - say, through faithfulness to one's partner - to just let go of the idea of that particular energy finding any expression. The energy may well still be there but it is not 'fed' in any way like a dog that runs up to you and wants to play. Yap! Yap! It wants attention. Sorry doggie but I'm not available. Chances are it sees it's not going to get attention right now and wanders off. There is also a need here to appreciate the principle of anatta - impersonality or not-self. The point is, it's not even my dog. The use of vinaya as part of the process of letting go applies not just socially in relation to 'bad habits' (the conditioning of the mind) but as a reflection on the impersonality of both the mind and the body.

The various thoughts, feelings and energies that we experience can be seen arising dependent on various conditions - they arise and pass away. Vinaya contains the habitual response and offers space for reflection. What is this thought? What is this feeling? Do I have to do anything with it? In the space created, one gets the opportunity to investigate and understand the nature of desire. With a relatively high level of renunciation in a monastery what is available becomes limited and it is often quite absurd to see the levels to which the desire mind will stoop.

Monks have alms bowls which sit on nice bamboo stands. Making these stands is quite a process and some can be real works of art. And you're sitting at the meal. The new monk comes in and sets up his bowl. And the bowl stands! Don't be silly, it's just a bowl stand, you're a grown man and you have a perfectly good stand already. Yes. You know the logic but the desire mind has no pride. It wants something, anything. Food is limited and one can find the mind coveting another monk's pear. It becomes so absurd sometimes that it suddenly falls into perspective. Let go. Relax.

The rules themselves can be roughly divided into four groups.

- 4 Rules of defeat - i.e. automatic excommunication. If one of the rules in this group is broken it is not possible for that person to reordain. They are obviously critical and are taught to a new monk literally within minutes of his ordination.
- 13 with some 'penance'. (Penance has the connotation of punishment which is not truely accurate here). This group is seen as major transgressions and the rectification involves quite a process which is aimed not at punishment but at increasing the monks' mindfulness around the particular area of fault. Many factors of this process require particular humility on the part of the transgressor

which tends to generate a sense of remorse and regret. He is on probation for six days, during which time he loses seniority, lives 'aside' from the community, is not trusted to go anywhere unaccompanied, and daily has to confess his offense to every monk who lives in or happens to visit the monastery. At the end of his probation, twenty monks have to be convened to reinstate him to his original status. What a hassle! Best be a good monk.

- 30 with forfeiture of some (inappropriate) item. This group deals largely with bowls and robes - significant items in a monk's life. Requisites generally that have been inappropriately acquired must be given up; some can be returned.

All the rest - these are 'confessable'. The word confession has associations with sin but the rules have no 'theistic' connection and are about sangha harmony, faith and mind training. The confession would usually take place fortnightly on the moon day although it can happen any time. Two monks would meet and the junior would pay respects to the senior. The formal ceremony is chanted in Pali but it is not uncommon for a monk to clearly indicate in English the particular rules that he has transgressed; the aim of the confession being to focus the monk's mind on his unskilful tendencies through body, speech and mind. The formla is a simple series of statements and responses repeated four times for each of four classes of rules:

'Venerable Sir, several times I have transgressed these rules and I now confess this to you.'

'Do you clearly see where you have transgressed?'

'Yes, Venerable Sir, I clearly see my faults.'

'In future you should practice restraint in these matters.'

'Well spoken Venerable Sir, I will indeed practice restraint.' [Repeated 3 times - to reinforce this intention

The rules are not primarily judicial but aim at illuminating the variety of unskilful mindstates we are suseptible to and, as many of them are minor, the hope is that any regular tendency to transgress - being regularly brought to light - will be clearly seen, understood, and let go of. For example, the second rule of defeat is about stealing and three parts of the definition have to do with the mindstate of the monk.

1. Object: anything belonging to another person, a group of persons, or a location.
2. Perception: One perceives that the object belongs to another person, etc.
3. Intention: One decides to steal it.
4. Effort: One takes possession of it.

Stealing under any circumstances is always an offense. However, the severity of the offense depends on another factor, which is:

5. The value of the object.

Of these five it is intention which acts as a major pivotal point. We all have a degree of mental delusion and do things out of habit or confusion in the 'heat' of a situation. Yes, you did it but, did you mean to do it? Were you quite clear in your mind about what you were doing? Often, with thought in retrospect, the answer is no. OK then, watch out for that tendency - don't do it again. Vinaya is meant to act as a mirror - to reflect the various mind states that occur - to highlight unskilful mind states (so they might be avoided), and to support the development of the skilful ones. The Buddha's first instruction about behaviour was on the full moon of Magha and is known as the Ovada Patimokkha.This was the foundation of vinaya. 'Do good, refrain from wrong and purify the mind.' Now, that's not difficult - is it?

8

The Buddha's Tooth

The Sacred Relic of the tooth of Buddha (Buddh-dantya) is venerated in Sri Lanka as a relic of the founder of Buddhism.

THE RELIC IN INDIA

According to Sri Lankan legends, when the Buddha died, his body was cremated in a sandalwood pyre at Kusinara in India and his left canine tooth was retrieved from the funeral pyre by Arahat Khema. Khema then gave it to King Brahmadatte for veneration. It became a royal possession in Brahmadatte's country and was kept in the city of Dantapuri (present day Puri in Orissa). A belief grew that whoever possessed the Sacred Tooth Relic had a divine right to rule that land. Wars were fought to take possession of the relic. 800 years after the Buddha's death, in the 4th century CE, the tooth came into the possession of King Guhaseeva of Kalinga, which roughly corresponds to the present day state of Orissa.

Kalinga had become a Buddhist and begun to worship the Sacred Tooth relic. This caused discontent among some of the citizens, who went to King Paandu and said that King Guhaseeva had stopped believing in god and that he had started to worship a tooth. King Paandu decided to destroy the relic, and ordered to it brought to the city. It is said that, as the tooth arrived at the city, a miracle occurred, and King Paandu converted to Buddhism.

When King Ksheeradara heard, he went with his army

to attack Paandu in the city of Palalus. The invaders were defeated before reaching the city, and King Ksheeradara died. A prince from the city of Udeni who had become a Buddhist came to worship the sacred tooth. King Guhaseeva was pleased with him, and let him marry his daughter. The prince was known as Dantha and the princess as Hemamala. When they heard that King Ksheeradara had died in the war, his sons raised a large army to attack King Guhaseeva and destroy the relic. They entered the city, but King Guhaseeva secretly sent Dantha and Hemamala out of the city, with the relic.

THE RELIC IN SRI LANKA

According to legend, Hemamali hid the relic in her hair ornament and the royal couple disguised themselves as Brahmins in order to avoid discovery. They set sail from Tamralipti, a port at the mouth of the river Ganges, and landed in Sri Lanka at the port of Lankapattana (now Ilankeiturei). It is said that Sri Lanka was chosen as the new home for the tooth relic because the Lord Buddha had declared that his religion would be safe in Sri Lanka for 2,500 years.

At the time of Dantha's and Hemamali's arrival on the island, King Kirti Sri Megavanna or Kithsirimevan ruled Sri Lanka. The King was overjoyed when he heard the news and warmly welcomed the royal couple and received the Sacred Tooth Relic with great veneration. He built a beautiful palace within the Royal Palace Complex itself and enshrined the Relic in it. Thereafter, he ordered that an annual *perahera* be held in honour of the Sacred Relic.

As time went on, as the land was threatened with foreign invasions, the seat of the kingdom was moved from Anuradhapura to Polonnaruwa, then to Dambadeniya and other cities. Upon each change of capital, a new palace was built to enshrine the Relic. Finally, it was brought to Kandy where it is at present, in the Sri Dalada Maligawa temple. The Sacred Tooth Relic came to be regarded as a symbolic representation of the living Buddha and it is on this basis that there grew up a series of offerings, rituals, and ceremonies. These are conducted under the supervision of the two Mahanayake Theros of Malwatte, Asgiriya Chapters, and Diyawadana Nilame of the Maligawa. These have a hierarchy of officials and temple functionaries to perform the services and rituals.

OTHER TOOTH RELICS

Aside from this specific tooth relic, another relic of the tooth of the Buddha is currently in Lingguang Temple in Badachu, Beijing, China. Fo Guang Shan monastery in Kaohsiung, Taiwan, the reliquary hall (*shariden*) of Engaku-ji in Kamakura, Japan, and the Buddha Relic Tooth Temple in Chinatown, Singapore are all also reputed to each contain a tooth of the Buddha. The Sri Dalada Maligawa or the Temple of the Sacred Tooth Relic is a temple in the city of Kandy in Sri Lanka. It was built within the royal palace complex which houses a relic of Buddha, a tooth, which is venerated by Buddhists.

The relic has played an important role in the local politics since ancient times; it's believed that whoever holds the relic holds the governance of the country, which caused the ancient kings to protect it with great effort. Kandy was the capital of the Sinhalese kings. Kings from 1592 to 1815 fortified the terrain of the mountains and made it difficult to approach Kandy. The city is declared by UNESCO to be a world heritage site, in part due to the temple. Monks of the two chapters of Malwatte and Asgiriya conduct daily ritual worship in the inner chamber Sof the temple, in annual rotation. They conduct these services three times a day: at dawn, at noon and in the evening.

On Wednesdays there is a symbolic bathing of the Sacred Relic with an herbal preparation made from scented water and flagrant flowers, called *Nanumura Mangallaya*. This holy water is believed to contain healing powers and is distributed among those present. The Temple has sustained damage from multiple bombings in the past. The first deadly attack was carried out by JVP (Janatha Vimukthi Peramuna), a Sinhalese nationalist, Marxist-Leninist organization which has now entered into parliamentary politics, split into JVP and NFF, in the late 1980s.

On January 25, 1998, Liberation Tigers of Tamil Eelam (LTTE), a banned terrorist outfit, carried out a deadly suicide attack inside the temple, killing 8 civilians and leaving 25 others injured, as well as causing significant damage to the temple structure. Fortunately, the temple has been fully restored each time. The worship of corporeal remains of the Buddha, as recorded in the Mahaparinibbana Sutta (the Record of the Demise of the Buddha), was sanctioned by the Buddha himself on the verge of his passing away. The Buddha declared that four noble persons are worthy of their bodily remains being enshrined and honored, the Buddha, the Personal Buddhas (Pacceka Buddhas), the Arahanths (Buddha's disciples) and the Universal Monarchs (Cakkavatti kings).

The bodily remains of the Buddha, after their distribution among various states, were enshrined in the funerary mounds known as stupa. However, the four canine Teeth were said to have been separately enshrined and worshipped. The right canine was worshipped in the heavenly domain of the king of gods, Sakra, while another was worshipped by the king of Gandhara in modern Pakistan. The third was taken away by the Nâgas and worshipped in a golden shrine room. The fourth, the left canine was removed from the funerary ashes by a monk and was handed over to the king of Kalinga in Eastern India, as recorded in the *Digha Nikaya.*

Thenceforth, the Tooth relic of the Kalinga became an object of great veneration by generations of Kalinga kings until it earned the wrath of brahmanical followers, and consequently several attempts were made to destroy the relic by fanatical rulers. Yet the Tooth relic was miraculously saved from such atrocities, which caused the kings of other states attempted to possess the Tooth relic for personal veneration. Thus, from the beginning, the Tooth relic came to be considered as an important symbol of veneration. The last Indian ruler to possess the Tooth relic was Guhasiva of Kalinga (c.4th century AD).

ARRIVAL OF THE SACRED TOOTH RELIC IN SRI LANKA

The final attempt made by a neighboring state to make war with Guhasiva for the possession of the Tooth relic caused this venerated relic to leave the Indian shores. By this time, Buddhism was well rooted in Sri Lanka, and the island rulers maintained close relations with the Indian states that fostered Buddhism. For this reason the Kalinga ruler, in imminent danger of losing in battle, decided to send the Tooth relic to the Sri Lankan king whose ascendants were from Kalinga, the present Orissa.

After about eight centuries of its existence in India, the Tooth relic was secretly taken away by Danta and Hemamala, said to be the son-in-law and daughter of Guhasiva. The literary works like Dathavamsa, Daladasirita and the chronicle Mahavamsa, record many and varied vicissitudes that the couple went through en route to Sri Lanka in order to safeguard the relic. It is recorded that the prince and the princess donned the garb of ascetics and carried the Relic hidden within the coiffure of Hemamala not to be noticed by passersby. A twentieth century wall painting of the well known monastery of Kelaniya (about 5 miles east of Colombo), depicts this episode in a classic style executed by a local artist (Solius Mendis).

Danta and Hemamala were said to have embarked on a ship at the ancient port of Tamralipti, a busy port at the time, located at the mouth of the river Ganges, and reached the shores of Sri Lanka at the port of Lankapattana (modern Ilankeiturei) in the Trincomalee District. The Relic was reported to have performed several miracles en route on the ship itself, thus being venerated by human and superhuman beings. The Tooth Relic finally reached the Sri Lankan capital, Anuradhapura, and according to the Sinhala text, Dalada Sirita, the Relic was kept at the Megagiri vihara in the park Mahameghavana.

At the time of its arrival, the Indian ruler Guhasiva's friend, king Mahasena had died and his son, king Kirti Sri Meghavanna (4th century AC), who himself was a pious Buddhist, had succeeded him. The Tooth Relic was well received by the king and placed on the throne itself with much veneration. The chronicle Mahavamsa reports that the king with great faith had the Tooth Relic enshrined in the edifice called Dhammacakkageha originally built by king Devanampiyatissa in the 3rd century BC, within the royal enclosure (Rajavatthu). The king built a special shrine and enshrined the Tooth Relic therein.

This shrine has now been identified as the ruined edifice lying almost next to the great refectory known as Mahapali. There are special religious programs conducted in the Maligawa on every Full Moon Poya day where large numbers participate. Apart from these daily, weekly and monthly ceremonies, there are four major ceremonies held every year. They are Aluth Sahal Mangallaya, Avurudu Mangallaya, Esala Mangallaya, and Karthika Mangallaya. Of these, the most important is the Esala Mangallaya. The relic is also one of the 80 treasures featured on Around the World in 80 Treasures series presented by Dan Cruickshank.

SACRED TOOTH RELIC IN SRI LANKA

From the time of its arrival in Sri Lanka in the 4th century until the end of the 10th century when the capital Anuradhapura was shifted to Polonnaruva, only a few instances are recorded in the chronicle Mahavamsa. Yet Fa-Hsien, the Chinese traveller monk, who lived in the Abhayagiri monastery in the 5th century, has left behind many details about the worship and rituals connected with the Tooth Relic. According to him, the procession instituted by King Kirti Sri Meghavanna in the 4th century, was continued in a grandeur scale.

The sacred Tooth Relic was taken in procession from the Tooth Relic shrine to the Abhayagiri Vihara where the Relic was exhibited for three months with elaborate ritual worship. Based on the descriptions of literary texts dealing with the sacred Tooth Relic, and also the sporadic references of the chronicle, it is possible to conclude that the sacred Tooth Relic was well guarded by the kings and considered it to be the palladium of kingship. Some of the kings even went to the extent of prefixing the term 'Datha' (Tooth) to their names, e.g. Dathopatissa, Dathappabhuti, Dalamugalan, etc., which indicates their close association with the sacred Tooth Relic.

The intrusion of South Indian Cholas and the internal disharmony in the ruling houses resulted in the Tooth Relic facing unsafe vicissitudes now and then. Yet, the historical records indicate that the Tooth Relic continued to be in the custody of the Anuradhapura rulers, until king Vijayabahu I shifted the capital to Polonnaruva in the 11th century. The present ruins of the Atadage at the Sacred Quadrangle (Dalada Maluva) in the ancient city of Polonnaruva, is identical with the Tooth Relic temple built by Vijayabahu. The Velaikkara stone inscription standing at the side of this edifice provides many details on the history of the Tooth Relic.

It appears that the Tooth Relic, together with the Bowl Relic, was brought down from the Uttaramula -ayatana monastery of the Abhayagiri Vihara and installed in the Atadage shrine. This shrine, according to the Velaikkara inscription, was placed under the protection of the Velaikkara mercenaries who were in the service of the king. The Atadage was well known for the ritual known as the Netra-Mangallaya. The eye-balls of the Buddha image located in the ground floor shrine room were washed annually with unguents, as recorded in the inscription. The architectural plan of the Atadage too, is significant in that this two-storied plan seems to have been the prototype followed in the later periods down to the present Dalada shrine at Kandy.

According to the text Sasanavamsa, king Vijayabahu I maintained friendly relations with his contemporary, king Anuruddha of Burma even to the extent of the latter request the Sri Lankan ruler to send him the sacred Tooth Relic. The wise king appeased the Burmese king's desire by sending him a replica of the Relic, which is said to be greatly venerated by the Burmese. The years following king Vijayabahu's death appear to have been quite calamitous in the political field. The country came to be ruled under separate rulers who were weaklings. Consequently, many Buddhist shrines were destroyed.

In this state of affairs, fearing the destruction of the sacred Tooth and the Bowl Relics, the monks secretly removed them to safer locations in the southern country, Rohana. With the accession of king Parakramabahu I in the year 1153 AD, Sri Lankan political scene assumed a firm basis again. While rebuilding the country's economy especially through vast agrarian schemes, he lost no time in bringing about a renaissance in the religious activities. Most of the existing religious edifices in Polonnaruva remain mementos to his immeasurable service to the cause of Buddhism.

Parakramabahu I managed to secure the possession of the sacred Tooth Relic and the Bowl Relic and enshrined the sacred objects in a new edifice built in the center of the city. He was also said to have had the exposition of the Tooth Relic in a circular shrine built at the Jetavana monastery, which is possibly the ruined edifice in proximity to the Tivanka Patimaghara image house in the northern extremity of the ancient city. The next great ruler to build a formidable Relic shrine for the accommodation of the sacred Tooth and Bowl Relics was Nissankamalla (1187-1196).

As recorded in his inscriptions, he had the Relic Shrine Hatadage built and, having offered his son and daughter to the Relics, redeemed them with the completion of the shrine. This edifice lying almost adjoining the Atadage, represents a larger version of the Atadage. By the beginning of the second quarter of the 13th century, the glory of Polonnaruva waned, and with the invasion of Kalinga Magha, the capital was shifted to the south-western part of the country in the wet zone. Thus, began the Damabadeniya period, which period saw the blossoming of an era of classical literary works.

By this time, the Tooth Relic and the Bowl Relic had again been taken away by the monks to a safer location in Kotmale in the central hills. Later, King Vijayabahu III was reported to have brought down the two Relics and enshrined them in a beautiful edifice built for the purpose on the hill top of Beligala. The king re-instituted the rituals connected with the Relics and handed over the custody of the Relics to his elder son, who succeeded to the throne under the name Parakramabahu II (1236-1270). Being an erudite scholar, he was well known for the compilation of classical literary texts, including the Kavusilumina.

Parakramabahu II brought down the Relics from Beligala in a procession with great veneration and placed them in a shrine built near the palace at the Damabadeniya rock According to the text Dalada Pujavaliya, Parakramabahu conducted the Relics to Srivardhanapura, the city of his birth, and held a great ritual worship. He was responsible for the building of the Tooth Relic shrine at the Vijayasundararama at Dambadeniya, where the Relic was deposited and festive rituals were conducted by the king. The peaceful and prosperous time under Parakramabahu was disturbed by the invasion of Chandrabhanu of Java.

However, the king was able to expel the enemy and bring back the country to a stable status again. It is recorded that during a severe drought, the sacred Tooth Relic was taken out of the shrine and a great procession held. He placed the Relic on the throne and having worshipped the Relic for seven days, offered the kingdom to the sacred Tooth Relic, which resulted in the termination of the drought. This incident indicates the esteem that the sacred Tooth Relic enjoyed as a symbol of kingship.

Even during the lifetime of Parakramabahu II, his son Vijayabahu as sub-king, renovated and enlarged the Relic shrine and conducted great ritual services. As the chronicle records, he restored the ruined religious edifices at Polonnaruva, including the Tooth Relic shrine and having placed the Tooth Relic therein, conducted an abhiseka (coronation) ceremony. Yapahuva (ancient Subha-pabbata) comes into prominence around this time with the appointment of his brother Bhuvanekabahu as the sub-ruler of this province.

This location, simulating the well known Sigiriya rock fortress, found itself to be a very secure place for the Relics. However, Chadrabhanu of Java invaded the country for the second time and after defeating the local sub-ruler at Yapahuva, demanded the Tooth Relic from Vijayabahu of Dambadeniya. Yet, the Sri Lankan ruler was able to defeat him and bring peace to the island again. Bhuvanekabahu built a shrine for the sacred Tooth Relic at Yapahuva with a grandeur stairway the ruins of which still portray the aesthetic achievement of the 14th century. As the chronicle records, he continued the tradition of paying homage to the sacred Tooth Relic daily.

Almost after his reign, Sri Lanka again faced severe droughts and also an invasion from the Pandyan country in South India, under the great warrior Arya Cakravarti. He devastated the country and plundered much wealth and treasure, including the Tooth and Bowl Relics, which he handed over to the Pandyan king Kulasekera. The next king, Parakramabahu III visited the Pandyan capital and after friendly discussions, brought back the Relics and initiated the traditional rituals. It is interesting to note that even at this late age, Polonnaruva Tooth Relic shrine was in existence, for the king is said to have brought the sacred Relics from India to Polonnaruva and enshrined them at the old Tooth Relic shrine at the ancient capital, which was abandoned by this time.

According to Marco Polo, the well known traveller, the Chinese Emperor, Kublai Khan, sent a messenger to obtain the Tooth, Hair and Bowl Relics from the king. However, the king was able to please the Chinese Emperor by dispatching two fake teeth, which were graciously received by the Emperor who established ritual worship for the objects. Bhuvanekabahu II (1293-1312) is reported to have brought the Tooth Relic from Polonnaruva and placed it within a shrine built at his capital, Kurunagala.

Next ruler was Parakramabahu IV, during whose time, there was a religious revival. He reorganized the rituals connected with the sacred Tooth Relic in a systematic manner as recorded in the text Dalada Sirita. Yet another significant factor was the handing of the responsibility of the security and conduction of rituals in charge of the chief prelate of the Uttaramula monastery, which institution originated from the Abhayagiri Vihara of Anuradhapura. The next ruler of note connected with the story of the Tooth Relic was Bhuvanekabahu IV, who selected a new capital, Gampola, in the central hills.

Yet, no mention is made of his bringing the Tooth Relic to this new city. It was possibly Vikramabahu III who had the Relic shifted to this hill capital and held a festival in honor of the sacred Tooth Relic. He is credited with the building of the shrine at Niyangampaya at Gampola, which comes closer to the 14th century Gadaladeniya temple in the decorative elements. Thereafter, Bhuvanekabahu V (1372-1408) shifted the capital to Jayavardanapura Kotte closer to Colombo. Although he did not bring the Tooth Relic to the capital, he is reported to have conducted many ritual performances for the Relic.

It was his successor, Virabahu, who brought down the Tooth Relic to Jayavardanapura Kotte from Gampola. China entered into Sri Lankan politics during his reign. The Chinese general, Chen Ho, invaded the island, captured the king and the family and took them before the Chinese emperor at the time, together with the Tooth Relic. However, conflicting and stronger reports conclude that the Chinese general did not take away the Relic and that he left the island after paying due homage and worship to the sacred Tooth Relic. This belief is corroborated by subsequent reports on the processions, festivals and rituals conducted by rulers like Parakramabahu VI, who was held in high esteem as the greatest ruler of the late medieval period.

He is said to have built a three-storied shrine for the Tooth Relic, had four golden caskets enveloping the sacred Tooth Relic and promulgated several regulations in the service of the Tooth Relic. The subsequent period, which saw the arrival of the first colonial power, the Portuguese, in 1505, brought about the deterioration of Buddhist activities. Further, the disturbances in the ruling power, missionary activities of the Colonial powers of the Portuguese and the Dutch and other calamitous situations resulted in the Tooth Relic being secretly carried away by the faithful monks to safer locations.

Thus, the Relic was shifted to the next kingdom, Sitawaka ruled by Mayadunne. According to Dathadhatuvamsa, prior to the bringing of the Tooth Relic to Ratnapura, it was taken as far south as the Mulgirigala Vihara and then to the Ridivihara in the Kurunegala District. The Tooth Relic was finally hidden in a coirn located in the Delgamuva Vihara in Ratnapura, and it was from this temple that the Tooth Relic was brought to its final and present resting place in Kandy by Vimaladharmasuriya I (1592-1603).

SRI DALADA MUSEUM

The latest institution added to the Dalada Shrine is the 'Sri Dalada Museum '. Ever since the Tooth Relic shrine was established in Kandy, different grades of visitors and devotees, ranging from the Roylty and Heads of States to the poorest of the general public, have been offering various gifts to the Sacred Tooth Relic, and these were preciously protected in specially built store-rooms by the successive line of Diyawadana Nilames.

On the initiative of the ex Diyawadana Nilame, Neranjan Wijeyeratne, it was decided that these valuable artifacts be made available for public display. On the invitation of the Diyawadana Nilame, the Museum has now been beautifully designed and organized by Prof.Leelananda Prematilleke, the Archaeological Director of the UNESCO-Sri Lanka Project of the Cultural Triangle, together with his team of officers.

The Dalada Museum is located on the first and the second floors of the new wing called the Alut Maligawa set up by one of the past Diyawadana Nilemes, T.B.Nugawela. The display on the first floor consists of historical records from the time when the Tooth Relic was brought to Sri Lanka to the time of the British rule, the 1765 Dutch Plan of the Palace Complex, Lists of the Chief Prelates of the two monastic establishments of Malwatta and Asgiriya, who were responsible for the protection of the Tooth Relic, Lists of Kandyan Kings and the portrait busts and lists of the long line of Diyawadana Nilames, the Royal garments of king Kirti Sri Rajasimha, the Pingo used by the king in the Buddha-puja service, and the most recent discoveries of mural remains that were exposed due to the bomb blast caused by Tamil Tigers in January 1998.

The photographic display includes some of the important sites where the sacred Tooth Relic was enshrined through the centuries and a large array of pictures depicting the immeasurable damage caused to the Dalada maligava due to the bomb blast. Among the items on view on the second floor are historical artifacts used in the daily ritual ceremonies of the Tooth Relic shrine, caskets, Buddha statues and typical Kandyan gold and silver jewellery studded with precious gem stones, all donated by the devotees. Also on view on this floor are some special exhibits of great historical and religious value.

These include (a) the silver water pot offered by king Kirti Sri Rajasimha , (b) Silver hanging lamp offered by king

Rajadhi Rajasimha, (c) the painted replica of Buddha's Foot Print sent by king Borom Kot of Thailand when he sent some monks to establish the Higher Ordination on Sinhala monks headed by Venerable Walivita Saranankara (who became Sangharaja subsequently), (d) The unique Relic Casket containing bodily relics of the great Thera Moggliputta who headed The Third Dhamma Council held by Emperor Asoka in the 3rd century BC, etc. Other significant exhibits include ancient flags, coins, carved ivory tusks donated by Burma, commemorative carved plaques, etc. A visit to this grandest display would evidently provide an insight into the splendor that was Kandyan Heritage, her Culture and the Arts.

Since the capture of the last king of Kandy, Sri Vikrama Rajasimha, in the year 1814, and the appointment of a lay custodian along with the two Mahanayakes as guardians of the sacred Tooth Relic, a long line of Diyawadana Nilames have served in this position. They are:

The Kandy Esala Perahera

The historic Esala Perahera in Kandy began on July 18, with the usual installation of the 'kapa' (sanctified log) at the devales dedicated to the four guardian gods Natha, Vishnu, Kataragama and goddess Pattini. It will be followed by the Devale peraheras from 18 to 21, and by the Kumbal perahera from 22 to 26.

The Randoli perahera, the most grandiloquent of the peraheras will parade the streets from 27 to 31. The ritual of the water-cutting ceremony will be held on August 1, followed by the Day perahera on the 2nd thus, bringing the grand spectacle to an end. Seven days after the Day perahera, as tradition holds, 'Waliyaknetuma'(an abridged form of Kohomba-kankariya) is danced at the Vishnu devale, by people of the 'balibat' caste, for seven more days, with masked dancing, to avoid malignant influences.

This is a general account of the Esala perahera in Kandy, which has changed in detail down the ages, e.g., during the Kandyan period two peraheras were held, one by evening and one by night, preferably during the Randoli perahera. The Associated Newspapers of Ceylon Ltd. (ANCL), will illuminate the Dalada Maligawa, during the perahera season, with due honour to the 'Dantadhatu'(the sacred Tooth Relic of the Buddha). The Esala perahera in Kandy, we see today, dates back to the reign of Kirti Sri Rajasinha (1747-1780). It is a combination of the Dalada perahera, and the four Devale peraheras dedicated to the guardian deities of the island.

Earlier, the Esala perahera was conducted exclusively to appease the divinities, and patronized by the Malabari kings of South India, who ruled the Kandyan provinces. They were Hindus. The month of Esala is reminiscent of 'Esala Dev-keliya' (play of the gods). How the band wagon of the Dalada perahera came to be merged with the four devale peraheras, has an interesting story. When the bhikkus from Siam (Thailand), headed by the Most Ven. Upali Maha Thera, came to Sri Lanka, to bestow the defunct 'Upasampada' (the highest ordination qualifying a bhikku), their arrival coincided with the Esala festival in Kandy, when preparations were under way to hold the Devale peraheras invoking the blessings of the gods for the king and his subjects.

The Maha Thera Upali, having heard the noise of jingalls (a kind of large Indian swivel musket), inquired from the king the reason for all that noise the king told the Maha Thera that arrangements were being made to hold the Devale peraheras, during the month Esala, to appease the gods and to receive their blessings. The Maha Thera immediately took umbrage over the news, and at the attitude of the king in giving preference to Hindu customs, in a land where orthodox Buddhism has gained ground for more than one thousand years.

The king, realising his mistake and using his wits, not to offend the Maha Thera, informed him that Dalada perahera will lead the procession followed by the Devale peraheras, in their order of importance. There had been, throughout history, processions of great magnitude which could be considered as the precursors of the present day Dalada perahera. When the 'danta dhatu' (Tooth Relic of the Buddha) was brought to the island by prince Danta and princess Hemamala of Kalinga (Orissa), during the reign of Kirti Sri Meghavarna (352-377), the three Buddhist fraternities in Anuradhapura (Mahavihara, Abahayagiri vihara and Jetavana vihara), claimed to possess it as the most revered object of worship.

The king, wishing not to displease the bhikkus of the three viharas, placed the Relic in a golden reliquary, and keeping it in his royal chariot, allowed to go to one of the three viharas. The chariot unguided went to the Abahayagiri vihara, and the bhikkus thera accepted it and enshrined it in a gaily decorated 'dhatugruha' (relic chamber). It later became the palladium of regal authority. The Mahaviharavasins and the Jetavanavasins did not claim it. Before the transfer of power from Anuradhapura to Polonnaruwa in 1058, the Tooth Relic was annually taken in procession from the vihara to the city of Anuradhapura and back to the vihara, with great pomp and ceremony. It was the beginning of the Dalada perahera in the island.

The significant and widespread belief regarding the origin of the Esala perahera is woven into the fabric of mythology, especially in regard to the water-cutting ritual. During the reign of Vankanasika Tissa alias Kasubu (109-112), a band of Cholians from South India, invaded the island, and having slain the king, took away 12,000 Sinhala captives to South India. His son, king Gajabahu, along with his herculian soldier Nila, crossed the Indian Ocean to India, by cleaving the waters of the sea with his massive iron rod. After peaceful negotiations with the Colian king Senguttuvan, king Gajabahu was able to bring back the captives, along with an equal number of Cholians, in recompense.

Later, they settled down in the villages of Hewaheta, Tumpane, Udunuwara, Yatinuwara, Alutkuruwa etc. The water-cutting ritual at the Getambe ferry reminisces the exploit of Nila in cleaving the sea to go to India. King Parakramabahu I (1153-1186) of Polonnaruwa, held a Dalada perahera, when there was a severe drought in the country threatening a famine. The following day, rains came down in torrents inundating the low-lying areas, and filling the lakes that had gone dry.

In the Dalada Siritha, a treatise on the Tooth Relic, it is said: "Vesi novasnakala mama lesin Dalada pooja karanawa isa". (When there is no rain, make offerings to the Tooth Relic in this manner). There is belief among the Buddhists that whenever there is severe drought, the Tooth Relic should be carried in procession.

History tells us that during the governorship of Sir Edward Barnes (1824-1831), a Dalada perahera was held in Kandy in 1829, on the advice of the Kandyan chiefs, to avert a severe drought. It resulted in a heavy downpour when the flood waters spilled over the Kandy Lake submerging the low-lying areas, and making roads impassable. The flood waters came to be known as the Dalada Watura (Relic water). The governor was surprised over the miraculous power of the Tooth Relic, about which a despatch was sent to the Colonial Secretary in England.

The Esala perahera ritual complex begins with the installation of kapa, a pole about four feet in height, within each devale. A few days before the new moon in August, the Basnayaka Nilames of the four devales, along with the kapuralas, go in search of a young jak tree (Artocarpus integrifolia), that has borne no fruit, and clear the ground around the tree. it is then fumigated with the smoke of burning resin and sprinkled with specially prepared sandalwood water. Flowers, betel leaves and a lighted lamp are placed at the foot of the tree, and the deity, whose abode, perchance, it may be, is implored to leave the tree, before it is felled. Earlier an asala tree (Cassia fistula) was selected, instead of the lactiferous jak tree, to make the kapa poles.

Once the tree is felled, it is cut into four equal parts and distributed among the four devales, the Natha devale getting the first kapa. The traditional procedure followed in felling the tree is mentioned in the Sinhala text Maimataya (Skt. Mayamata). Each log is carried in procession and planted inside the devales. Earlier they were installed outside the devales, but now having reduced in size, they occupy an elevated ground inside each devale, specially built for the purpose. It is known as kap-situweema. For five days from the date of installation of the kapa, the kapurala of each devale take around the log every evening (formerly twice a day), accompanied by music and drumming, flag and canopy bearers and spearmen and the sacred insignia of the gods (ranayudha).

This takes the form of a little procession in each of the devales, and is known as Devale perahera. On the fifth day, the insignias are taken out of the devale premises and borne inside a dome like structure, known as the ranhilige, on the back of an elephant, accompanied by the Basnayaka Nilame and his retinue. The Devale peraheras come at the appointed hour and assemble in front of the Dalada Maligawa. The Relic casket, which is a substitute for the Tooth Relic, is placed inside a ranhilige, which is tied on to the back of the caparisoned Maligawa elephant.

The Maligawa perahera joins the waiting Devale peraheras in front and gives the lead in moving on. The perahera consist the Maligawa and Devale peraheras march through the prescribed streets, and it is called the Kumbal perahera. Randoli perahera is an expanded version of the Kumbal perahera, to which are added palanquins (randoli) of the four devales. These contain the ornaments of the goddesses, sword and pitcher of each devale. On the 5th day of the Randoli perahera, after a short break up, reassembles and makes its way to the Asgiri vihara, where the casket is placed, and the Devale peraheras return to their respective devales.

Later in the night the four Devale peraheras make their way to the water-cutting site at Gatambe ferry. At the river the kapuralas of the devales are led in a decorated boat to some distance, from where they cleave the waters with the sacred sword, and collect a pitcher full from the place where the sword touched the water, to be stored in the devales for one year, to be fed back into the river, at the next water-cutting ceremony. On their way, the peraheras stop at the Ganadevi Kovil, Kandy, where the assembled crowds received the blessings of the gods, in the form of a tilaka (prasada) of sandalwood paste on the forehead.

In the afternoon, the peraheras of the four devales form into one unit and go to Asgiri vihara to join the Maligawa perahera. Thus, the full procession is formed again and the Day perahera takes a prescribed route and goes back to the Maligawa, where at the prescribed auspicious moment, the casket is replaced at the sanctum sanctorum. The introduction of Ves dancing to the perahera is of recent origin. Ves is a sacred dance. The ves-tattuwa (the magnificent head dress of the Kandyan dancer) is a sacred object guarded by a system of taboos and traditions. As a form of dancing Ves is considered fit for the gods.

The Diyawadana Nilame, Punchi Banda Nugawela Nilame (1916-1937), who introduced it to the Maligawa section of the perahera, has made this great change. In 1828, when Governor Barnes participated in the Dalada perahera, the Maligawa perahera consisted of the following: (1) Peramune Rala riding the Yahalatanne elephant. (2) Gajanayaka Nilame carrying the symbolic goad. (3) Kodituwakku Nilame and his retinue. (4) Disava of Four Korales. (5) Disava of Seven Korales. (6) Disava of Matale. (7) Disava of Sabaragamuwa. (8) Disava of Walapone and (9) Disava of Udapalatha, each carrying their respective flags.

Today, the provincial representation has been forgotten. The Kodituwakku department is absent. The Peramune Rala and Gajanayaka Nilame are solitary representatives. The extinction of old elements and the substitution of new elements have, doubtless, harmed the original integral symbolism of the Esala festival. The elephants are less in number than in the old days, when more than one hundred elephants participated in the perahera. The winds of change have affected the old customs and rites to a reasonable degree.

9

Vajrayana Buddhism in Southeast Asia

Vajrayana Buddhism, also known as *Tantric Buddhism,* found its way to the Indonesian islands of Java and Sumatra before 700 C.E., which predates its presence in Tibet. Vajrayana is an extension of Mahayana Buddhism consisting of differences in the adoption of additional techniques (upaya, or 'skillful means') rather than in philosophy. Some of these *upâya* are esoteric practices which must be initiated and transmitted only through a skilled spiritual teacher. The Vajrayana is often viewed as the third major 'vehicle' (Yana) of Buddhism, alongside the Theravada and Mahayana.

The Buddhist Empire of Srivijaya in Palembang, Sumatra was for more than 600 years, the centre of Vajrayana learning in the Far East. Yi Jing (635-713) praised the high level of Buddhist scholarship in Srivijaya and advised Chinese monks to study there prior to making the journey to Nalanda, India. He wrote:

> In the fortified city of Bhoga, Buddhist priests number more than 1,000, whose minds are bent on learning and good practice. They investigate and study all the subjects that exist just as in India; the rules and ceremonies are not at all different. If a Chinese priest wishes to go to the West in order to hear and read the original scriptures, he had better stay here one or two years and practice the proper rules.

The temple complex at Borobudur was built as a Mandala, a giant three dimensional representation of Vajrayana Buddhist cosmology. All of the Buddha statues on each of its four sides have the same mudra, corresponding to one of the Buddhas of the cardinal compass directions.

Tang Dynasty Buddhist scholar Yi Jing travelled to Srivijaya in 687 CE. He stayed there for two years to translate original Buddhist scriptures from Sanskrit to Chinese. Yi Jing's visits to Srivijaya gave him the opportunity to meet with others who had come from other neighboring islands. According to him, the Javanese kingdom of Ho-ling was due east of the city of Bhoga at a distance that could be spanned by a 4-5 days journey by sea. He also wrote:

Buddhism was flourishing throughout the islands of Southeast Asia. Many of the kings and chieftains in the islands of the Southern Sea admire and believe in Buddhism, and their hearts are set on accumulating good actions.

He was also responsible for the translation of a large numbers of Buddhist scriptures from Sanskrit into Chinese. He translated more than 60 sutras into Chinese, including:

- Saravanabhava Vinaya
- Avadana, i.e. *stories of great deeds* in 710 CE.
- Suvarnaprabhascottamaraja-sutra, i.e. Sutra of the Most Honored King in 703.

The Account of Buddhism sent from the South Seas & Buddhist Monks Pilgrimage of Tang Dynasty are two of Yi Jing's best travel diaries, describing his adventurous journey to Srivijaya and India, the society of the society of India and the lifestyles of various local peoples.

ATISA DIPANKARA SHRIJNANA (982-1054 CE)

In the eleventh century, the Buddhist scholar Atiœa Dipankara Shrijnana who was responsible for the revival of Tibetan Buddhism after its repression by King Langdarma (838-841 CE), studied in Srivijaya under the eminent Buddhist scholar Dharmarakshita of Sumatra. In a sense, Tibet owes its

Buddhism to Sumatra since it was almost wiped out under King Langdarma's brutal repression.

DHARMARAKSHITA

Serlingpa or Dharmarakshita was a renowned 10th century Sumatran Buddhist teacher and a member of the Srivijayan imperial family who composed an important Mahayana text called the *Wheel of Sharp Weapons* (Tib. *blo-sbyong mtshon-cha 'khor-lo*). He was the teacher of Atisha, who was instrumental in establishing a second wave of Buddhism in Tibet.

BUDDHISM IN THE PHILIPPINES

Buddhism, specifically Vajrayana, gained a foothold in the Philippines with the rise of the Indianized Buddhist Srivijaya Empire centered in Sumatra in the 7th century. Archaeological finds in the Philippines include a number of Buddhist images common to Vajrayana iconography that dates back to this period. These include a number of Padmapani images and the Golden Tara found in 1917 at Esperanza, Agusan.

PRE-COLONIAL PERIOD

In the 9th century, Butuan (in Mindanao, southern Philippines) and Ma-i (Mindoro, central Philippines) began extensive trading with the kingdom of Champa (now southern Vietnam), an Indianized state then undergoing a period of strong Buddhist influence.

In 1001 AD, the Buddhist ruler of Bhutan (P'u-tuan in the Sung Dynasty records), Sari Bata Shaja, made the first tributary mission to China and this was followed by the rulers of Basilan (in southern Philippines) and the Luzon Empire more than two hundred years later, and by Mindoro, Sulu and Pangasinan (northern Philippines) four hundred years later. However, according to the *Sung Shih* (‹[òS), the official History of the Sung Dynasty, Butuan made regular tributary missions to China since 1001 AD, and that it rulers usually arrived at the same time as the rulers of Tibet, Champa (Southern Vietnam), and the Mongols.

SPANISH COLONIAL PERIOD

With the advent of Spanish colonialism via Mexico in the 16th century, the Philippines became a closed colony and cultural contacts with other Southeast Asian countries were closed. In 1481, the Spanish Inquisition commenced with the permission of Pope Sixtus IV and all non-Catholics within the Spanish empire were to be expelled or to be "put to the question" (tortured until they renounced their previous faith). With the refounding of Manila in 1571, the Philippines became subject to Spanish law and the Archbishop of New Galicia (Mexico) became the Grand Inquisitor of the Faithful in Mexico and the Philippines.

In 1595, the newly appointed Archbishop of Manila became the Inquisitor-General of the Spanish East Indies (the Philippines, Guam, and Micronesia) and until 1898; the Spanish Inquisition was active against Protestants, Buddhists, Hindus and Muslims. As was the case in Latin America and Africa, forced conversions were not uncommon and any attempt not to submit to the authority of the Roman Catholic Church was seen as both rebellion against the Pope and sedition against the Spanish King, which was punishable by death.

Buddhist practices, festivals and iconography had to be converted and adopted to Catholicism if they were to survive Spanish persecution. A good example of this was is the *saniculas* biscuit of Pampanga that has its roots in Buddhism. Syncretism (the blending indigenous religions such as Hinduism, Buddhism, Catholicism and indigenous folk religions) became necessary. This can be seen instantly with statues of the Virgin Mary, including the depiction of the halo, hand poses, and rainbow-arches, look almost identical to statues of Tara especially in Binondo and other areas. In time, Buddhism seemed to have virtually disappeared during the 400 years of Spanish rule.

AMERICAN COLONIAL PERIOD

With Revolution of 1896 against Spain and later with the coming of the American colonial regime in 1898, religious freedom was instituted. Mahayana and Zen Buddhist temples began to be built in the 1920s and 30s. Davao, due to the large number of Japanese residents, and Cebu, due to the large number of Chinese settlers had the largest Buddhist populations in the Philippines. After World War II, most Japanese were expatriated to Japan and the Chinese and Chinese-Filipinos became the predominant Buddhist ethnic group. In the 1960s, Vietnamese refugees arrived and established a temple in Palawan. At the same time, Japanese Buddhist temples and organizations began to re-emerge such as Sokka Gakkai International.

BUDDHISM TODAY

Today, Buddhists account for about 1-3% of the Philippine population. Currently, only the Mahayana and Zen are present in the Philippines. Theravada Buddhism is now only confined to nationals from Sri Lanka, Thailand and Myanmar, as well as Cambodia and Laos.

Language

However, the linguistic influence left its most lasting marks on every Philippine language throughout the archipelago with the following Buddhist and Hindu concepts directly from the original Sanskrit. About 25% of the words in many Philippine languages are Sanskrit terms:

From Tagalog:

- *budhi* "conscience" from Sanskrit *bodhi*
- *dukha* "one who suffers" from Sanskrit *dukkha*
- *guro* "teacher" from Sanskrit *guru*
- *sampalataya* "faith" from Sanskrit *sampratyaya*
- *mukha* "face" from Sanskrit *mukha*
- *laho* "eclipse" from Sanskrit *rahu*
- *maharlika* "noble" from Sanskrit *mahardikka*

From Kapampangan:

- *kalma* "fate" from Sanskrit *karma*
- *damla* "divine law" from Sanskrit *dharma*

- *mantala* "magic formulas" from Sanskrit *mantra*
- *upaya* "power" from Sanskrit *upaya*
- *lupa* "face" from Sanskrit *rupa*
  sabla "every" from Sanskrit *sarva*
- *lawu* "eclipse" from Sanskrit *rahu*
- *galura* "giant eagle" (a surname) from Sanskrit *garuda*
- *laksina* "south (a surname)" from Sanskrit *dakshin*
- *laksamana* "admiral (a surname)" from Sanskrit *lakshmana*

From Tausug:

- *suarga* "heaven"
- *neraka* "hell"
- *agama* "religion"

Sanskrit and Sanskrit-derived words common to most Philippine languages:

- *sutla* "silk" from Sanskrit *sutrc*
- *kapas* "cotton" from Sanskrit *kerpas*
- *naga* "dragon or serpent" from Sanskrit *naga*

TIBETAN BUDDHIST LINEAGES

- Nyingma-pa Tracing its origin to the Indian adept, Guru Padma-sambhava, who came to Tibet in 817 C.E. at the invitation of King Trisong Detsen (742-797) in order to subdue the evil forces then impeding the spread of Buddhism. This lineage of Buddhism is uniquely Tibetan in that many aspects of the traditional Bon religion are mixed together with more properly Buddhist beliefs and practices to form a unique expression of Buddhist piety. This lineage emphasizes the move towards more advance stages of enlightenment through "preliminary practice" that comprises the beliefs and practices of Buddhism before the advent of Tantra, and through the "higher practices," which involve the attainment of enlightenment through the chanting of magical spells, special hand gestures and mystical diagrams.
- Sakya-pa- The lineage has descended intact up to the present time from Khon Könchok Gyelpo (1034-1102),

founder of the Sakya tradition. From the doctrinal point of view the tradition traces its origins to the Indian Yogin Virupa through Gayadhara. His disciple Drogmi Shakya Yeshe (992-1074) travelled to India where he received teachings on the Kalachakra, the Path and its Fruit, and others from many Indian masters and returned to Tibet. Later, Khon Könchok Gyelpo, one of his main disciples, built a monastery in the Tsang province of central Tibet and named it Sakya, or Grey Earth monastery. So the school took its name, Sakya, from the location of the monastery. Succession to the position of head of the Sakya tradition has been hereditary since the time of Khon Könchok Gyelpo. The present incumbent is the 4lst occupant of the Sakya Throne. The central teaching and practice of the Sakya-pa, called Lam-dre (Lam-bras), the Path and Its Fruit, ultimately leads a practitioner to the state of Hevajra. The Path and Its Fruit is a synthesis of the entire paths and fruits of both the exoteric and esoteric classes of teachings.

- Kagyu-pa- The lineages of the Kagyu school of Tibetan Buddhism derive primarily from two sources: Marpa Chökyi Lodro (1012-1099) and Khyungpo Nyaljor (978-1079). Marpa received the lineage of tantric teachings called the Four Commissioned Lineages - concerning the Illusory Body and Consciousness Transference, Dreams, Clear Light, and Inner Heat directly from Naropa (1016-1100), who had been given them by his teacher Tilopa (988-1069). Mahamudra, the unique feature of Kagyu tradition, can be explained according to interpretations of sutra and tantra. Both aspects of the teachings are aimed at direct understanding of the real nature of the mind. The approach to Mahamudra, which differs slightly within each Kagyu school, generally follows through the stages of foundation, path and fruit. Tantric practices unique to Kagyu tradition are the Six Yogas of Naropa, Chakrasambhava and Mahakala. In the context of tantric practice, the application of Mahamudra becomes much more profound and sophisticated.
- Gelug-pa- Founded by Tsong-kha-pa (1357-1419) as a reform movement within Tibetan Buddhism, followers

acclaimed the third teacher as an incarnation of the bodhisattva Avalokiteshvara, thus inaugurating the line of the Dalai Lama, the fourteenth and most recent of whom was born in 1935. Emphasis in this lineage is on a strict monastic discipline and on the conviction that the bodhisattva, a Buddha who has foregone final nirvana out of compassion for all sentient beings, is continually present. This tradition remains dynamic even after coming into exile. The major Gelug monasteries, Sera, Drepung, Ganden, and Tashi Lhunpo monasteries and Gyumey Tantric College have been re-established in various Tibetan settlements in Karnataka, and Gyutö Tantric College has been re-established in Bomdila, Arunachal Pradesh, all in India.

Vajrayana is also found in Japan, where it is represented by the Shingon and Tendai traditions. Both were established around the end of the eighth century/beginning of the ninth, a period known as the Heian era (794–1185). Shingon is focused on Vajrayana practice, while Tendai divides its practice between Vajrayana and Lotus sutra. Shingon: Established by Kukai (774–835) following his study of the rituals and texts of the two mandalas, Vajra world and Matrix world. The two mandalas represent the two bodhisattva qualities of wisdom and compassion.

Upon completion of his studies under Huiguo in China, he returned to Japan. He was given the responsibility to oversee one of the most important temples in Kyoto, Toji Temple, which remains important for the Shingon tradition. He also established a training center on Mt. Koya, which flourishes today as the main center of Shingon in the world. Tendai: Established by Saicho (767–822), who during his trip to China in pursuit of the Tiantai teachings also received tantric initiation? Upon his return, the emperor directed him to create a dual tradition, that is one that incorporates both exoteric, Lotus sutra based teachings, and esoteric, Vajrayana teachings.

The main center of Tendai is Mt. Hiei, located just outside of Kyoto, which was established by Saicho as the main training center for Tendai. Later Tendai priests, particularly Ennin,

Enchin and Annen, further developed the Vajrayana dimensions of Tendai in Japan. The word Zen is an abbreviation of the word zenna (also zenno), the Japanese way of reading Chinese ch'an-na (short form, ch'an). This is turn is the Chinese version of the Sanskrit word dhyana, which refers to collectedness of mind or meditative absorption in which all dualistic distinctions like I/you, subject/object, and true/false are eliminated. Zen can be defined both exoterically and esoterically.

Exoterically regarded, Zen, of Ch'an as it is called when referring to its history in China, is a school of Mahayana Buddhism that developed in China in the 6th and 7th centuries from the meeting of Dhyana Buddhism, which was brought to China by Bodhidharma, and Taoism. In this sense Zen is a religion, the teachings and practices of which are directed toward self-realization and lead finally to complete awakening or enlightenment as experienced by Shakyamuni Buddha after intensive meditative self-disciple under the Bodhi-tree. More than any other school, Zen stresses the prime importance of the enlightenment experience and the uselessness of ritual religious practices and intellectual analysis of doctrine for the attainment of liberation. Zen teaches the practice of zazen, sitting in meditative absorption as the shortest, but also the steepest, way to awakening.

The essential nature of Zen can be summarized in four short statements: (1) "(a) special transmission outside of the orthodox teaching"; (2) non-dependence on sacred writings; and (3) "direct pointing to the human heart; leading to (4) realization of one's own nature and becoming a Buddha". The pregnant characterization of Zen is attributed by tradition to Bodhidharma, its first patriarch; however, many modern scholars suspect that it originated rather with the later Ch'an master Nan-ch'uan P'u-yuan. According to legend the "special transmission outside the orthodox teaching" began with the famous discourse of Buddha Shakyamuni on Vulture Peak Mountain.

At that time, surrounded by a great host of disciples who had assembled to hear him expound the teaching, he is said only to have held up a flower without speaking. Only his student Kashyapa understood and smiled-as a result of his mater's gesture he suddenly experienced a breakthrough to enlightened vision and grasped the essence of the Buddha's teaching on the spot. With this, the first transmission from heart-mind to heart-mind took place. In Zen, which is often also called the "School of Buddha-Mind," sudden enlightenment has played a central role.

Esoterically regarded, Zen is not a religion but rather an indefinable, incommunicable root, free from all names, descriptions, and concepts, that can only be experienced by each individual for him-or herself. From expressed forms of this, all religions have sprung. In this sense Zen is not bound to any religion, including Buddhism. It is the primordial perfection of everything existing, designated by the most various names, experienced by all great sages, saints, and founders of religions of all cultures and times. Buddhism has referred to it as the "identity of samsara and nirvana." From this point of view azan is not a "method" that brings people living in ignorance to the "goal" of liberation; rather it is the immediate expression and actualization of the perfection present in every person at every moment.

Bibliography

Auboyer, Jeannine, *Buddha: A Pictorial History of His Life and Legacy*. New York: Crossroad, 1983.

Bapat, P. V., ed., *2500 Years of Buddhism*. New Delhi: Government of India, Publications Division, 1956.

Basham, A. L., *History and Doctrines of the Ajivikas*. London: Luzac, 1951.

Basham, A. L., *The Wonder That Was India*. New York: Grove Press, 1959.

Bechert, Heinz and Richard Gombrich, eds., *The World of Buddhism: Monks and Nuns in Society and Culture*. London: Thames and Hudson, 1984.

Bharati, Agehananda, *The Tantric Tradition*. New York: Weiser, 1975.

Cabezon, Jose Ignacia, ed., *Buddhism, Sexuality, and Gender*. Albany: SUNY Press, 1992.

Charles S. Prebish, ed., *Buddhism: A Modern Perspective*. University Park: Pennsylvania State University Press, 1975.

Chattopadhyaya, D. ed., *Taranatha's History of Buddhism in India*. Delhi: Motilal Banarsidass, 1970.

Conze, Edward, *Buddhism: Its Essence and Development*. New York: Harper Torchbooks, 1965.

Dasgupta, Shashibhusan, *An Introduction to Tantric Buddhism*. Berkeley, Calif: Shambhala, 1974.

Dowman, Keith, *Masters of Mahamudra: Songs and Histories of the Eighty-Four Buddhist Siddhas*. Albany: SUNY Press, 1985.

George, Christopher S., *The Candamaharosana Tantra*. New

Haven: American Oriental Society, 1974.

Guenther, Herbert V., *The Royal Song of Saraha.* Berkeley, Calif.: Shambhala, 1973.

Hattori, M., trans., *Dignaga on Perception.* Cambridge, Mass.: Harvard Oriental Series, 1968.

Kinsley, David. *Tantric Visions of the Divine Feminine: The Ten Mahavidyas.* Berkeley: University of California Press, 1997.

Kvaerne, Per, *An Anthology of Buddhist Tantric Songs.* Oslo: Universitetsforlaget, 1977.

Lorenzen, David L., *The Kapalikas and Kalamukhas: Two Lost Saivite Sects.* Berkeley: University of California Press, 1972. Pathbreaking study of the Saivite sect that formed the model for the Unexcelled Yoga Tantras.

Mookerjee, Satkari, *Buddhist Philosophy of Universal Flux.* Delhi: Motilal Banarsidass, 1980. On the school of Dignaga.

Pott, P. H., *Yoga and Tantra.* The Hague: Martinus Nijhoff, 1966. Helpful work for the study of Buddhist Tantra.

Prebish, Charles S., ed. *Buddhist Ethics: A Cross-Cultural Approach.* Dubuque: Kendall/Hunt, 1992.

Robinson, James B., *Buddha's Lions: The Lives of the Eighty-Four Siddhas.* Berkeley: Dharma, 1980.

Shaw, Miranda, *Passionate Enlightenment: Women in Tantric Buddhism.* Princeton: Princeton University Press, 1994.

Singh, Amar, *The Heart of Buddhist Philosophy: Dinnaga and Dharmakirti.* New Delhi: Munshiram Manoharlal, 1984.

Snellgrove, David L., *The Hevajra Tantra.* Part 1, Introduction and Translation. London: Oxford University Press, 1959.

Stcherbatsky, Theodore, *Buddhist Logic,* 2 vols. Leningrad, 1930. Reprint, NewYork: Dover Books, 1962.

Tucci Guiseppe, *Tibetan Painted Scrolls. Vol. 1, The Religious Ideas: Vajrayana.* Rome: Libraria cello Stato, 1949.

Wayman, Alex, *Yoga of the Guhyasamajatantra.* Delhi: Motilal Banarsidass, 1977.

Index